D1667069

B

Claus-Dieter Brauns
Lorenz G. Löffler

Mru

Hill People on the Border of Bangladesh

Birkhäuser Verlag
Basel · Boston · Berlin

Colour photographs by Claus-Dieter Brauns
Text by Lorenz G. Löffler
Translated from German by Doris Wagner-Glenn

Frontispiece:
Harvest festival. Beating the drum and three plate-shaped gongs, four men circumambulate the place of sacrifice in front of the open platform of the field house. Three bamboo poles have been decorated with tassels, thread squares, and double-funnelled spirit traps. At their foot – a miniature altar flanked by swallow-tailed bamboo tubes.

Endpaper:
Map of the southern Chittagong Hill Tracts, 1961.

Library of Congress Cataloging-in-Publication Data

Brauns, Claus-Dieter.
[Mru. English]
Mru : Hill people on the border of Bangladesh / Claus-Dieter Brauns, Lorenz G. Löffler : translated from German by Doris Wagner-Glenn.
p. cm.
Revised translation of: Mru, Bergbewohner im Grenzgebiet von Bangladesh.
Bibliography: p. 245–247
ISBN 0-8176-1816-3 (U.S.) : 70.00F (est.)
1. Mru (South Asian people) – Social life and customs.
2. Chittagong Hill Tracts (Bangladesh) – Social life and customs. I. Löffler, Lorenz G. II. Title.

CIP-Titelaufnahme der Deutschen Bibliothek

Mru : Hill people on the border of Bangladesh / Claus-Dieter Brauns ; Lorenz G. Löffler. Transl. from German by Doris Wagner-Glenn. – Basel ; Boston ; Berlin : Birkhäuser, 1990
Dt. Ausg. unter dem Titel: Mru, Bergbewohner im Grenzgebiet von Bangladesh
ISBN 3-7643-1816-3 (Basel...) Gb.
ISBN 0-8176-1816-3 (Boston) Gb.
NE: Brauns, Claus-Dieter [Ill.]; Löffler, Lorenz G. [Text]

This work is subject to copyright. All rights are reserved, whether the whole or part of the material is concerned, specifically those of translation, reprinting, re-use of illustrations, broadcasting, reproduction by photocopying machine or similar means, and storage in data banks. Under §54 of the German Copyright Law where copies are made for other than private use a fee is payable to 'Verwertungsgesellschaft Wort', Munich.

Original publication in German
© 1986 Birkhäuser Verlag Basel
© 1990 of this edition Birkhäuser Verlag Basel
Concept/Cover/Typography: Albert Gomm, Basel
Layout: Helga and Claus-Dieter Brauns/L. G. Löffler
Printed in Germany
ISBN 3-7643-1816-3
ISBN 0-8176-1816-3

Table of Contents

Introduction
Author's concern: Claus-Dieter Brauns 19; author's concern: Lorenz G. Löffler 21; previous studies 22

The Chittagong Hill Tracts and their Inhabitants
Landscape and climate 25; major ethnic groups 26; colonial administration 30; minor ethnic groups 32; population figures and development 36

House and Home
Hamlets 61; paths 62; houses 64; house construction 69; baskets and other utensils 72

Food and Clothing
Swidden farming 109; selecting, slashing, and burning 110; planting and weeding 113; hunting and trapping 118; harvesting 122; food 125; domestic animals 130; cotton, textiles and jewelry 133; harvest festival 141

Kinship and Life Stages
Clans and marriage rules 169; premarital life 173; wedding and marriage 181; birth and childhood 187; illness and death 195

Cattle Ceremonies and Feasts of Merit
Women's work: alcoholic beverages 226; men's work: mouth organs and decorations 228; the sacrifice 231; interpretations 235; feasting 238

Epilogue

Bibliography 245
Glossary of Terms Related to the Administrative Structure 247
Glossary of Mru Terms 248
Picture Credits 248

The three standard patterns of decorative bamboo weaving. The motifs appear also in beaded jewelry and the embroidery of women's skirts.

Right side:
First meeting with the strange white man at the bazaar in Lama.

Next page:
Morning fog in the valley of the Matamuri.

Above and right:
Mru young people attach much importance to a smart appearance. On festive occasions, particularly, they take great pains in adorning themselves.

Next page:
A group of people gathers around a warm fire during the cold season.

◀
It works like this, too: the flower in the mouth and the cigar in the ear.
▶
The bamboo flute is the musical instrument of young girls.

Next page:
Menyong-Para at dusk – the Mru village where C.-D. Brauns lived.

Introduction

This book offers a glimpse into the world of the Mru — a world which is unknown and inaccessible to us. It shows pictures which can be seen nowhere else and describes a culture which has been described nowhere else. Apart from the two authors — Claus-Dieter Brauns, as photographer, and the writer, as anthropologist — there is no one who could have written or illustrated this book. And this book will be for many years, if not for ever, the only document of its kind about the Mru, since the culture of the Mru documented here — a people residing in the southeast corner of Bangladesh — is threatened with extinction.

Author's concern: Claus-Dieter Brauns

That this book itself materialized is due above all to the efforts of C.-D. Brauns, who spared himself neither trouble nor money to erect a monument to the Mru. Motivated by a deep longing to break out of the pressures of technological society and to return to nature by experiencing "the unbridled freedom of primitive people," he travelled in various parts of Southeast Asia during the '60s and '70s. In the area between India and Burma he expected to find a land far away from all civilization, where wild tribes enjoyed a natural existence and went on head-hunting expeditions.
Since World War II, however, much in this region had changed. To be sure, it was still an area outside well-ordered statehood, yet it was no longer a region outside European influence. On the contrary, within this broad mountainous area which was divided up between India, Burma, and East Pakistan (today Bangladesh), colonially-trained elites mobilized the indigenous peoples against the unconditional seizure of power by the new nation-states. Especially India, whose government had little idea with whom it was actually dealing, feared for her territorial integrity; and the country soon exchanged the arrogance of its administrative officers for a persistent jungle war — a war which soon found international participants. The area which until the 1960s had been least affected by this unrest was the small mountainous strip which at the partition of British India in 1947 had been handed over to Pakistan as part of the hinterland of Chittagong.
In 1963 in the southernmost part of this relatively low chain of mountains, the so-called Chittagong Hill Tracts, C.-D. Brauns came upon an ethnic group which fascinated him. In comparison with the Bangali people of the plains, who are predominantly Muslim, or other ethnic groups of the Chittagong Hill Tracts — particularly the Buddhist Marma, who are related to the inhabitants of Arakan on the other side of the border with Burma — these "Murung" (as they are called by the Bangalis) appeared to represent a tribal culture still closely tied to nature. In contrast to their "civilized" Bangali neighbors, who consider them to be naked savages, these people were sparsely clothed, the men with a loin-cloth and the women with a miniskirt. In their villages, so it was said, they celebrated bloody rites in which cattle were sacrificed.
C.-D. Brauns found a helper in Karim, a Bangali who was somewhat acquainted with the hill people and who knew enough English to act as interpreter. Additionally, he made himself useful as a cook. In one of the local dugouts, they travelled upstream on the Matamuri (one of the largest rivers in the southern part of the Chittagong Hill Tracts). As the Bangali boatman poled the canoe hour after hour upstream along the meandering course of the river, the banks of which were often overgrown with high elephant grass, the hectic state of modern, mechanized civilization remained farther and farther behind in the West. Two porters

◀ Shall I string beans — or put on my jewelry?

were hired in Lama, a small administrative center and market town which is surrounded by the first hills, but which, as an enclave, still belongs to the plains district. With these porters, the travellers made their way southwest into the mountains, toward the Mru.

Claus-Dieter Brauns reports: "While thick fog still covered the Matamuri Valley, our group set out following the course of a small tributary. At first the paths were pleasant, leading through dry shrubbery and grassland, past harvested fields which ran up the sides of the slopes. Soon, however, the path led upwards into the mountains, becoming steep and difficult. The hot sun beat down from a cloudless sky. I began to perspire, my legs ached, and it was difficult to breathe; but the sight of the hilly landscape, which during the dry season turns a yellow-brown color, was wonderful. In the east, as one followed the course of the Matamuri, one saw the blue shimmering of still higher mountains; in the west, the coastal plain glistened, and the Bay of Bengal appeared like silver glitter on the far horizon. Finally, after hours of marching, the goal was in sight: Menyong-Para, a particularly picturesque Mru village. One could count twenty-one houses on the side of the hill overlooking a gorge which was already in the shade. First to greet us were the barking and whining dogs. The women and young girls, who could expect only the worst from Bangali troops moving through the area, fled in fear into the houses; the children, who were afraid yet curious, bunched together in small groups behind the corners of the houses; the men stopped where they were and stared at us in cold silence. I felt uneasy and began to doubt that things would go well."

In the beginning the village head made no secret of the fact that he was little pleased; however, he assigned the visitors a small fieldhouse at the edge of the village as a place to stay. No one wanted to feed them though — not even for payment. The harvest had been poor. In addition, no one wanted to have himself photographed. C.-D. Brauns tried by means of gifts to overcome the mistrust, but without much success. Help finally came from Menlong, the younger brother of the village head. Menlong had once been in a mission hospital where he had been treated by a white doctor. Since that time, he ventured to trust white people. He understood and spoke Bangla (the Bangali language) and Marma; he considered himself a Buddhist; and he used this opportunity to learn some English. He introduced the guest to the Mru culture, showed him where there were things to photograph, and fetched him on various occasions — for example, when a sacrifice was being offered, when young girls were washing or fishing in the stream, when women were dyeing or weaving cotton, when men were going hunting, and so forth. After a while the inhabitants of the village accepted the unusual visitor; and when he returned in the following years, he was greeted as an old acquaintance and good friend who could feel safe and secure among them. In 1964 the Chittagong Hill Tracts were declared off-limits for foreigners. In spite of this, Karim managed to arrange (without government permission, however with the knowledge of the local police) additional visits to the Hill Tracts — visits which lasted several months (1965, '69, '71, and '74). One of the things which prompted C.-D. Brauns to continue such a risky undertaking was the interest shown his work by the editorial board of the American National Geographic Magazine. The board constantly encouraged him and consented to publish parts of his work.

Claus-Dieter Brauns remembers: "1971 was the year of the Bangali war of independence — the separation of Bangladesh from Pakistan. I wanted to complete my documentation and, in spite of warnings, travelled in August to that tormented land in order to experience harvesttime with the Mru. While fear and terror ruled the land, Karim arranged things in his own way with the military and brought me to the Mru village. Rain poured down in streams; everything grew profusely, dripping-wet and green. The paths were slippery. My clothing was constantly soaking wet. I was concerned about my cameras and films — and also about my health. All around us there were mosquitoes, sand fleas, leeches, scorpions, and snakes. Life in the cloud-covered jungle mountains seemed like hell."

"In October the periods between rain showers

became longer, as the rain itself subsided. The nights were noticeably cooler and therefore more pleasant. Then the thing happened which I had always feared: policemen came in order to take me from the village. In Lama a West Pakistani security officer awaited me. He appeared to be well informed about my photographic activities and indicated that it was forbidden to do mission work in the mountains and to take pictures of 'unclothed natives.' The only thing which might be permitted, he said, was the taking of group pictures at the bazaar. I showed him a few black-and-white photographs, which were immediately burned. As far as the remainder of the interrogation is concerned, the Punjabi revealed to me his high regard for the Germans and then released me; he even warned me about the next police station. I managed to get to Chittagong by bus without being checked; and from there I flew to Dhaka, the capital city. At the hotel, however, two special officers appeared; they confiscated my passport and demanded that I hand over all film materials. I handed over ten rolls. As a precautionary measure, on the previous evening I had given the others to friends for safekeeping. These were later brought to Bangkok. Only at the intervention of the embassy was I given my passport back and allowed to leave the country on the last day before the bloodbath of the West Pakistani troops."

The pictures for this volume were chosen from some 6000 slides of C.-D. Brauns and complemented by a few pictures from my own collection. They are not intended to be purely scientific and functional documentary photographs, but rather seek at the same time to convey feelings — including all of those exotic and romantic sentiments which the Mru can awaken in occidental people. Brauns has captured these sentiments through the medium of exquisite and artistic photography — a photography which exploits the play of light and shadow, resulting in high drama and brilliant color.

Author's concern: Lorenz G. Löffler

The photographs show many things which are not mentioned in the text, but then many things are described in the text which are not documented in the pictures. Text and pictures should contrast and complement each other, not only from the standpoint of content, but also in their manner of perceiving and understanding. In contrast to the photographer, the ethnographer is in danger of going beyond the visible, not merely through his description of things which cannot be documented by photography, but more particularly through his choice of data and his interpretation of his own experiences. By means of these things he may convey impressions not necessarily in harmony with reality as experienced by members of another culture. I have, therefore, taken great pains to restrict my report to the facts as far as possible.

Yet no description can avoid a certain amount of interpretation or translation. The culture of the Mru is different from ours. Quite a few things are absent from their culture which are present in our own, but then there are also many things in their culture which are missing from ours. Because our language reflects the things of our own culture, we lack many concepts and terms which are needed to portray Mru culture. I shall try as best I can to paraphrase those things for which we have no proper term. However, in the course of description a few items will have to be referred to repeatedly, so pharaphrasing becomes cumbersome. In such cases, it is felt more convenient to use the Mru terms. Information regarding the pronunciation of Mru words is found at the beginning of the Glossary on page 248.

By the 1950s, the climatic, economic and political environment within which the Mru lived was far from ideal. Yet if my health had not failed, I would have gladly lived among them for many more years — and those in "my" village would have very much liked for me to stay. The 10000 German marks which I had received from the German Research Council and which were intended to cover the expenses of my stay were, however, almost exhausted, though I had been quite economical; and even after one and a half years of instruction, I was still far too ignorant to make my own livelihood in the manner of the Mru. I could not plant one field, build one house, cut up one animal; I could not even build an evenly-distributed fire on a Mru stove. Like every other person in our culture,

I only understood — and understand — how to *buy* those things which are essential for life. In the Hill Tracts, on the other hand, one must traditionally be able to produce almost everything one needs. To be sure, this ability means greater independence and autonomy, but also a greater limitation regarding what can be produced. In effect it means living without many things which we ourselves could not imagine living without. The living standard of the Mru is not like ours, but then their abilities are also different. Apart from my better understanding of the external economic conditions with which the Mru had to contend, I had little reason to feel myself superior to them. All the things I had learned never measured up to their everyday knowledge. That I could write and was constantly making notes for myself they simply excused with the explanation that my memory was poorer than theirs. On the following pages one will find some of those things which I was able to take away with me in this manner. Perhaps I have made an error here or there — may my teachers forgive me for this.

When I wrote my doctoral dissertation on the cattle ceremonies of Southeast Asia, I did not yet know that I would later have the opportunity to do research among one of the peoples I had briefly mentioned in this thesis. The ideas I had developed in this purely literary study proved rather useless for an actual understanding of the Mru, and the Bangla (i.e. the Bangali language) I had learned before setting out on my trip corresponded little to that spoken in the Chittagong area. A young Marma had learned enough written Bangla in school to be able to help me better understand local Bangla and Marma as time went on; he also took care of my physical needs. After a few months I also found a Mru teacher, who, apart from his own language, had a good command of Bangla, Marma and Lushai. This teacher subsequently became my major informant and accompanied me on long trips to other Mru groups. Without him I would have learned little in these unfamiliar villages. He explained to the people who I was and what I wanted; that I was not a representative of the government; that they therefore could trust me; that I was on their side; and that I wanted to learn as much as possible from them, in order to pass it on to future generations. Yet not everyone understood that I could do nothing *more* for them. Had not white people the power to help them against their new rulers?

Previous Studies

I was, however, only a guest in this country, even if the secret service did occasionally suspect me of organizing rebel groups: no one could imagine that any civilized person could possibly have any interest in the life of savages. What would there be to study? To be assigned to a post in the Chittagong Hill Tracts was for a Bangali of good standing something like being sent into exile. Among the educated stratum of Chittagong society, one knew little more about the Hill Tracts (lying barely thirty kilometers to the east) than the fact that they were supposedly inhabited by monkeys; and this bit of knowledge originated in a corruption of the name of the main place in the southern circle — Banderban. The name was understood to be Bandor-bon: "Forest of Monkeys." Even the *rajas*, who levied taxes and administered justice upon the various ethnic groups within their territories, knew little more about these peoples than what they could learn from a report published in 1869 (second edition, 1870) by Captain Thomas H. Lewin, one of the first British administrators of the Hill Tracts. One of Lewin's successors, R. H. Sneyd Hutchinson, wrote a newer summary in 1906 (second edition, 1909). Since this latter report contains several ethnographic errors, however, it is less reliable than Lewin's; the earlier report may even today be counted among the best and most reliable existing descriptions of the culture of the hill peoples. Both authors dealt mainly with the larger ethnic groups residing in the major valleys: the Chakma, the Marma and the Tippera. Less information is offered on the smaller groups: the Mru and the Khumi, the Bawm and the Pangkhua, the Khyang and the Sak. Two German collectors of ethnographic materials, E. Riebeck and J. Konietzko, visited the Hill Tracts around the turn of the century — Riebeck at the end of last century and Konietzko at the beginning of this century. (The Riebeck collection may be found in the Völkerkunde-Museum Berlin-Dahlem, Konietzko's, in the Museum für Völkerkunde Hamburg). During the years 1925 and 1926, J. P. Mills (author of several monographs on the Naga of the mountainous area of eastern Assam; later Deputy Commissioner of the Naga Hills) was assigned to study the role of the *rajas* in the Chittagong Hills. In the course of his travels, he also visited the villages south of Banderban; from these trips come the first photographs of the Mru — some of them were later most kindly placed at my disposal by J. P. Mills himself. Regarding the gathering of further ethnographic data in the Chittagong Hills, almost nothing else was done until 1950. In that year the French anthropologist, Claude Lévi-Strauss, who since has become quite famous, paid a short visit to the central Hill Tracts; yet the findings which he later published are in no way reliable. In 1951/52, however, and again in 1959/60, one of Lévi-Strauss' former students, Lucien Bernot, along with his wife, a linguist, did fieldwork in the southern Chittagong Hill Tracts; thanks to the work of the Bernots, we have an excellent monograph on the Marma and a small book about the Sak. We have nothing comparable on the Chakma or the Tippera. Although single studies on the history, the social organization and the ceremonial life of the Chakma have in the meantime been done — studies which offer at least a partial picture of this people — we know little more about the Tippera than what is contained in Lewin's account. In 1954 a research project among the Tippera in India and Pakistan was planned by Dr. Hans E. Kauffmann, an academician well-known for his 1930s' research and publications on the Naga; I was to be allowed to accompany him. After a long delay, though, only the Pakistani government granted the necessary visa; this necessitated a reorientation toward the southern part of the Hill Tracts. At the end of 1955, shortly after research had begun, Dr. Kauffmann became ill and had to return to Europe in the spring of 1956; all that was left of the project was my one-and-a-half-years' stay among the Mru. During a second stay in the area in 1964, three of my students were able to make contact with the Bawm; however, the visit was cut short when the Hill Tracts were declared a restricted area. The contacts with the educated Bawm could be maintained to a certain degree up until today; those with the illiterate Mru were of necessity broken off. What follows, then, are memories of the past. Just how vital or alive the Mru culture still is today, I do not know. However, one thing I know for sure: the Mru are not — and never were — happy children of nature, isolated in some delightful and idyllic corner of the world; they are rather honest human beings whose conditions of life were never easy. For more than a century they have been subjugated, denied their rights, harrassed, and exploited. Their chances for survival, however, were never more precarious than they are today; for today their right to their traditional homeland, the environment in which they have lived and made their living, is being contested by their Bangali neighbors — a people far more numerous and far more powerful than they.

The first photographs made in Mru villages south of Banderban – taken by J.P. Mills in 1926. Khaitung-Kua: the village square with sacrificial posts (above right), a woman hulling rice (above left), and winnowing (middle right). Yimpu-Kua: a man with earrings and bracelet (below left); houses, seed-plot, and the enclosure of a young fruit tree (below right).

The Chittagong Hill Tracts and Their Inhabitants

Among the few indisputable things which can be said about the Chittagong Hill Tracts are those which relate to their geographical location and more recent history. The Hill Tracts are bounded on the west by the narrow Chittagong Plains running along the Bay of Bengal, on the north and east by the Indian states of Tripura and Mizoram respectively, and, finally, in the south and southeast by the Burmese region of Arakan; they lie between 91° 45' and 92° 50' East longitude and 21° 35' and 23° 45' North latitude. At the partition of British India, the Chittagong Hill Tracts became part of the eastern wing of Pakistan; since Bangladesh gained its independence, they have been considered part of that country's territory.

Landscape and Climate

The chains of large mountains which reach the sea in Arakan are part of the extension of the Himalayas which bends southward, cutting through Assam and Arakan. From a very modest height in the backcountry of Chittagong, the mountains rise gradually toward the east in three or four ranges. Running approximately north to south, the hill and mountain ranges are occasionally traversed in a westerly direction by the rivers which flow down between them. The Feni river is found in the north (it also forms the border with Tripura); the Kornofuli, fed by many tributaries, forms the largest river and cuts across the central area; the Songu and the Matamuri rivers respectively are found in the central and extreme south. Unless one wishes to climb the mountains, these few rivers offer the only access to the Hill Tracts. At the mouth of the Kornofuli lies Chittagong town, the largest port in Bangladesh.

Whoever chooses the route over the mountains must master considerably steeper slopes in the south than in the north. In the southeast, the highest point—Kyokra-Tong (Burmese for "stony mountain"), which peaks at about 1300 meters (4034 ft.)—marks the place where three countries come together: India (Assam), Bangladesh and Burma (Arakan). Generally, however, the ranges rising from a low elevation climb to an altitude of only 500 to 700 meters (1500 to 2000 ft.). The hills are formed of poorly consolidated sandstone and shale which conglomerate into a harder stone only in certain places; where the slopes were exposed, they were quickly eroded by the monsoon rains and converted into scree. Cultivation on the hillsides is therefore possible only as long as the soil itself is not broken up or moved. How such cultivation is done will later be described.

Between October and April the sky is almost always bright; from May to September the monsoon rains, which are occasionally accompanied by typhoons, sweep across the area, with the heaviest rains occurring in June and July. With an average yearly rainfall of 2.5 meters (100 in.)—an amount which, however, has declined due to progressive deforestation— the Hill Tracts belong to those areas receiving an extremely high amount of precipitation. Cherrapunji, which receives the highest annual amount of precipitation in the world (more than 10 meters [400 in.]), lies somewhat north of the Hill Tracts in the mountainous area of west Assam. Not only during the rainy season does the relative humidity of the Hill Tracts lie almost always between 90 and 100%; during the dry season the valleys are also covered by a fog so thick that it is normally penetrated only briefly by the noonday sun. At night the fog is so heavy that water drips from the trees. Over the mountain ridges, in contrast, the dry northeast monsoon wind blows; nights on the mountains are generally clear and the temperatures five to seven degrees *warmer* than those on the plains and in the valleys. (During the cold months of January and February, temperatures in the valleys and on the plains can sink below 10°C.) During the hot season, though, from the end of March to the beginning of the rains, the temperatures on the ridges are a few degrees *colder* than below. In April, around the middle of the day, temperatures in the valleys can go above 40°C. Since the humidity decreases at the same time, however, these midday periods are comparatively pleasant when likened with the afternoons and evenings; for even during this season fog reappears in the afternoon and evening. Far from reminding a European of November weather back home, this fog seems more like a sauna — but with one small difference: in the valleys there is no door through which to escape; and in the civilized steam of the sauna there are no frolicking clouds of sand flies and malaria mosquitoes.

The oncoming monsoon rains bring some relief with respect to the heat. During the months of the monsoon, the temperature generally hovers around 28° to 30°C. day and night, though continual rainfall may push it down even a little lower. At the same time, however, the rains wash up all kinds of refuse which during the dry months was hardly able to penetrate the earth's surface. Everyone has intestinal troubles, mostly in the form of amoebic dysentery; and small children die during this season due to the resulting dehydration. It should therefore be obvious, not only that everyone in the Hill Tracts suffers from malaria, but also that, during the cold months, colds and respiratory diseases are likewise universal (at night one can even hear the monkeys in the trees coughing). This is not to mention the fact that tuberculosis is fairly common; that until a few years ago cholera and smallpox epidemics belonged to the annually-recurring plagues; and that persons suffering from leprosy are also occasionally found. Chronic malaria leads periodically to a painful enlargement of the spleen; yet these periods, like mosquito and leech bites, are tolerable. Amoebas, on the other hand, can in the course of time eat through the walls of the intestines and, by way of the spinal cord, enter the brain, causing insanity. The most commonly used remedy against dysentery (at times officially prescribed by doctors) is opium, well-known to be addictive and to ruin a person's physical health. In addition, the Mru claim that it will destroy a person morally; and they complained bitterly that the government withheld from them the healing remedies, so that it could instead sell them expensive poison. To this political tendency we shall return shortly.

In view of the climatic conditions and related health problems just described, it is not surprising that an earlier author described the climate of the Hill Tracts as "deadly." Yet the population increased yearly by some two percent. This rate of increase is, to be sure, substantially lower than that of the Bangali plains; but it has been high enough over the last hundred years to have effected a fivefold increase in population, in spite of some emigration during past decades. If the valleys were in places almost free of people one hundred and thirty years ago, today, under the present conditions of land utilization, they are overpopulated. Except for a few places in the governmental forest reservations, what was once virgin forest has long disappeared; and in many places an infertile grassland is already spreading — a fact which, however, did not deter the government from moving hundreds of thousands of landless Bangalis from the plains into the hills where, under military protection, they compete with the indigenous people for land.

Major Ethnic Groups

The fundamental opposition just hinted at — namely, between the plains people and those of the hills — has a long history. To be sure, the Hill Tracts can be geographically considered the hinterland of Chittagong; yet thirty years ago one crossed from South to Southeast Asia when one moved from the plains into the hills. There was a striking difference in culture between the plains people of Caucasoid race (speaking an Indo-European language) and the hill people of Mongoloid race (speaking Sino-Tibetan languages). The disparity was further accentuated by the fact that the inhabitants of the

Chittagong and the Chittagong Hill Tracts

—·—·— International borders since 1947
------ Borders of the Hill Tracts and the Reserved Forests (R.F.)
········ Subdivision (now: District) boundaries
· · · · · Circle boundaries (if not identical with those of the Subdivisions)

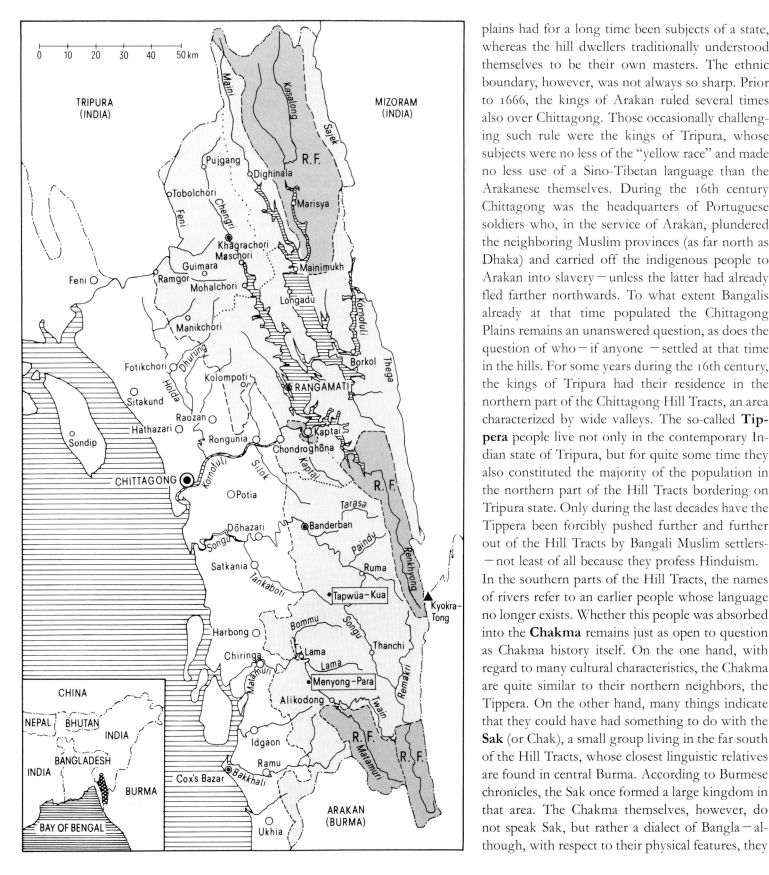

plains had for a long time been subjects of a state, whereas the hill dwellers traditionally understood themselves to be their own masters. The ethnic boundary, however, was not always so sharp. Prior to 1666, the kings of Arakan ruled several times also over Chittagong. Those occasionally challenging such rule were the kings of Tripura, whose subjects were no less of the "yellow race" and made no less use of a Sino-Tibetan language than the Arakanese themselves. During the 16th century Chittagong was the headquarters of Portuguese soldiers who, in the service of Arakan, plundered the neighboring Muslim provinces (as far north as Dhaka) and carried off the indigenous people to Arakan into slavery — unless the latter had already fled farther northwards. To what extent Bangalis already at that time populated the Chittagong Plains remains an unanswered question, as does the question of who — if anyone — settled at that time in the hills. For some years during the 16th century, the kings of Tripura had their residence in the northern part of the Chittagong Hill Tracts, an area characterized by wide valleys. The so-called **Tippera** people live not only in the contemporary Indian state of Tripura, but for quite some time they also constituted the majority of the population in the northern part of the Hill Tracts bordering on Tripura state. Only during the last decades have the Tippera been forcibly pushed further and further out of the Hill Tracts by Bangali Muslim settlers— — not least of all because they profess Hinduism.

In the southern parts of the Hill Tracts, the names of rivers refer to an earlier people whose language no longer exists. Whether this people was absorbed into the **Chakma** remains just as open to question as Chakma history itself. On the one hand, with regard to many cultural characteristics, the Chakma are quite similar to their northern neighbors, the Tippera. On the other hand, many things indicate that they could have had something to do with the **Sak** (or Chak), a small group living in the far south of the Hill Tracts, whose closest linguistic relatives are found in central Burma. According to Burmese chronicles, the Sak once formed a large kingdom in that area. The Chakma themselves, however, do not speak Sak, but rather a dialect of Bangla — although, with respect to their physical features, they have little in common with the Bangalis. (They are rather clearly of "eastern" origin.) This Bangla dialect is to a large extent unintelligible for the Bangalis of the Chittagong Plains and was traditionally not written in Bangali characters but rather in a script peculiar to the Chakma alone (and unknown to the Sak). This script, at times wrongly classed with the Khmer script of Cambodia, is actually closely related to the Burmese script. In those cases where Hindus and Muslims use different words to denote the same things, the Chakma follow the Muslim usage; however, they, like the Tippera, make use of Hindu first names. Other Hindu influence may also be found, although the Chakma, like the Marma who came from Arakan, officially confess Buddhism.

According to their own traditions, in the 17th century several Chakma clans lived on the upper Matamuri, that is, in the southern Hill Tracts. During the two preceding centuries, however, Chak or Sak probably constituted the majority of the inhabitants of the southern plains. There they became involved at various times in the struggle for control over Chittagong — a struggle carried on between Arakanese and Muslim rulers. Chittagong was definitively incorporated into the Mogul empire in 1666. Yet until the beginning of the 18th century Chakma chiefs still sought to have their position confirmed by the Arakanese king; and only at that time did an ancestor of the present chiefly line, who was coming from exile in Arakan, move his residence as far north as Rongunia on the Kornofuli.

While the history of the Chakma still poses many unsolved questions, there can be little doubt about the origin of the **Marma**. Their name for themselves is already suggestive of their connection to Arakan and Burma: "Marma," like "Burma," can be traced back to the old designation "Mranma," which the Burmese used for themselves. In older sources the Marma are referred to as "Mogh" (also written "Magh"), a pejorative term still used today by Bangalis. In the most ancient sources on Chittagong and Arakan, however, the use appears to be mixed with a certain amount of fear and respect. "Mogh" is probably to be derived from the same

Ethnic Migrations

Prior to 1600, Sak, Marma, Tippera, and Bangali immigrated into the Chittagong region. Later on, the Chakma emerged, the Mru moved from north Arakan into the southern part of the Chittagong mountains. After 1750 Marma fled from Arakan and entered the Hill Tracts; Lushai and Bawm moved westward.

- - - Borders since 1947
⊙ Old capital of Arakan
Ⓐ Marma centers, 16–19 C.
⟨S⟩ Sak prior to 15 C. (?)
Ⓢ Sak since 16 C.
⟨C⟩ Chakma prior to 1700 (?)
Ⓒ Chakma residence, 18–19 C.

◀◀
Marma-*ruatsa*. His son became headman.
◀
Chakma medical officer.

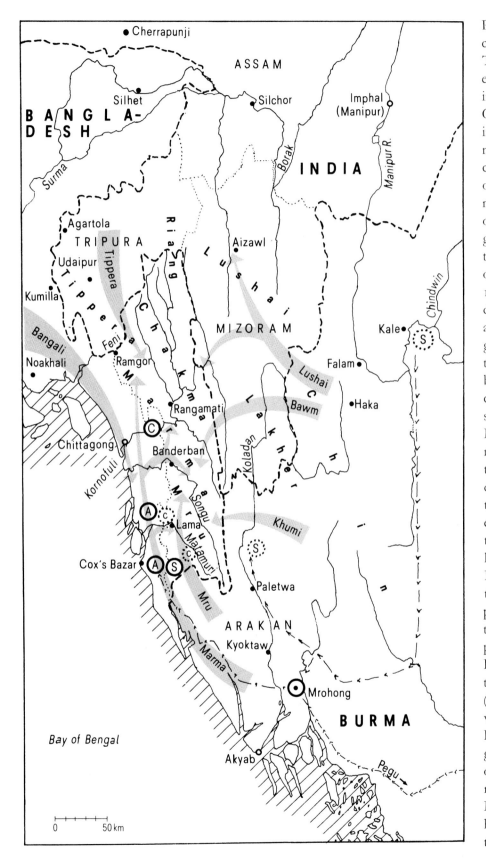

Persian source as our word "magician" and, in our context, denoted the "infidels" of Buddhist creed. To state that all Marma came from Arakan, however, is not to say that all contemporary Marma are indeed descendants of the erstwhile rulers of the Chittagong Plains — even if the *raja* of the Marma in the southern Hill Tracts, the so-called "Bohmong" (field marshall), may claim to have descended from the brother-in-law of the former king of Arakan. (This brother-in-law, incidentally, was not a Marma, but a descendant of the Mon dynasty of Pegu in lower Burma; and he was appointed governor of Chittagong by the king.) On the contrary, most of the forefathers of the Marma moved out of Arakan as that kingdom declined and was in 1784 incorporated into the Burmese empire, that is, during a time when the East Indian Company had already taken over the administration of the Chittagong region (1760). Repeated, but futile, attempts to throw off the yoke of the new Burmese rule brought more and more refugees into the English-controlled area. For the year 1798 alone a report speaks of 10,000 refugees; and in addition to the Marma, the Chakma and other hill tribes are also mentioned. One Marma group migrated from a tributary of the Koladan in Arakan; after intermediate stops on the Matamuri and in the low hills of the plains north of Chittagong, it reached its present place of residence in the northwestern part of the Hill Tracts around 1830. Marma, however, also lived on the southern Chittagong Plains: in Cox's Bazar and its backcountry. There the Bangalis are the new-comers; and since the end of the colonial period, more and more Marma have relinquished their possessions to these new-comers and sought protection and security once again in Arakan and Burma. A witness to this exodus is the deterioration of the once-magnificent Buddhist temples (made of teakwood), occurring simultaneously with the erection of new mosques. Not that Buddhists, as such, are persecuted. On the Chittagong Plains one finds a not insignificant minority of Buddhist Bangalis, who in the older sources are related at times to the Marma and are referred to as Marma-gri. These Bangalis refer to themselves, however, as **Borua**; and under this designation they have made a name for themselves in Calcutta

as cooks. In other places, though, they tend to belong to the more educated and highly respected strata of the Chittagong Plains. A Borua appears also in the chronicle of the royal house of the Chakma, as one of the *rajas*.

Colonial Administration

The three major ethnic groups living in the valleys of the Chittagong Hill Tracts are 1) the Tippera in the north (without a *raja* of their own, as long as one does not want to relate them to the *raja* of the Indian state of Tripura), 2) the Chakma (with their own *raja*) in the central and northeastern regions, and 3) the Marma with a *raja* both in the south and the northwest. The order in which they have just been mentioned corresponds approximately to the order of their movement into the Chittagong Hill Tracts. With respect to the history of the royal houses of the *rajas*, prior to 1750 it fades into darkness. In the case of the Chakma, it seems that the position of the *raja* was not consolidated before the Mogul rule; in the case of the Marma, as late as the English administration. Prior to that, each of the regional groups of both peoples had its own representatives. For both Muslim and English administrations, the Hill Tracts produced an interesting raw material: cotton. The inhabitants of the Hill Tracts were, at the same time, dependent on the plains for iron and salt. By throttling the free flow of these goods from the plains, permitting such trade only against payment of a tribute of cotton (and even leasing a monopoly of trade to the highest bidder), the rulers of the plains contributed to the gradual subordination, or elimination, of the minor group leaders who had acted as middlemen. Those coming out on top were those chiefs who had built their places of residence at the main gates of entry to the Hill Tracts, that is, at those places where the Kornofuli and the Songu flow onto the plains. After the British had set up their own administration over the Hill Tracts in 1860, it was these chiefs — namely, the Marma Bohmong and the Chakma Chief — who were held ultimately responsible by the British for the collection of taxes from all inhabitants of the southern and central regions. Only a few years earlier, the northern Marma had established themselves in such a way as to select their own *raja*; and because the British did not want to concede too much to the reigning *rani* of the Chakma, who was less than subservient, they eventually turned over the northern region to this "Mong Raja" (from the Burmese word "màng," meaning ruler), although the area was peopled mainly by Tippera.

Thus was created the Mong Circle in the north

A young Marma headman has had his inaugural celebration. Now he and his wife receive the blessings and congratulations of their relatives, who strew puffed rice over the celebrants' heads and slip white cotton threads onto their right hands.

◄◄

Flanked by the (British) Deputy Commissioner of the Hill Tracts and the (Bangali) Commissioner of Chittagong, the Marma Chief (Bohmong) of Banderban (in 1955) collects the field tax delivered to him by the headmen.

The three Chiefs of the Chittagong Hill Tracts (form left to right: Mong, Chakma, and Bohmong) with the then president of Pakistan, Ayub Khan.

(with the center of administration in Ramgor and the *rajbari* in Manikchori); the Chakma Circle, in the central region (with administrative center and *rajbari* in Rangamati, the principal city of the Chittagong Hill Tracts); and the Bohmong Circle, in the south (with administrative center and *rajbari* in Banderban). In addition to the portion of tax revenue to which these *rajas* were entitled — by that time these leaders were officially called "Chiefs" — the jurisdiction over minor legal matters and the selection of "headmen" for the newly-created smallest administrative units (the *"mouza"*) were also entrusted to them by the colonial administration.

The fact that in the course of these duties the *rajas* feathered their own nest did not escape the attention of the administration; yet in spite of suggestions for fundamental modifications, the system survived the colonial period. The Marma Chiefs particularly were looked upon by their subjects (including the Marma themselves) more as exploiters than leaders. One of the Chakma groups, the Tongcengya, does not traditionally recognize the Chakma *raja* as its representative. Yet a Chakma Chief was even able to legitimate democratically his position as representative for the entire Hill Tracts. In 1971 when all of Bengal voted for the Awami Party of Mujib-ur-Rahman, thereby signifying the commencement of the struggle for independence, the voters of the Hill Tracts chose the Chakma Chief, Tridiv Roy, as their representative to the Pakistani parliament. With his election, the Chakma Chief accepted his exil into Pakistan, while those who had elected him were, against their wills, incorporated into the new state of Bangladesh.

But we have rushed ahead of events. Let us return again to the beginning of the colonial era. Surely the *rajas* owed their rise to power to their role as middlemen between the inhabitants of the Hill Tracts and the representatives of what for them was a foreign state in Chittagong. Yet they were anything but zealous civil servants. They handed over hesitantly and irregularly the tributes they were required to pay. East of their region lived hill tribes, generally referred to as "Kuki" in the old sources, who made a name for themselves by raids reaching even into the district under British administration. The *rajas* received money and weapons in order to defend themselves against such attacks, but occasionally they made a pact with the raiders. This gave the British an excuse to extend their own system of control over the mountains, which they did in 1860. The area was placed under the jurisdiction of a Superintendent (from 1919, Deputy Commissioner) and was henceforth known as the "District of the Hill Tracts of Chittagong". In 1880-83 one-fifth of the region was declared forest reserve — most probably at that time there was almost no one living in these lands bordering on Lushai and "Shendu" country. Around 1900 the remainder was divided up into more than three hundred administrative units, called *"mouza"*. These units were meant to correspond to the village administrative bodies of the plains; in the mountains, however, they incorporated rather arbitrarily into one unit a varying number of hamlets, or villages, irrespective of ethnic affiliation. (Since official usage tends to regard the *mouza* as the equivalent of a "village," the several small villages included within the borders of a *mouza* will be called hamlets or settlements in order to avoid confusion.) It was the task of the "headmen" who oversaw these *mouza* to collect taxes — part of which they were entitled to keep — and settle minor disputes. In the hamlets of the *mouza*, which otherwise were independent, so-

◀◀
Pangkhua youth in festive dress.
◀
A Bawm man in traditional dress.

called *"karbari"* (managers) served without pay; these men were named to this post by the villagers themselves. The control was effective, and the inhabitants of the Hill Tracts proved to be peaceful people.

Minor Ethnic Groups

The free hill tribes of the east, however, continued to cause trouble. These tribes included above all the **Lushai** and the so-called "Shendu" (Lakher, Poi, and others). The Lushai were at the time expanding toward the northwest, superimposing themselves on the so-called "Old Kuki" group of tribes; the Shendu peoples were located south of the Lushai. The raids of these tribes were feared not only in the Chittagong region, but also in Arakan, Tripura, Kachar and Manipur. The weakness of the Lushai and other related groups was their practice of fighting each other in shifting alliances, as well as their willingness to include the British in this game. After fifty years of what were partially painful experiences in guerrilla warfare, the British eventually dispatched large units of troops from the west, north, and east and burned down every village whose chief they considered untrustworthy. Since the hill people could harvest only once a year, this policy helped to starve them out and thereby force the insubordinate Lushai to their knees. In 1898 the land of the Lushai was added to the province of Assam. Twenty years later the "Shendu" settling south of Lushai land—namely, the Lakher—also had to surrender; and for the sake of control, in 1924 their land was divided between the Chin Hills, the Arakan Hills and the Lushai Hills. This meant that at the 1947 partition of British India the Lakher, too, were apportioned to two countries: India and Burma.

After the "pacification" of the hill region by the British, the Lushai turned very quickly to Christianity and set out, with the Bible rather than armed violence, to bring their new culture to their neighbors. The fellowship of believers grew quickly and eventually had to face the consequences. The Lushai had once been nothing but a tribe; now it was made up of hundreds of thousands of Christians. Their old name seemed, therefore, inappropriate; so a new and more comprehensive designation was introduced. They became "Mizo" — in English something like "highlanders." As Lushai, they had been forced to accept the sovereignty of the British; as Mizo Christians, they reasserted their equality with the British. When they did not also receive *their* independence at the time the British pulled out and British India was partitioned, but were rather subordinated to India, the Mizo eventually took up arms again. In doing this they followed the lead of their northern brothers, the Naga, who also resorted to arms in their struggle for independence. In their armed fight the Mizo were supported by the other partner of the partition, namely, Pakistan.

Those people of the Chittagong Hill Tracts standing culturally closest to the Lushai are the **Pangkhua** and the **Bawm**. Linguistically, the Pangkhua are probably to be grouped with the so-called Old Kuki; ethnographically, however, very little is known about them. By absorbing parts of other tribes, the Bawm came into being during the 18th C. under the leadership of a "Shendu" aristocracy. ("Banjogi," the name by which they are called in the older literature, actually means "forest yogi" and is nothing but a Bangali corruption of "Bawm-Zo", the name these people use for themselves.) The aristocratic dynasty which united the Bawm had already died out by the beginning of this century, and the social hierarchy weakened. This was due not least of all to the missionary work of the Lushai. If the border had not been drawn between India and East Pakistan (now Bangladesh), the Bawm would surely in the long run also have been absorbed into the Mizo. Meanwhile, however, between 1960 and 1970, that is, during the Mizo struggle for independence, this small ethnic group doubled its some 3500 people as a result of newcomers fleeing the war-torn neighboring country. The mission work which the Lushai introduced into the Hill Tracts during the 1920s is now being carried on independently by the Bawm and the church they founded, the Christian Church of the Chittagong Hill Tracts. Those most likely to be attracted to the work of the mission are the other

Below:
A Lushai family (living in a Christian Bawm village), in festive dress. The women wear their long, homemade skirts which can also be used as wraps.
▶▶
Tongcengya woman.

small ethnic groups of the Hill Tracts: the Khumi, the Tongcengya, the Hill Tippera, the Khyang, and, finally, also the Mru.

These small ethnic groups are generally found in the transitional areas — that is, in small river valleys and on the lower crests of hills — between those unmistakable hill dwellers of eastern origin and those who are clearly valley dwellers. The hill dwellers include the Lushai, the Pangkhua and the Bawm. They are never attracted to the valleys and their villages are therefore nearly always found on hill tops and the spurs of hills. The Chakma, the Marma and the Tippera are, on the other hand, valley dwellers who will settle in higher regions only when pressed for lack of land.

The largest of the smaller ethnic groups mentioned above is the **Mru**, called "Murong" or "Murung" by the Bangalis, and "Mro" by the Marma. "Mru", as the people call themselves, denotes 'men' in general; in order to set themselves apart from others, "Mru-tsa" ("children of man") may also be used. They inhabit a relatively closed area in the southern part of the Hill Tracts, an area to which, according to their own tradition, they immigrated from Arakan several hundred years ago. Perhaps more than half of the Mru still live there today. The Arakan chronicles mention them as early as the first millennium and speak even of a Mru ruler of Arakan.

The language of the Mru can be assigned neither to the group of Burmese languages nor to the Naga-Chin languages. (In addition to Lushai, the Naga-Chin languages include Bawm and Pangkhua, Khumi and Khyang.) It rather claims an independent status within the framework of the Tibeto-Burman family. The Mru of the Chittagong region divide themselves into five linguistically and culturally distinctive groups: the Anok, the Tshüngma, the Dömrong, the Dopreng, and the Rümma. Anok means "West," although today this is the most northerly group south of Banderban; the northern section of the Tshüngma ("Mountain People") has joined the Anok, while its southern part in the upper Songu valley has adopted Khumi practices of house construction and festival celebration and calls itself "Longhu", the Khumi word for the Mru; the Dömrong, or "Lowlands" group, is at home north of the Matamuri; and, finally, the Dopreng and the Rümma ("Forest People") live in the far south and on into Arakan.

The ethnic group which is culturally most closely related to the Mru is the **Khumi**. In the Hill Tracts this people is represented by a relatively weak contingent in the far southeast; in Arakan, however, the Khumi comprise several 10,000 people. We know little about them, however. A small group of Khami, a tribe closely related to the Khumi, must

Hill Tippera (Mrung) women wear unique ear decorations and numerous necklaces.
◀◀
Sak women with the characteristic, large earrings.

also have come out of Arakan; these people have been absorbed today, as Rengmittsa, into the Mru living on the upper Matamuri. Though they still know some of their old language, they know nothing of the Khami in Arakan.

As far as the small group of **Khyang** is concerned, they claim, according to one source, to have always lived in the Hill Tracts; yet their language relates them to the most southerly Chin group in Arakan. ("Chin" is the anglicized form of the High Burmese pronunciation of "Khyang".) The Khyang live surrounded by Marma in the area between the Bohmong and Chakma Circles; and they have more or less taken over the culture of the Marma. It is also quite possible that the two groups came into the area together at the time the Burmese empire was expanding.

Finally, there are two groups of hill people who in the census enumerations are normally subsumed under groups whose language they share. On the one hand, there are the Hill Tippera, who are called **Mrun(g)** by the Marma and therefore occasionally confused with the Mru, who are called "Murung" by the Bangalis. The Hill Tippera also include the **Riang**, a group living in the northern Hill Tracts and above all in the Indian state of Tripura. All Tippera groups speak a language belonging to the Tibeto-Burman Bodo group in Assam; their culture, however, is not uniform, and the valley Tippera, as members of the Hindu caste system, do not recognize the Mrung and Riang as their equals. On the other hand, we have the **Tongcengya** (also written "Tanchangya", etc.), who are often called "Doi(n)gnak" in the older sources. ("Tong-cen" is a Marma word for "mountain clans"; "Doingna(k)" is the Marma pronunciation of the Mru designation for the Tongcengya, namely, "Dengnak"). Like their neighbors, the Chakma, the Tongcengya speak a local dialect of Bangla; but there are differences in culture, e.g., in their house form and style of dress. Also, the Tongcengya attach much importance to their *not* being subsumed under the Chakma. They are found both in the Kornofuli area, on the hills between Chakma and Marma, and, along with the Marma, in the southernmost part of the Hill Tracts on the border of Arakan. (An old source tells of Dengnak who came out of the mountainous area of Arakan, but who then returned). The Mrung, on the other hand, live spacially separated from the Tippera, widely scattered over the southern part of the Hill Tracts. As they came from the north, they possibly settled down in that area wherever they could still find unclaimed land.

It is improbable that these two groups were originally Tippera or Chakma who over time "degenerated" into hill people. It is more likely that they

Below:
Khumi girls dancing. Their skirts are somewhat longer than those of the Mru, their earpegs somewhat larger.
▶▶
Khyang man carrying a beer pot.

have largely assimilated themselves to the more civilized valley dwellers, but actually represent the "aboriginal people" of the Hill Tracts — with the Riang/Mrung being formerly located in the northern, and the Tongcengya/Dengnak in the southern, part of the Tracts. This distribution corresponds to the spheres of influence of the Tippera and Chakma prior to the massive influx of the Marma, that is, roughly in the seventeenth century. Because by that time, however, Mru may well have already moved into the southern Chittagong hills, while Dengnak may have migrated into Arakan, such early relationships between the two ethnic groups would help to explain the existence of an isolated Mru village which, though located in the middle of the Dengnak in the Chakma Circle, still preserved an exceedingly large number of old traditions. It is not at all impossible, however, that Mru were also absorbed into the Dengnak, though the two cultures today have little in common.

Population Figures and Development

After this short, historical overview of the ethnic groups of the Chittagong Hill Tracts, let us enumerate them again. There are 1) the Chakma and 2) the Tongcengya/Dengnak, both of whom speak a dialect of Bangla; 3) the Tippera and 4) the Riang/Mrung, both speaking a Bodo language; 5) the Marma, who speak a Burmese dialect; 6) the Bawm, 7) the Pangkhua, and 8) the Lushai, whose languages are classed as Central Chin; 9) the Khumi and 10) the Khyang, whose languages are classed with the Southern Chin; and, finally, 11) the Mru and 12) the Sak, with comparatively isolated languages, but languages which, nevertheless, like Burmese, Chin, and Bodo, are to be placed in the large Tibeto-Burman — or the even more comprehensive Sino-Tibetan — language family. To these twelve ethnic groups have been added in more recent times a few Santal, some Assamese, and, above all, Bangalis. (The Santal are representatives of a people whose home is in West Bengal and whose language belongs neither to the Indo-European, nor the Sino-Tibetan, language family.) Most of the Bangalis are Muslims, but some are Hindus or Borua, that is, Buddhists. All of these peoples are gathered in an area, including the forest reserves, of only 13,000 km², which is approximately the size of Connecticut.

If there is anywhere on earth where one can find within an area of a few square miles several different ethnic groups exhibiting distinctly different cultures, then it is in certain regions of the southern Chittagong Hill Tracts. Here, within one and the same *mouza*, one may find four groups speaking completely different languages, building different types of houses, wearing different clothing, and following different customs and different religions (Buddhism, Hinduism, Christianity and Animism). In order to be able to communicate with each other in spite of these differences, one must master sufficiently at least one additional language. This is particularly true for members of the smaller ethnic groups. Some Bangla, in the form of a reduced Chittagong dialect, is understood by most. In the Bohmong Circle, however, Marma is often preferred. English, the language of their erstwhile colonial masters, is common only to those who have a higher education, that is, above all the better-off social strata of the Chakma and Marma. English, however, is also mastered by a growing number of representatives of the Christianized ethnic groups, particularly the Bawm.

The diversity which is evident in a mere listing of ethnic groups and languages is, however, deceptive if it does not take the size of the groups into account. In order to compare group sizes, we would have to have accurate figures at our disposal. The official census, however, which was begun by the British in 1871 and which has been repeated every ten years since that time, has more and more neglected ethnic identification the closer one comes to the present. If the census of 1931 contained interesting material, those of 1941 and 1951 were, under the circumstances, not particularly informative; in 1961 notes on ethnic affiliation seem still to have been taken but are not to be found in the published report. The census of 1971 fell at the time of the Bangladesh war for indepencence. The official figures published in 1981 may not be fully reliable; but, in any case, they come much closer to my own extrapolations than privately published, imaginary figures.

Distribution of Ethnic Groups

The map shows the distribution in 1965. Highest densities are reached in the Chakma circle, where the people were pushed together as a result of the flooding in connection with the manmade lake. The borders drawn between the signs for the ethnic groups (each sign stands for ca. 500 persons) are meant to facilitate the orientation; they exist neither officially nor inofficially – the heterogeneity is actually much greater.

A Marma
B Bangali
C Chakma
D Tongcengya (Dengnak)
H Khyang (Hyou)
K Khumi
L Lushai
M Mru
P Pangkhua
R Riang/Mrung
S Sak
T Tippera
Z Bawm-Zo
Ⓑ 5000 persons, mostly Bangali

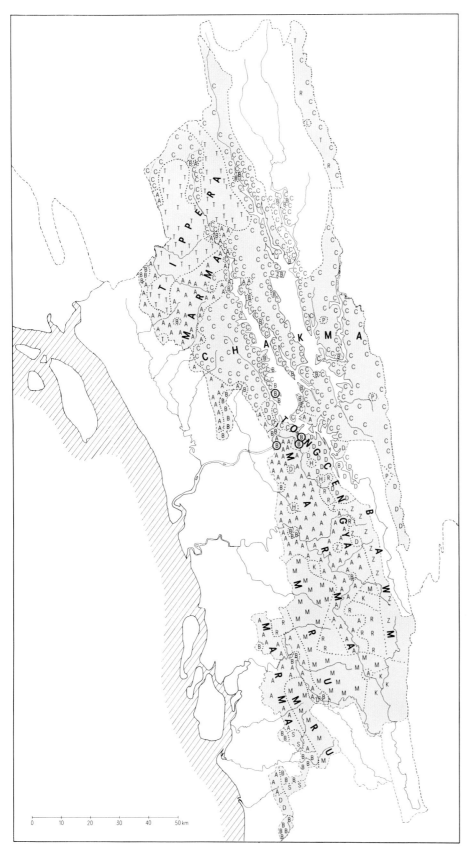

During my first period of field research in the Hill Tracts (1955-1957), the leader of the expedition, Dr. H. E. Kauffmann, secured the field-tax lists from the office of the Bohmong in Banderban. These lists recorded, by name and village, the household heads charged with the tax. From the names one can with some certainty determine the ethnic affiliation. Summing up the number of ethnically-identified households and multiplying the sum by the average number of persons per household, one gets the approximate strength of the ethnic groups (although in each case a few households which were not obliged to pay the tax will be missing). I myself was able to view the lists for the central and northern Circles. Difficulties, however, arose in relation to name identification, since both the Chakma and Tongcengya, as well as the Tippera, have Hindu names. The ethnic affiliations were eventually established by means of additional information and were finally checked against the census data, inasmuch as the religious affiliation — though not the ethnic affiliation — was included; and most of those persons classified as members of Hindu castes are probably Tippera. The figures given here for 1981 are rough estimates, which need not be accurate.

Ethnic Group	1901	1956	1981
Chakma	44500	140000	230000
Tongcengya		15000	20000
Marma	35000	80000	120000
Sak		2000	1500
Khyang	500	1000	1500
Tippera	23000	30000	40000
Mrung/Riang		7000	10000
Mru	10500	17000	20000
Khumi	1500	2500	1000
Bawm	1500	3500	8000
Pangkhua	200	1500	2000
Lushai	?	500	1000
	118000	300000	455000
Bangali	7000	30000	290000
Total	125000	330000	745000

Taking all uncertainties regarding the estimates into account, the table still shows that the Chakma, who once made up one-third of the indigenous

population, now account for at least one-half of the indigenous population. The expansion is due primarily to the constantly growing number of children over the past decades. This growth, however, is no sign of wealth, but rather of increasing poverty. The comparatively small growth rate of the Tippera, which contrasts the high one of the Chakma, is to be explained by the fact that the Tippera, as Hindu, have increasingly been driven from their homeland. The Marma and the Tippera seem to be the smaller ethnic groups when compared to the Chakma, but only because their areas of settlement were cut up by the political boundaries established at the partition of British India. If the Bangalis today want to force these ethnic groups back into their areas of origin, then it should be pointed out that when the Chittagong Hill Tracts were first consolidated as a political territory by the British, the one and only people who were positively not yet settled in the Tracts were the Bangalis themselves. The present government would like to transform the Hill Tracts into a home for Bangalis, in spite of the unpleasant fact that the one and only ethnic group already speaking a Bangla dialect is the selfsame group offering the most obstinate resistance to the government's policy.

The British pursued completely different goals. When they began from 1789 onward to require the representatives of the Hill Tracts to pay their tribute in money rather than in cotton, as had formerly been the case, they could not have known what the consequences would be. Surely the money economy would in time, and without such measures, have displaced the barter economy. The forced use of money, however, resulted immediately in an increasing indebtedness to Bangali moneylenders, since money was obtainable only through trade with the plains dwellers. The goods imported from the plains increased in number and kind, and the volume of produce obtained by the hill dwellers from their traditional agriculture was substantial enough to enable them to buy luxury goods. But the hill dwellers did not understand much about market trading. As far as the traditional agriculturalists are concerned, this is still true today, even though, in the meantime, successful traders and entrepreneurs also appeared among the Chakma and Marma. Lending businesses were not part of the traditional culture. 'Debts' were in the form of long-term mutual obligations; only the aristocrats among the valley dwellers and eastern ethnic groups grew rich by turning debtors into slaves. Price fluctuations and usury, which enabled clever moneylenders, for example, during the 1950s to squeeze annually up to 500% of a loan out of their debtors, was – and still is today – something far

Bangali traders on the Songu transport the export products of the Chittagong Hill Tracts: cotton in dugouts, thatching grass on long bamboo rafts.

◄◄

Bangali trader weighing dried tobacco leaves.

beyond that with which a simple farmer can come to grips. Since such lending and borrowing relationships are understandably loaded with tension, the common man generally tries to avoid giving a loan to a person of his own ethnic group. This means, however, that those suddenly finding themselves in need almost inevitably fall into the hands of foreign moneylenders. Against the exploitative manipulations of such persons, the debtors are again unable to defend themselves, since all legal means are in the hands of those who also control the market, namely, the Bangalis.

As early as 1870 Lewin described the numerous tricks and types of chicanery used by Bangali moneylenders who attempted in court to extract all they could from some inexperienced hillman – a hillman who had gotten deep into debt due to a poor harvest or a wedding. In such cases, it was not rare for a debtor to suddenly find himself in a situation of lifelong dependency. Lewin, therefore, fixed the annual interest rate at 12%; and whenever a court had validated a claim, the outstanding debts had to be collected immediately or they were written off. The efforts of the British, however, appear in the long run to have changed little. When in the 1950s the courts were for a time supervised by the Pakistani military government, a certain Bangali moneylender was, against all expectations, condemned to pay back the debtor. The moneylender, however, had already wrangled an exhorbitant payment out of the Marma involved. Over a period of three years, the moneylender had collected ten times the amount of rice originally lent, and as settlement for the remaining debt was now demanding more than the man's entire harvest.

When a few Bangali policemen were finally disciplined for blackmail and rape, the inhabitants of the Hill Tracts recognized the Pakistani government as their new friend; and it is no wonder that Bangali endeavors to attain independence elicited little positive response from the hill people. The simple hill dwellers would have much preferred to have again been placed under the protection of the British, even if the British had demanded multiple taxes. Such statements, voiced by the people themselves, throw some light on the close connection between economy and politics.

When the British administration recognized that it could not solve the region's problems through the courts alone, it drew up special regulations for the Hill Tracts. The initial Rules of 1892 were followed by the Chittagong Hill Tracts Regulations of 1900; in 1921 the Hill Tracts were declared a "backward tract", and in 1935, by receiving the status of a "totally excluded area", they were withdrawn from the central and provincial legislature. Besides laying down special functions for the Chiefs and headmen, these regulations, by means of special rules regarding land acquisition and residence rights, provided for an effective check on a further influx of Bangalis. The markets which had in the meantime grown up were, likewise, placed under special supervision, in order to prevent the intrusion of "dishonest" traders and merchants. During the Pakistani era, however, in spite of the resistance of the Chiefs, the special status was partially revoked and immigration became possible again. The Bangali government completely eliminated the discrimination against its own people, abrogated in 1981 all special privileges of the Chiefs, and in 1989 finally abolished the Regulations of 1900 altogether.

Prior to 1900, though, the British administration had already taken measures which inadvertently furthered the influx of Bangali settlers. The tradi-

The "Karnafully Paper Mills Ltd." in Chondroghóna, the first factory on the border of the Chittagong Hill Tracts and once the largest paper mill of Asia. Here, wood and bamboo extracted from the Hill Tracts are processed.

tional method of tilling a field, slash-and-burn cultivation (which will be discussed in Chapter 3), had seemed to the British a harmful practice — all the more so since the easy mobility it afforded the farmers was thought to be politically risky. In 1870 slash-and-burn cultivation was therefore forbidden on the plains; however, sedentary plowing, which in the meantime had become the ideal and generally-practiced method on the plains, could not be introduced in the mountains. Only in the wide valleys of the central and northern Hill Tracts were there a few places where plowing appeared possible. The first "development-aid" money was used to help purchase the tools and animals needed for plowing, and what the *rajas* already practiced on their estates on the plains now gained entry into the valleys: plowing done by Bangali share-croppers. Even though the hill farmers at first seemed rather reluctant to set their own hand to the plow, after 1900, a growing number of Chakma, Tippera, and Marma turned to plow cultivation; and this changeover indicates that land was already becoming scarce. The traditional slash-and-burn method of cultivation brings higher yields as long as ample fallow periods are possible. Fields which are plowed but not regularly irrigated yield less; yet because they may be cultivated every year, plowed fields allow for a substantially higher density of population.

During the first half of this century, land in the valley regions was brought under the plow. The largest part of this land was located in the Chakma Circle (the rapid growth of the Chakma has already been mentioned); and precisely this land in the valleys of the Kornofuli and its tributaries had to fall victim to a new project, namely, an artificial lake. This "Kaptai Hydroelectric Project" was to produce the badly needed energy for the electrification of Chittagong. Of the some 85,000 people whose land disappeared in 1960 under the new man-made lake — among them approximately 70,000 Chakma — 46,000 lived primarily from plow cultivation. To replace the lost 585 km², the government allowed 40 km² of forest-reserve land to be taken over by farmers and turned into plowed fields, and relocated Bangalis received preference. Following the resettlement of the Bangalis, the remaining "available" land was mostly land already under slash-and-burn cultivation. The shortage of suitable land resulted therefore in massive unrest and overexploitation of existing resources. In search of new land, some Chakma migrated all the way to north Assam and the foothills of the Himalayas. The Pakistani military government, however, under whose protection this whole process had taken place, knew very well how to blame all mismanagement on subordinate Bangali officers; the blame placed on these officers only contributed to the traditional Chakma mistrust of Bangalis, a mistrust which was subsequently transformed into bitter hostility.

Living in an area already strongly influenced by the economic system of the plains, the concerned Chakma and Marma were surely not people with whom other hill people would have felt any particular solidarity. Similarly, the valley dwellers, with their *raja*, had always considered the less civilized hill people to be quite different from themselves and not in the least tied to them by a common origin. The fact that they now had to contend with these people for land only added to their feeling of separateness and a lack of common interest; thus the building of the Kaptai dam had no further political repercussions. It is true that in the European embassies in Dhaka the rumor went around that Christian Chakma were being persecuted; yet if D. E. Sopher, an American geographer interested in the transition from slash-and-burn to plow agriculture, had not almost accidentally been eyewitness to the 1960 flooding, we would not know even today what really happened there. The government prevented further research by declaring Sopher a *persona non grata*. A few years later, in 1964, the entire Hill Tracts were closed to foreigners; and up until today they have not been reopened. What has happened in the area since that time was not supposed to be known to the outside world. The information which in spite of these measures has managed to make its way out of the area will be briefly discussed in the final chapter.

▶
Perched on high poles closed toward the outside world – the back of a Mru house.

Next page:
Women returning to the hamlet with harvested cotton.

◀
Water is being bottled in gourds straight from a spring which during the rainy season has turned into a small waterfall.

▶
Young girls wash their hair in the small pond below the spring.

Next page:
Men bind split rails and rafters to a thick bed of bamboo leaves with which they have covered the roof.

◀
Growing girls help early around the house. An older sister cares for her small brother: she carries him in a shawl (like the one hanging on the platform railing in the background) or, when he is older, on the hip.

▶
A young man with a fancy headdress sits in the door of his father's house. After dyeing cotton, his hands are the color of indigo.

The large living room, with a view of the door leading to the private quarters: at the left, the fireplace; under the roof, the loft where bamboo mats and baskets are stored; bathed in the light coming through the door, the small sewing basket of the young woman seated at the loom.

Standing in the entrance to the house, a young girl winds the spun thread onto a manual spindle.

With the help of long headbands, the women carry baskets weighted with water-filled gourds as they return from the spring. The platform of the house looms high against the blue December sky.

Right side:
The wall of the bamboo cane can be split into thinner and thinner strips. One needs straps and thongs of various strengths to tie together the building components of a house, to weave a basket, etc.

Next page:
All of the building components of a Mru house are tied together with bamboo thongs. Two men are just lashing bundles of thatching grass onto the rafters.

It takes a lot of practice to be able to use the hewing knife skillfully.

Right side:
A simple storage basket is under construction.

Next page:
In the evening sun, a man is weaving a large basket which will be used to transport cotton.

House and Home

As has already been mentioned in the preceding chapter, Mru hamlets are not found at any fixed elevation. The most important consideration has to do with the available water supply: there must be a water source near the hamlet which does not run dry even in the dry season. This may be a small brook or stream. That a settlement is located above a stream is unavoidable; that it, however, is also always found above a spring — so that water must be carried *up* to the village — surely indicates that higher residential locations are preferred whenever available. If the source runs dry too often, one has a reason to move; illnesses which occur too frequently may also prompt the relocation of a settlement.

Hamlets

In general, however, hamlets remain in the same place for decades, although the inhabitants may well change. Whenever official statements all too gladly characterize the hill dwellers of the Hill Tracts as semi-nomads, they paint a false picture, but one which is supported by the official government practice of recognizing a hamlet under the name of its *karbari* or headman. This practice results in the constant "disappearance" of old settlements and the "appearance" of new ones, although it is the settlement *names* only which actually disappear. Some hamlets may not have their own proper names; in such a case the settlement is known by the name of its founding sib or the name of the stream on which it is located. "My" hamlet, which was situated on the crest of a hill, was bisected by the boundary of a *mouza*; and each of its two parts was registered in the tax lists under the name of its respective *karbari*. The people living in the other *mouza*, the majority of whom were members of the Atuang sib, called the entire hamlet "Atuang-wüa-Kua"; in my *mouza*, however, the hamlet was known as "Tap-wüa-Kua" ("Village of the Fortress-People"). This latter name recalls a previous time, more than a hundred years ago, when the settlement was still fortified. The last traces of even earlier inhabitants were found in the form of an old tombstone located just outside the hamlet. (Incised on this stone was a head with feather decorations.) These inhabitants were no doubt the Bawm, who for a short time pushed into the mountain chain west of the Songu valley. According to their own traditions, however, the Bawm retreated again to the eastern chain of mountains because of too many diseases.

It is generally difficult to identify a Dengnak hamlet, since their houses stand isolated in the middle of the fields. On the other hand, one may find hundreds of Lushai houses grouped into one village; and the paths to their fields are correspondingly long. The Mru hit a happy medium between the two extremes: five to twenty houses generally make up a hamlet. Among the Marma, who have larger settlements and therefore longer paths to the fields, entire families often move into the field-houses during the time of cultivation. The Mru walk each day to and from their fields; and often two or three families will join together, working the field of one family one day and the field of another family the next. Among the Marma such forms of cooperation are rare. The correlation between cooperation and settlement size is, however, not so simple. The Lushai and Bawm also prefer to cooperate in the fields rather than live there as single families, even though they must walk longer distances. In the past when warring was common, large villages could better defend themselves against attack; isolated families in the fields had to fear for their own safety. Today, on the other hand, people would like to have churches and schools in the villages; and such can be afforded only when settlements are large.

Small hamlets does not mean isolated hamlets. Unmarried Mru rarely find proper marriage

◀ If a man needs a new blade for the hewing knife, he must buy it from a Bangali trader at the bazaar. One rarely has enough money to buy more than what will fit into a shoulder bag or a man's carrying basket.

partners in their home hamlet; during the dry season, therefore, young men may occasionally leave their hamlet in order to pay an evening visit to some neighboring hamlet. If a celebration should happen to be taking place in one of the hamlets, young girls also go along. Married persons may also be especially invited for one reason or another. It can happen, however, that two neighboring hamlets are not on particularly good terms. Hamlet boundaries are not officially marked — only the *mouza* boundaries are clearly set; and as land becomes more and more scarce, people more frequently plant their crops on a plot which is also claimed by a neighboring hamlet. Should someone from that neighboring hamlet then answer the encroachment by a similar invasion, the relationship between the two hamlets can be permanently damaged. In such a case, the footpath connecting the two settlements grows over.

Paths

It takes only one rainy season for a path to grow over, and the only footpaths always kept cleared are those leading to the hamlet of the *mouza* headman. Wherever relationships between neighboring hamlets are good, however, villagers agree upon the boundary up to which each hamlet is obliged to keep the connecting path cleared; most of the time this boundary corresponds to the dividing line between the fields being worked by the inhabitants of the two hamlets. Once a year, after the paddy has been cut and the rainy season has almost come to an end, every household supplies one man; and together these men clear the connecting paths. The footpath to one's own field is cleared by the person himself, and it is cleaned up to four times a year: before the fieldwork begins; in July, during the weeding period; before the rice is harvested; and, if necessary, again before the cotton harvest. Footpaths used frequently by many people doubtless grow over less easily or quickly than private ones. If an obstacle, such as a fallen tree or a landslide, blocks a public path, however, no one takes the trouble to remove it if he or she can go around it in less time or with less trouble. Should a really lovely path leading along the crest of a hill suddenly take a sharp, unpleasant turn downward and continue so for some distance before turning up again, one can be sure that there was once a cultivated field located on that spot below the ridge. (Why should people take the trouble to keep a comfortable or pleasant public path cleared, when someone is going to keep the footpath to his own field cleared anyway?) If a person cuts bamboo close to a footpath, without any hesitation he leaves the cut-off branches and chips on the path, in spite of the fact that these bamboo chips, which are as sharp as arrows, can be dangerous for even the most thickly-calloused Mru feet. During the earlier days of warfare, two bamboo sticks sharpened on both ends were used to "mine" a footpath. The sticks were twisted tightly together in such a way that, no matter how they fell, one point always stuck upward over the other three. Dozens of these mantraps were hidden on a path, if possible under leaves; and whoever stepped on one of these points could count on its going straight through his foot.

In spite of all the discomforts they offer, Mru footpaths are laid out in a truly masterful way. First of all, one makes sure that during the rainy season the paths are not washed out by the rain and thereby transformed into slopes of scree. Wherever it is possible, therefore, the paths run along the top of a watershed, even when this leads down the slope; and at places where this is not feasible, paths are moved to the right or the left for short stretches. One does not by any means always choose the shortest route. Smaller valleys and depressions, for example, are often circumvented by walking around the rim. Steepness, however, is no obstacle; if necessary, one uses a notched tree trunk as a staircase — like the one used at home. The most popular paths, though, are those which do not have to be cleared, those which nature herself, so to speak, makes freely available. These are the waterways. Path and riverbed are often more or less identical. Most of the time during the dry season, only a small trickle of water flows over these paths made of scree; but it does not in any way disturb a Mru to have to wade through water up to his waist. A Mru, however, cannot swim. For this reason he prefers to walk along the edge of a river — even a large river — rather than use the dugout of one of

A mantrap — made from two small, sharpened bamboo sticks which have been twisted together.

A Mru hamlet located on a spur of the chain of mountains west of the Songu.
▶

The path to the fields is often difficult, yet with a tree-ladder even steep slopes can be child's play.
▶▶

Bamboo is absolutely necessary for the construction of a house. Strong young men are needed to carry the heavy bundles of bamboo canes from the jungle to the village.

◀◀
A young man brings big bundles of thatching grass (*Imperata*) into the hamlet.
◀
Formerly, in times of war, the Mru reinforced their village gates with long spikes. Today one finds only symbolic representations of this practice. They, as well as the monkey armed with bow and arrow towering over the village gate, are intended to repel epidemics. Strangers are not permitted to enter a village marked in this way.

the river dwellers. Walking is, first of all, cheaper, since one would have to pay to be ferried across. Secondly, it is safer, since a Mru would constantly fear that the boat might capsize. Under such circumstances, riverbed paths are much preferred by the Mru. For me they were horrible: slipping from the slick stones and scrapping my ankles on the scree, with shoes full of water and, often enough, with wet trousers, I could never keep pace with the Mru.

Until I had made the Mru whistle technique of breathing my own, I also had some trouble keeping pace when climbing uphill — whistling enables one to better control the rhythm of breathing, thus preventing the mucous in the mouth from drying out. Steep descents, however, remained problematic. The footholes which offered Mru toes a secure foothold did not give my boots much help; and the two times I attempted in desperation to go unshod, thinking it might work better, I failed due to the relative instability of the soles of my feet. The fact that Bangali police and military personnel all wear shoes and, in addition, know nothing about mountain climbing has proved an advantage for the hill dwellers: they have been protected from too many unwanted visitors. (This will also continue to protect them until the roads necessary for "the opening up of the Hill Tracts" have been constructed with development-aid money.) During the last world war, the attack of the Japanese on India, which was launched from Burma, got stuck in these "hills" — and already on the Arakan side. I have walked hundreds of miles on Mru footpaths and have heard even the Mru complain that their footpaths are "not fit for a dog," but the Mru love their land and can with justification become enthusiastic about its beauty. Why should they construct paths which would offer easier access to the foreigners who want to snatch their land from them?

Houses

In earlier times Mru settlements were fortified. Today a gate reinforced with bamboo spikes will still be constructed in order to signify the symbolic closing of a hamlet, e.g., in the case of a "bad

Below:
Many springs dry up during the dry season. Wherever even a little water seeps out, however, the water hole is sealed off by a barricade, so that neither animals nor people can stumble into it and thereby transform it into a mudhole. Women use half of a split gourd as a ladle, in order to fill their water bottles.

▶▶

In a brook or stream women wash dishes and clothing, as well as themselves. A mass of bamboo threads may be used for scrubbing pots; it is more pleasant to clean one's skin with a soapstone – something also used to do the wash.

death." Under normal circumstances, however, everyone may enter freely, though Mru settlements are not particularly inviting to outsiders. Whenever one approaches a Mru village, particularly when climbing up the slope, one is confronted with the solid backs of houses. These solid walls tower on posts far above the head and are broken only occasionally by narrow slits or lookouts. A person finds admittance only from the side of the village square; and where the ground is in fact very uneven, one may get the impression that the houses are built in complete disarray. There is nothing to suggest the clear order which is found among the Chakma — the Chakma turn all of their houses toward the east because they love to have the morning sun on their platforms. Mru houses, however, are much larger than those of the Chakma. Compared with Mru houses, for example, the dwellings of the simple Bangali plains farmers are nothing but huts. In contrast to the Bangalis, though, the Mru and the Chakma have something in common: their houses stand on stilts. (This is a practice common to much of Southeast Asia where traditional cultures still prevail.) In a country of monsoon rains, the Mru would consider it quite unwise to build their houses directly on the ground as the Bangalis do. Due to the natural unevenness of their land, they would, in addition, be obliged to move a considerable amount of soil.

As a general rule, trunks of hardwood trees, from which the bark has been removed, serve as the main posts and major crossbeams of Mru houses. (The better the wood, the more durable and long-lasting the house.) Other posts may, if necessary, be replaced by bundles of bamboo. The choice of material is dependent upon availability, since increasing deforestation has reduced the constant supply of large hardwood trees; and in some places even bamboo has become scarce. Whereas in former times one needed only go to the edge of the village to cut whatever one wanted, today one is often obliged to seek materials in neighboring villages. Before one is allowed to chop down what one needs, however, one must attain the consent of the villages concerned; otherwise, they might file a complaint with the headman, and the transgressor

may be fined. On top of that, one has the inconvenience of carrying the supplies home over long distances; and if villagers assist in the cutting and carrying of materials, they must be paid for their labor. Since the floor and walls of a Mru house are made of bamboo, a shortage of bamboo means that houses can be refurbished less often. After a few rainy seasons, the original yellow-brown color of the bamboo walls is transformed into a speckled gray; and the village begins to take on a dowdy and poor appearance — no mere deception when the means of renovation is no longer available.

Houses situated on exposed slopes are more subject to wind and rain than those lying in protected valleys. Generally speaking, however, bamboo and softwood pieces should be renewed every 5 to 10 years, though this depends much on location. In the past, when building materials were plentiful and when one was allowed to cut wood anywhere except in official forest reserves, purely hardwood constructions would surely have made for more durable houses. One could, for example have used teakwood boards. Yet even the Marma, whose Buddhist temples were made of teakwood, preferred bamboo for their homes. This was not without reason. A floor made of boards is hard, whereas one of woven bamboo strips is flexible. (With a simple blanket, one sleeps on a bamboo floor as on a mattress.) Similarly, a board wall means a dark room, whereas a bamboo wall may be penetrated by hundreds of narrow beams of light. Bamboo also allows fresh air to enter; so even an inside room of a bamboo house having small windows is never dark or stuffy.

A Mru house consists of three basic parts. First, there is a large room, the *kim-tom* (ca. 7 × 7 m. [23 × 23 ft.]), with an outside entrance. This room is a kind of living room in which people cook and eat, receive visitors, and accommodate guests. Children and the unmarried members of the family also sleep in the *kim-tom*. Secondly, there is a narrower and somewhat lower room, the *kimma*, with a separate roof. Though being situated on the side of the village square and in front of the *kim-tom*, this room is accessible only from the *kim-tom*. At night the *kimma* serves as a bedroom for the marri-

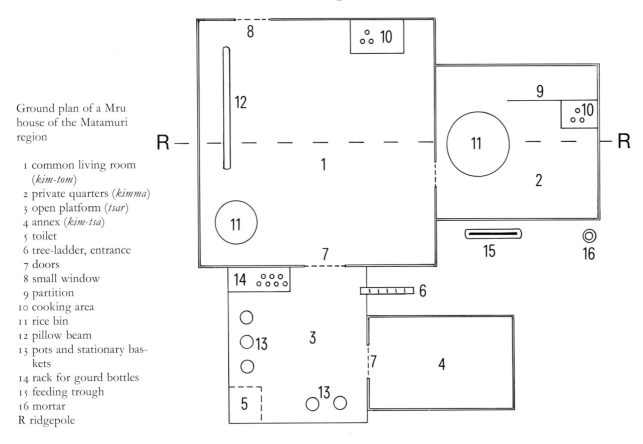

Ground plan of a Mru house of the Matamuri region

1 common living room (*kim-tom*)
2 private quarters (*kimma*)
3 open platform (*tsar*)
4 annex (*kim-tsa*)
5 toilet
6 tree-ladder, entrance
7 doors
8 small window
9 partition
10 cooking area
11 rice bin
12 pillow beam
13 pots and stationary baskets
14 rack for gourd bottles
15 feeding trough
16 mortar
R ridgepole

A Mru house. The *kimma* is turned toward the village square; here the women hull the family's daily supply of rice. The roof of the *kim-tom* juts out over the *kimma*. To the left is the *tsar*, which is almost hidden by the *kim-tsa* built in front of it. The latter serves as a storeroom or an additional *kimma* for a younger brother.

ed couple and their smaller children; in the frontmost part of the room, where there is a second fireplace, children are born. Strangers are not permitted to enter the *kimma*; and if the door to the *kimma* is open, they should not even look inside. The view is blocked anyway, though, by the large, round storage bin placed directly behind the door. (This large basket holds the year's rice harvest.) Spears, cloth, and other things of value, as well as cotton and vegetables, are also kept in the *kimma*. If a stranger would still like to look into the *kimma*, in spite of the prohibition, he must be prepared to get an eye disease. It is therefore better to wait until the wall of the *kimma* must be renewed; for at that time one has a full view of the room for an entire day — and a view which embarrasses no one. During the period of repair, the married couple sleeps in the *kim-tom*; and no one would renovate a house at the same time that a birth is expected. The prohibition then is really intended only as a defense against the "evil eye": it will return to its sender. Finally, there is the open platform, the *tsar*, approximately 5 × 5 m. (ca. 16 × 16 ft.), which is built onto the right or left side of the *kim-tom* and is accessible only from that room. If one wishes to dry the rice — which one must do in order to avoid mold — one spreads it out on a large bamboo mat on the *tsar*. If there are vegetables to be cleaned and washed, animals to be carved up, vessels and dishes to be washed, or other work to be done which would dirty the inside of the house, this is also done on the *tsar*, since water runs immediately through the bamboo slats and, thereby, off the floor. On the *tsar* one rinses one's mouth out after eating; on this platform one could also wash clothing or oneself. Since water for washing or bathing must first be fetched in gourds from the spring or brook, however, one generally prefers to wash or bathe at the water-source itself. (Using warm water for washing is consequently rare.) Finally, if a corner of the *tsar* is particularly isolated — or even if not — it serves as a toilet. Even if this area of the *tsar* is not specifically marked, one recognizes it immediately by the bamboo strips placed there to be used as toilet paper, as well as the opening left in the slat grid-work. Generally, the designated corner serves only as a urinal. (The women do their business standing, the men squatting — just the opposite, therefore, from our practice). In an emergency, however, it may also be used for defecation. One normally prefers to do the latter, though, in a place on the backside of the village. At night, when the path to this outside toilet is dark, one could unexpectedly step on a poisonous snake or, apart from that, meet an evil spirit. Children particularly, then, cannot be expected to go out at night!

Now, one might think that this practice would create a stench in the neighborhood of every house, but that is not the case. The pigs, which are allowed to run loose, demolish all kitchen trash and human faeces; and the slanting incline which is always found under the *tsar* sees to it that all water runs off quickly. The only disadvantage of the *tsar* is the fact that its thin bamboo slats rot quickly, since they are often washed over with water. Unless the slatting is annually repaired, one is occasionally in danger of stepping down into open space. This disadvantage, however, means once again that the *tsar* never becomes very dirty, for its renovation sooner or later becomes imperative.

Wealthy people occasionally build themselves an additional storage room, a *kim-tsa*, on the other side of the *tsar*. This room is shaped like a *kimma* and, when a son of the family marries, can also be used as such. Houses with three *kimma* are unusual. (The *kimma* of the household head is always the one built directly onto the *kim-tom*.) A French sociologist, P. Bessaignet, had the bad luck of landing in just such a house and therefore came to the conclusion that the Mru live in extended families. This is, however, completely false, since, generally speaking, every married Mru male values greatly being the head of his own household. A widow or a widower who lives with a married son must again, like the unmarried, sleep in the *kim-tom*; in such a case, a room is often partitioned off by a special wall. A private sleeping compartment may also be constructed for the oldest unmarried daughter still living at home. The *kim-tom*, with its floor-space of approximately 50 m.² (500 ft.²), is always large enough to take care of the everyday needs of any Mru family — as well as those special needs on festive occasions.

Bamboo work

Bamboo is the most essential rawmaterial for house construction. For the preparation of floors and walls, bamboo canes are fashioned into flat, wide strips. In order to be able to roll out the cane, one must first notch well the knotted joints. This is done with a hewing knife, first on the outside (above), then after slowly spreading the cane open, on the inside (below).

Since the central village square is often the highest point of the locality, the front wall of the *kimma*, which faces the square, usually stands on lower stilts (or poles) than the back wall of the *kim-tom*. This means that the distance of open space under the two walls can vary from one-half to five (or more) meters. The smaller space (under the *kimma*) is panelled laterally with small bamboo canes; at night the front part of this basement serves as a pigsty and the back part as a chicken coop. Firewood is stacked in the large, open space beneath the *kim-tom* and testifies to the industriousness — or lack of such — of the housewife and (possibly) her marriagable daughter.

House Construction

The building of a house is a communal undertaking involving all the village men and lasts several days. First of all, trees and bamboo must be selected, cut, and carried to the village. Long tree trunks which have a diameter of more than 20 cm. (8 in.) are so heavy that no one person alone could transport them or lift them up into place. Neither cars nor machines are available to the Mru; given the circumstances, such conveniences could not be utilized anyway. The ax and the hewing knife are the only two tools suitable for the work at hand. First, the main ten posts of the *kim-tom* are set into position. The holes for these posts, dug with hewing knives converted into digging sticks, are dug in two parallel rows about 4.20 m. (14 ft.) apart. Each row has four posts spaced about 2.10 m. (7 ft.) apart; then two posts are placed between the rows, at the front and back. These two posts tower above the others and will later support the ridgepole of the roof. All of these posts will later stand within the interior of the house, only 20 cm. (8 in.) from the back wall but 1.40 m. (4.6 ft.) from the side walls. Slightly inside the line of the wall, somewhat thinner and shorter posts are set up. These are notched on the outside of the top end; and a pole which will later serve as the purlin is tied lengthwise in the notch.

Additional rows of posts are set up still closer to the edges; these posts, which are notched at the top, reach up only to the bottom of the floor and

Next, one smoothes out the inside (above). Finally, the resulting strips are woven together to make the floor (with the outsides turned upward) (below).

The wall panels are made in the same way. First, the vertical strips are placed close together; then the horizontal strips are woven in between them. This time, the inside of the bamboo is turned toward the interior of the room, since the hard and smooth outer side is better suited to repel rain and moisture.

support the lowest beams of the floor, which are approximately 10 cm. (4 in.) in diameter. Upon this lowest layer, which runs lengthwise, eleven pieces of wood are placed crosswise: in the middle between, and on either side of the main posts. They are supported by perpendicular posts staggered with the main posts. The perpendicular posts, moreover, are propped up from left and right — and the crosswise, horizontal posts, from front and back — by still other wooden pieces some 10 cm. (4 in.) thick. Then follow a layer of bamboo poles lengthwise, a layer crosswise, and then a second layer lengthwise. (The poles laid out crosswise are placed about 30 cm. [12 in.] apart, and those of the second lengthwise layer, some 5 cm. [2 in.] apart). The floor itself, which consists of woven bamboo strips (15-20 cm. [6–8 in.] wide), is finally laid out on the third and last layer of poles.

In order to prepare these bamboo strips, one splits open one side of a bamboo cane so that the inner side of the knotted joints can be reached; these joints are then notched in such a way that the canes bend completely open and can be freed of all remainders of the knots. In the construction of the foundation, all points of intersection (where perpendicular posts come together with poles, bamboo, or wooden pieces running lengthwise or crosswise) are secured by thongs cut from bamboo bark. No use is made at all of nails, screws, or wire. Props and thong bindings offer ample support for a Mru house. Not only can dozens of people sit on the floor at the same time; they can also dance on it and jump on it in rhythm. During the monsoon season these houses hold up repeatedly to storms. In some villages, however, special typhoon houses are also built. Consisting only of a roof made of tree trunks, these shelters serve as protection in case of an emergency.

Across each of the two rows of four main posts a pole is laid out lengthwise; upon these poles four thick beams are placed crosswise. These beams, in turn, may carry a purlin on both ends. Then come the rafters of the roof; they run from the ridgepole, which is supported by the two central posts, to about half a meter past the side purlins. Upon these rafters one places the split-bamboo rails to which bundles of thatching grass or bamboo leaves are

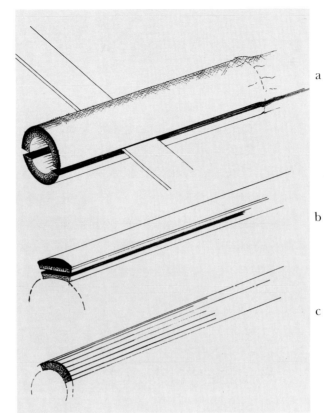

Bamboo canes can be split into halves (a) – and then into smaller and smaller tangential (b) and radial (c) segments.

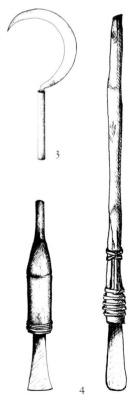

Tools

Iron instruments must be bought; the Mru do not forge metal, but they do provide their tools with shafts or handles.

1. ax – for felling larger trees and chopping wood
2. hewing knife – the most widely used work-tool; bamboo or wooden shaft with inserted iron blade; shaft length ca. 20 cm. [8 in.], blade (of various forms) ca. 35 cm. [14 in.]
3. sickle – for cutting thatching grass and harvesting rice
4. dibbling sticks – the blade of an old hewing knife, wich has been refashioned like a chisel, stuck into a thick bamboo shaft or a wooden shank

Above:
Bamboo strips are being cut with a hewing knife into thin thongs. All parts of the house will then be tied together with such thongs.

Below:
Constructing the *tsar*. The second layer of bamboo canes is being tied perpendicular to the first by means of bamboo thongs.

Above:
The cane siding of a basement is being secured: the two ends of a thong are twisted together into a knot. At night pigs and chickens are kept in this basement.

Below:
On the *tsar* bamboo segments are being used to clamp downsplit-bamboo rods on top of the second layer of bamboo canes.

◄◄ Bundles of thatching grass, over-lapping like tiles, are tied progressively onto the roof rails from the edge of the roof to the ridgepole.

◄ A young man fastens a roof rail above the purlin, wich runs from the front to the back of the roof, and the rafters, wich lead from the ridgepole to the edge of the roof. With his right foot he stands on one of the heavy crossbeams which has been notched on the end and bound to the purlin.

► A young father secures the support-frame on the bottom of a new carrying basket; his small daughter is watching.

tied; the thatching material is then secured against wind damage by an outer layer of rails which is tied with bamboo thongs to the lower parallel-running layer. A layer of leaves or grass which is scarcely 10 cm. (4 in.) thick can keep even a heavy monsoon rain out; an extra thick crosswise layer protects the ridgepole. Finally, the walls are added. They consist of vertical bamboo strips (20 cm. [8 in.] wide) which are woven together with horizontal strips (5 cm. [2 in.] wide). The walls of the *kim-tom* are secured from without to horizontal rails which have been attached to the outside of the wall posts. The *kimma* walls are put up in precisely the opposite manner, that is, the woven wall is secured to the inside of the posts.

Windows can be cut out of the walls. Generally, only one window is constructed on the back side of the house; and this window can, if necessary, be closed with a piece of bamboo matting. Doors also consist of woven pieces of bamboo matting. They hang on one of the rails of the upper part of the door frame and can be moved to one side. Among the southern Mru groups, one enters the house from the *tsar*; this platform is reached by climbing up a tree-ladder (a tree trunk with notched steps). Among the Anok-Mru, the *tsar* is accessible only from the *kim-tom*, which in turn is accessible directly from the outside — again by way of a tree-ladder. (The ladder leads to a small landing on the narrow front side of the *kim-tom* at the point where the *kim-tom* joins the *kimma*.) According to early sources, it was at one time customary to pull up the tree-ladder at night; but today one leaves it down. One could not possibly enter the house unnoticed anyway, since the door can be locked from the inside; in addition to that, it would be impossible to open the door without making some noise.

Baskets and other Utensils

Between the floor and the ridgepole of the roof there is no ceiling; however, a kind of loft is customarily suspended in this area just above head-height. It sometimes rests on the purlins of the wall; often, though, the loft is simply tied up by means of long, looped ropes to the crossbeams between the main posts. This loft is used primarily for storing large rolls of finely-woven mats — mats which, in various shapes and forms, are used as sleeping pads or for drying rice. Small baskets are also stored in the loft; larger baskets are placed against the walls inside the house or on the *tsar*. There are baskets for seeds, others for harvesting; there are baskets for women, others for men; there are portable baskets and stationary ones; baskets for clothing or for chickens. There are very small and very large baskets. Mru baskets range from delicate, lidded baskets in which women keep their jewelry to the simply woven baskets which serve to transport cotton to market — unless, of course, the cotton is used at home. The baskets used to transport cotton are crude, however, only because they go with the cotton. Baskets made for one's own use are always of high quality. They are both stable and flexible and, therefore, capable of forming themselves to a person's back even when heavy loads are being carried. A very poor Mru may weave mats and baskets to sell to Bangali peddlers, but Mru do not buy and sell basketware among themselves. Similarly, no trading takes place between the ethnic groups. Every man weaves his own baskets — weaving is a man's job; and the baskets a man weaves are peculiar to his own ethnic group. The Marma may well recognize that the Mru have better baskets than they, but they stick to their own forms even if these fulfill basically the same kinds of functions as among the Mru.

The Longhu-Mru, as well as the Khumi and the Bawm, use an additional form of basket in which they thresh rice with their feet. The other Mru groups use one of their many types of mats for this activity. The Bangalis have still another form of basket — a basket with handles which together with a carrying pole is used to transport goods. In the Hill Tracts no one uses a carrying pole unless he happens to have a large game animal which must be carried by two people — or unless he must transport a pig during a wedding ceremony or a corpse to a place of cremation. If possible, hill people always carry their load in a basket on their back. The basket, however, is not suspended from a shoulder strap, but rather from a headband which is grasped by the hands between forehead and basket. This, of course, helps to lighten the load. The headband is fashioned from the inner bark of a tree (*Sterculia villosa*), or it may be woven out of fine bamboo thongs. There are no animals used for transport — the *rajas* alone kept elephants; so the only thing left which can be used for overland transport is man and his baskets. In baskets, har-

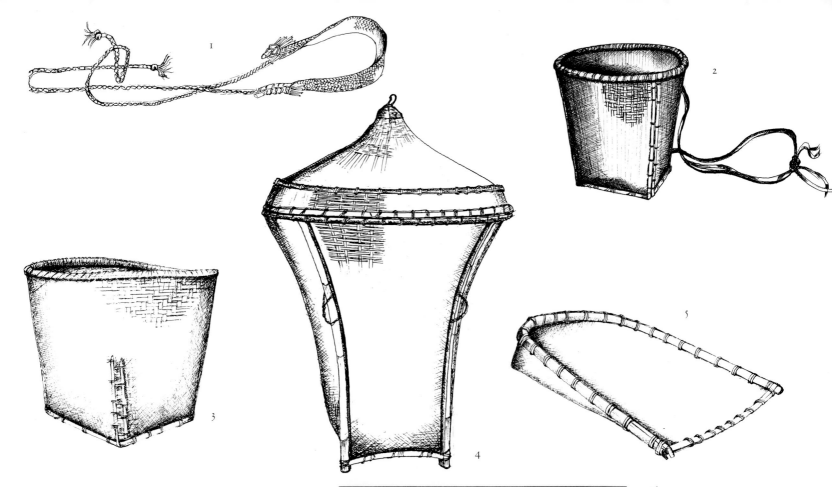

vests are carried home, and in baskets women fetch their daily water, which beforehand is poured into gourd bottles. Children learn to carry baskets at an early age; however, when young girls must begin helping their mothers carry water, their necks hurt until their muscles become strong. As grown women, though, they, like the men, are able to carry very heavy loads up the steep slopes.

Among the Marma, women prefer to fetch (and preserve) water in the round, earthen pots made by Bangalis. The great disadvantage of these pots is the fact that they break much more easily than the gourd bottles; and the gourd bottles, unlike the pots, can simply be stoppered with a piece of banana leaf. These gourds, which have the form of a thick-bellied bottle, are grown in the fields for no other purpose. Before the gourds can be used as water containers, however, one must allow the soft insides to rot out until only the hard shell remains; for if they are not completely clean inside, water kept in them will soon taste foul. After each use the gourds must again be allowed to dry out as completely as possible. In order to dry them, one places

◀ A young woman wades across a brook on her way to the nearby spring. In the basket she carries gourd bottles into which she will fill drinking water; some of them are stoppered with banana leaves. Camera-shy, she covers her mouth with her hand.

Gourd bottle stoppered with a piece of banana leaf.

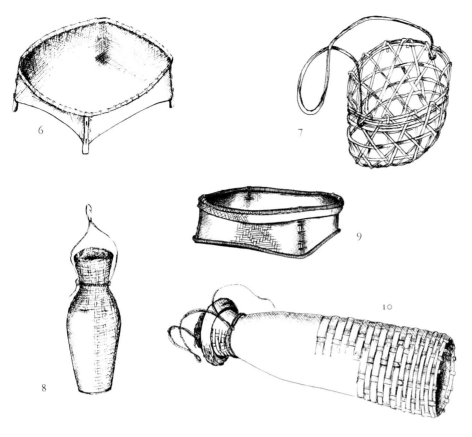

Basketry

1 Carrying strap made of finely woven bamboo thongs (cf. p. 79).

2 Man's carrying basket (cf. p. 60), linen binding, with carrying strap made of the inner bark of the *Sterculia* tree; height 28 cm. [11 in.].

3 Basket (*klai-puk*) used as a temporary container in daily and ceremonial life (cf. pp. 94, 126, 233). Worn-out specimens (p. 155) are still useful for collecting kitchen garbage or (after hulling and winnowing the rice) bran and husk, which will later be cooked as pig feed. Patterned twill weave, height 32 cm (12.6 in.).

4 Big storage basket, with lid and short legs: solid, double-walled woven container in which clothes and things of value are kept; height ca. 100 cm. [ca. 40 in.].

5 Shovel-shaped tray, 45 x 45 cm (18 x 18 in.), with two rounded corners on the side of the raised edge. The upper rim is reinforced by two bent bamboo slats. Used primarily for winnowing (cf. pp. 82, 94, 126), but also for preparing and depositing odds and ends (cf. p. 195).

6 Flat basket with small legs, used by women to store cotton balls and smaller weaving utensils (cf. p. 51).

7 Openly-woven basket made for carrying chickens and storing kitchen plates (cf. p. 97); carrying strap made from the inner bark of the *Sterculia* tree.

8 Small, vase-shaped basket with linen binding: used to collect small fish and shrimp (cf. p. 86) or to preserve fruit seeds.

9 Small, square jewelry basket: made of dark red and black bamboo strips woven like twill; height 5 cm. [ca. 2 in.].

10 Fish trap: a woven body with linen binding and strongly reinforced edges; on the inside one finds a cone-shaped piece of netting about half the height of the trap, the warp threads of which are partially exposed; an egg-shaped piece of basketry is used as a stopper for the smaller upper opening; used to catch small fish and shrimp; diameter 11 cm. [4 in.], length 42 cm. [16 in.].

Round earthen pots must be purchased. Mru women always wear their cloaks to the bazaar; the cloaks also come from the market, sometimes as a gift of a young man for his girlfriend.

them upside down in a rack over the stove; this means that in time the gourds turn black on the outside. If the fire inadvertently gives off too much smoke, the water which is afterwards fetched in the gourds will also take on a smoky taste. The clay pots may well keep the water cooler; for this reason, the Mru occasionally store water in such pots after it has been brought into the house. In general, though, the Mru use clay pots for one purpose only: the brewing of beer. Since rice beer has an important role in all ceremonies and since the clay used in making the pots is not found in the hills — and neither the Mru nor any other ethnic group of the Hill Tracts knows how to make pottery — these pots may well be among those items which the Mru have always been obliged to acquire from the plains peoples.

Another long-imported commodity important to everyday life has already been mentioned: iron. Without hewing knives a Mru cannot cut and splice bamboo; without bamboo he would have no house and no baskets. The hewing knife, which the Mru carries with him with the regularity that one of us would carry a purse, is at the same time his universal tool. He carries it, however, not in his pocket, but in a basket or, in the case of men, in the belt of his loin-cloth. With the hewing knife the Mru cut everything, from the largest to the smallest object, in the most varied ways possible. When the cutting edge becomes worn down by repeated sharpening on a hone, the blade is given the form of a chisel. Fitted with a longer handle, it then serves as a dibbling, or digging, stick. Spear points are also made from iron, and there are arrows and spears made completely of iron. Except for the spear which is occasionally used to kill a cow, these weapons are no longer used in everyday life. A cow is killed with a spear, however, only for celebrations — the very context in which the erstwhile weapons still play a strategic role in the ceremonial exchange of gifts.

A set of three plate-shaped gongs, which is used for several important ceremonies, is also among those metal objects imported by the Mru. Only the wealthier households, however, possess such instruments — and the knobbed gongs which are made in Burma are even rarer. It is just as rare to find tables, stools, or cupboards in normal households. The only wooden furniture — if one wishes to call it that — is a tree-trunk "pillow," that is, a split tree trunk which has been smoothed off on the rounded side and is used like a pillow. Likewise made of wood are the pig trough and the large mortar and pestle used daily in every household. But we are now moving into the field of nutrition, which is to be the subject of the next chapter.

▶
The rainy season is almost over. The paddy has been harvested and is now being carried home from the field hut over slippery mountain paths. On top of the paddy are a few gourds.

◄
The Mru use their feet to thresh the paddy. As the bundles are tumbled, the grains are separated from the stalks.
►
Ears of paddy are piled high in the large harvesting basket which the cutter carries on her back. The basket is carried with the help of a finely woven bamboo band.

Next page:
On woven bamboo mats spread over the platform of the field house, men tumble and sift paddy which was cut in the field by a workgroup of women.

A light breeze helps to separate the remaining pieces of stalk from the grains.

If the wind does not help, the winnow serves as a fan as one kicks a bunch of grains into the air.

After the paddy has been gathered, there are still several things in the field to harvest – here, for example, the sour fruits of the rozelle. The rozelle, which is a type of hibiscus, is not sown together with the paddy, but separately on the edges of the field.

At the beginning of May new seeds are being sown in a field which has already been slashed and burnt. Trunks of cut trees which survived the fire have been laid out crosswise on the ground, so that it will be less easy for the coming rains to wash away the soil.

Women's open-work baskets serve not only as a means of transport, but also as a means of catching small fish and shrimp which hide under the stones or in the sand of shallow water.

Right side:
If one wishes to eat a meal during a fishing expedition, one simply spreads out a large banana leaf. Small fish and shrimp, which have been cooked on the spot, serve as a side dish for rice which has been brought from home.

◀
Taking a bath.
▶
In larger streams, as here in the Twain, one can fish with a net. The nets are bought at the bazaar.

◀
A tree squirrel has been caught in a spring-pole trap which was tied to a bamboo cane.
▶
With a tree branch, a young boy skewers beetles which he dug out of the ground. Grilled and salted, the insect food tastes similar to nuts.

Every day the women and girls pound the daily portion of rice for the family – in front of the house in the dry season, inside the house during the rainy season.

Right side:
Under the blue sky of a December day, a Mru house located in the chain of mountains south of the Matamuri – at the front, the open platform; to the right of the platform, a storehouse; to the left, a little down the slope, a second house.

◀
Afer rice has been hulled and winnowed, remaining impurities are picked out by hand.

▶
The rice which was hulled in the mortar inside the house is now being winnowed on the open platform. In the background, paddy spread out on mats to dry in the sun.

A small rodent was caught in a trap near the field. It is roasted immediately over a fire below the field house.

Everyday food is cooked in a fireplace located on the side wall of the main room. The floor and walls of the fireplace are smeared with mud; above it, there is a suspended rack upon which, among other things, bottle gourds are dried. On the right side against the wall, firewood; in loosely-woven baskets, plates and bowls.

Next page:
Menlong's family at mealtime – the women kneeling, the men squatting. In addition to the rice, there are vegetables and hotly-spiced dried fish. Water is drunk from gourds. The dog waits patiently for the scraps.

Threading tiny beads onto self-spun thread is tedious work. All beads are bought at the bazaar, but their transformation into jewelry is work done exclusively by young girls.

Left side:
White, green, black, and, above all, red strands of beads are among the most popular decorative items used by young Mru women and girls. Occasionally, young people who wish to make a particularly striking appearance color their entire faces red.

Mru women use the tension loom for weaving. From the warp, which has been dyed indigo, a new skirt is being created. The weaver is presently inserting the threads of the pattern.

Right side:
To gin the cotton, Mru women use a simple machine.

Not only is the cotton retained for one's own use carried in baskets, but also that cotton which is transported to the market for sale. Such transport baskets hold some 40 lbs. of cotton.

A length of material for a work jacket is being made. The weaver has created the countershed by lifting up the heddle, and she holds the shed open with the sword turned edgewise. The broken woof thread had to be removed from the warp and then re-tied. Now she passes the shuttle again into the shed at the crucial place.

Right side:
This woman weaves material for a blanket. Her husband squats in the doorway, weaving a basket.

Food and Clothing

As already mentioned in the introduction, the inhabitants of the Hill Tracts are primarily swidden farmers. Fields which are plowable — whether they can be irrigated or not — are possessed only by a few Chakma, Marma, Tippera and Sak. On the Matamuri there are also a few isolated Mru who plow; all others lay out their fields on the slopes of the hills where no type of plow agriculture is possible. Terracing as one finds in Sri Lanka and on Luzon is not found anywhere in the Chittagong Hill Tracts. That it would be completely impossible is doubtful; in most places, however, the stone which would be needed to reinforce the ground is simply nonexistent. If one wishes to prevent the monsoon rains from washing away the thin layer of humus, one cannot clear the ground in such a way as to remove the roots of the old growth. One therefore cuts and burns only that vegetation standing above ground; the root system is left intact. In contrast to the type of cultivation where old growth is uprooted, however, this so-called swidden farming puts a double burden on the soil; for in addition to the old root system, new plants are also put into the ground. The available soil nutrients diminish quickly, and the yields decrease accordingly if a field is cultivated in this manner two years in a row. In order to at least partly restore the former fertility fallow periods of many years are necessary, during such periods a secondary forest grows up under which the nutrients can replenish themselves.

Swidden Farming

Scientists no longer doubt the fact that, where the farmer's own consumption is concerned, swidden farming is indeed a method well-suited to the sandstone slopes of the tropics. It is well-known, however, that swidden farming — also called slash-and-burn or shifting cultivation — has been opposed by governmental authorities. The colonial administration, for example, saw only valuable timber going up in flames. Since it has become known that it is possible to combine farming and forestry, as long as there is enough land available to allow sufficient fallow periods, the argument against swidden farming has been limited to one, namely, that it belongs to a backward civilization incapable of further development. This is obviously not true, since with this same method cash-crops (such as cotton, tea, etc.) can be cultivated. It is true, though, that swidden farming could never sustain the high density of population which plow agriculture can sustain. This has nothing to do with the method itself, however, but rather with natural conditions. Still, in the face of a growing population, swidden farming in fact proves to be an extremely precarious way to utilize land — as we shall presently see.

The natural qualities of soils can vary considerably. In the Hill Tracts, the only soils which permit cultivation two years in a row are those which, prior to cultivation, rested at least 12 years; nowadays such soils are found only in the forest reserves where, however, swidden farming is forbidden by law. No swidden field — not even one cultivated for only one year — escapes the general rule: the shorter the fallowing period, the lower the yields. As long as there is enough good land available then, the farmer is also interested in fallowing land as long as possible. However, when poorer soils have increasingly to be drawn into the area being cultivated — as is the case with a growing population — it is only rational also to shorten the fallowing periods of the better soils. Shorter fallowing periods and poorer soils mean lower yields from the same piece of ground; consequently, in order to maintain the level of production, the cultivated area should be expanded. Once again, this is only possible when lower-quality soils are utilized and when fallowing periods are further shortened. This spiral, however, cannot continue forever, for larger fields also mean more work; sooner or later the family will not have enough man-power to keep up with the weeding. The shorter the fallow periods, the more quickly a

◀
Spinning. Concentration is put entirely on the thread. After the manual spindle hanging on the thread's lower end has been set in motion by the right hand, the thread is held high by the left hand.

type of weed (*Imperata*) grows up alongside the original growth (the roots of which were left in the ground). The roots of this weed spread like those of couch grass; its blades, however, can grow much higher than a man's head and become so hard and sharp that they cannot even be used as cattle feed. Apart from its utilization as a roof-covering — and bamboo leaves can serve the same purpose — this grass is useless. If a family is not able to keep up with the weeding, *Imperata* grass immediately overgrows the paddy and smothers it. If an area is burnt off only every five or six years, there is no danger that it will be taken over by the grass, although the bamboo will slowly die out. If, however, an area is burnt off three years in a row, other growth will also be unable to maintain itself against the grass. In such a case, a grassy slope grows up which is lost to cultivation for at least ten years, due above all to the fact that the grass uses those soil nutrients needed by the rice. The strategic importance of the quality of soil is seen in the yields: the yields from well-fallowed soils may reach up to eighty times the amount planted, whereas those from exhausted soils — under unfavorable rain conditions and an infestation of insects — can drop to less than five times the sowing. When a farmer reaps hardly more than he sowed, hunger is unavoidable. This is particularly true nowadays, since today's farmer reaps small return from those endeavors formerly resorted to in case of a bad harvest: the gathering of wild roots and the hunting of wild animals. These undertakings are possible only as long as there is a relatively large amount of uncultivated land, which is no longer the case today; and even such resources can not be tapped too extensively every year.

Selecting, Slashing and Burning

Under the circumstances, much of a farmer's success depends upon how well he can estimate the productive potential of available land. On fallowed plots, his main criterion for judging actual soil fertility is the condition of the secondary growth. By cultivating more than one swidden field *(üa)*, he can reduce the risk of crop failure. On small plots pests spread less easily and the reforestation during the fallowing period is accelerated. Preparing one's field in the immediate neighborhood of another person's is therefore not appreciated. A farmer is not completely free to do as he pleases; he must also respect the wishes of other persons. There is, traditionally, no such thing as privately-owned land. If there had been such a thing, there would long have been land speculation and the buying and selling of land; there would be rich families with lots of land to lease and others owning nothing. The government has in fact made it possible for a person to own land. Mru farmers, however, know what the inevitable consequences of landownership would be, and most of them insist that every person should have access to land. There is, however, a kind of unwritten law related to land claims; according to this law, the person having first claim to a piece of land is the one who earlier cultivated it. Still, the sizes of families fluctuate over time; hence one farmer needs more land and another less, possibly due to the setting up of separate and independent households by adult children. Such new households would then need land for themselves. Additionally, any person who harvested too little one year and consequently went into debt should be allowed to cultivate a larger area the following year — but still no more than his family can weed.

Other factors must also be taken into consideration. First of all, there is the general concern with the maintenance of a wood and bamboo reserve for the village. Secondly, the distribution of old and new plots in relation to each other must be carefully considered; for under no circumstance, even accidentally, should old plots be burned off twice. Finally, when all organizational questions have been settled among the household heads, the spirits *(tshüng-nam)* may still exercise their veto power. Each farmer puts up a mark (a bamboo cross) on the edge of his future swidden field and observes the signs in his dreams the following night. In former times, if the signs were negative, a new plot was selected; today the chosen site is only slightly altered.

As soon as everyone is in agreement, the slashing of the field can begin without further delay. The time needed for this task can vary greatly, depend-

▶
Against a background of burning and smoking fields one sees a field which has already been burnt off but not yet cleared. The sky is gray with smoke.

▶
A swidden plot after burning.
▶▶
With the help of a dibbling stick, a young man puts a mixture of paddy and cotton seeds into the earth. In his ear he sports a champaca bloom; stuck between hairknot and turban, his pipe.

ing upon the stage and amount of old growth; however, the period between January and March offers ample time to get the job done. The first time the field is gone over, the undergrowth is cut progressively from bottom to top; women and children assist in this phase, each armed with a hewing knife. Larger trees are cut only during a second round of slashing, done exclusively by the men. The ax is also used for this job. Earlier it was customary to fell all of the trees, even the larger hardwoods — the Mru love a neatly cleared field. Today, however, after lopping off the larger branches, one leaves the major trees standing. They will, perhaps, be needed later; in the meantime, they may also serve to speed up the process of reforestation (provided they survive the burning).

By the first days of April — April is the hottest month of the year — the cut wood has dried sufficiently to be burned. In order to prevent the fire from jumping uncontrollably from one field to another, the exact days for burning are agreed upon, not only within a given hamlet itself, but, even prior to that, among the various settlements in the neighborhood. The dates are decided upon by the *karbari*, who meet together in the village of the headman. If public paths lead through the fields which are to be burned, they are blocked off with special signs. Around the concerned area wide lanes are cleared as far as possible of everything ignitable; and bundles of long, split bamboo canes are laid ready — they will serve as torches. Outside the boundary of the field a small fire is finally made and the torches are lighted; then men run with the torches as quickly as possible around the area to be burnt, setting the fire in several places on the outside edges. (When the fire is set in such a way, the blaze becomes stronger and stronger as it moves inward.) The burning is done either in the morning or evening, since at such times the wind is normally still. If the plot to be burned is very close to the village, people may even wait until it has become completely dark, so that flying sparks can be more easily observed. Flying sparks on a roof, which at this time of the year is even drier than the field itself, can set an entire house aflame — and, spreading from there, the entire village. Since all food supplies and all seeds are kept in the house, such a fire would mean, in addition to everything else, the loss of food for the next half-year. As a precautionary measure, therefore, men equipped with water cans and ladels, as well as banana leaves (we would use blankets), are stationed on the roof of every house.

If in spite of the surrounding cleared corridors, flying sparks and smouldering ashes cause the fire to spread across the jungle floor, no one is particularly concerned. The smoulder spreads only among dried leaves and grass and goes no further than the next path. Live bushes and trees remain basically undisturbed by a fire of this type; for in spite of the preceding six months of dry season, the nightly fog still prevails and the humidity is high enough to keep green wood from catching fire. Even in the field, trunks and branches may have only been scorched by the fire, but not reduced to ashes. During the days following a burning, when the sky over the Hill Tracts is so gray from the smoke that the sun is hidden, the dirtiest work of the entire year begins for the men. Like black pixies they climb around in the field in order to gather the remaining charred wood. This wood is then stacked up at the field's edge — it will later serve as firewood whenever one wishes to prepare a meal while working the field. If there are fallen trees which cannot be hauled from the field through collective effort, even after all remaining branches have been chopped off, these are usually placed diagonally across the slope. They then serve two purposes: on the one hand, they act as barriers against possible erosion; on the other hand, they serve as paths through the field once the seeds have come up. The ashes left on the field fertilize the soil, presupposing that the first rains are not long in coming and that they are not too heavy once they do come. If the rains are delayed, the ashes may well be blown away by the wind, since prior to the rain they cannot penetrate the hard ground. Similarly, if the first rains are too heavy, the ashes are simply washed away.

Without the ground being softened — something accomplished by the first rains — it would be extremely difficult to get the seeds into the earth. At this point, in fact, the farmer becomes totally dependent upon those powers which, even with the most intimate knowledge of the soil, he cannot control. In the hope of putting these powers or spirits into a favorable mood, the farmer sacrifices a piglet just prior to the planting; and he asks the spirits about his prospects for a good harvest. The stumps of four certain species of trees come under consideration for a kind of sacred spot, known as *tur-tut*, where all rituals take place. It is here that planting begins.

Planting and Weeding

The selection of seeds begins during the previous harvest. At those places in the field where the harvest is unusually good, the fully mature and evenly-proportioned paddy ears are harvested separately, according to variety; they are then dried, threshed, winnowed, and finally put into baskets lined with special leaves. Before these paddy seeds are used for planting, they are cleaned of empty hulls and spread out on the *tsar* (the open platform) to air in the sun. One generally keeps back more seeds than are eventually utilized. The surplus is consumed by the family, but never sold — on the one hand, for the practical reason that it is the best quality of rice, whereas the buying price is set according to weight only; on the other hand, because of the belief that the sale of any remaining paddy seeds could result in lower yields at harvesttime. If for any reason a person lacks the carefully selected seeds generally held back for planting, he must be content with the quality of paddy normally used for consumption, namely, a mixture of different varieties.

The varieties of paddy range from large-kerneled, good-tasting white rice, which requires fertile soils, to small-kerneled, hard, red rice which can thrive even in poor soils. The Mru naturally prefer to eat the large, good-tasting rice; yet they must be increasingly content with the inferior varieties, depending on the quality of the soils at their disposal. In all cases, however, the paddy utilized is paddy which requires no watering apart from the monsoon rains and which matures fully in about five months. If a person knows ahead of time that his rice supply will not last until the next harvest, he may prefer to plant one section of his field with

Prior to the sowing, a piglet is sacrificed on the *tur-tut*, the special spot next to a tree trunk where field rituals are held.

a variety of rice normally grown in the watered paddy fields of the plains, since this "water-rice" matures in only three months. On swidden farms, however, this variety brings only one-third the yields of "dry-rice". Whereas such water-rice is planted only in an emergency situation, some sticky rice is always planted; for sticky rice must be present at all special and ritual occasions. At such times, the rice is not prepared in pots, but rather in quiver-shaped bamboo cookers; even without additional sugar this rice tastes somewhat sweet and, as the name indicates, is very sticky. (Sections of bamboo may have served generally as cooking vessels before metal pots were introduced. When they are held over an open fire, they may be charred on the outside only, without actually catching fire. They can be used only one time, however).

On one and the same plot of ground several varieties of rice can be planted side by side; and on this selfsame plot a whole series of other fruits or vegetables may also be found – no ethnic group practices monoculture on swidden farms. The question of what, and how much, is to be mixed in with the paddy is largely left up to the individual's own judgment. Only in the case of cotton – which, however, is not planted over the entire field, but only in the humid lower end – is a given proportion used for the mixture: 10 lb. cotton seeds to 20 lb. paddy kernels. Seeds of different types of squash and cucumber – the vegetables most commonly eaten by the Mru – as well as beans, sweet cane, and indigo, are also mixed in with the paddy. The seed mixture is prepared at home and taken to the field in large baskets; there it is divided up into smaller baskets which can be hung around the waist of each person.

As always, the work begins on the lower end of the field; if several families are working together in mutual-aid groups, the field is divided up between the sexes. Each person takes a dibbling stick in the right hand and a handful of seeds in the left – a dibbling stick is an old hewing knife, the blade of which has been resharpened into the form of a chisel. He or she shoves the blade into the ground, yanks the handle downward so that a hole is wedged open, throws in 10-15 seeds, and, finally, pulls the blade out again. As the person moves

An old form of tobacco pipe is still used by Mru, Khumi and Bawm men. The bowl is of wood; the inside is in the form of an hourglass with an aluminium ring inserted in the top; on the bottom, there is a softwood plug which can be removed for cleaning. The stem is inserted at an angle. It consists of a thin bamboo internode, which need not be cleaned, since it can easily be replaced.

gradually up the hill, this procedure is repeated over and over again about every 30 cm. (12 ins.). The planter may haphazardly cover the holes by pushing earth over them with his feet; but most of the time, as the person proceeds up the hill, enough loose soil falls back into the hole of its own accord. If ten people work together in this way, they can plant 20 lb. of seeds in less than two hours, thereby cultivating an area of about half an acre. Crops such as Indian corn, Indian lentils, and rozelle are also planted with the dibbling stick; their seeds, however, are never mixed in with the paddy seeds because their plants would overpower the paddy seedlings. Creepers – certain species of *Luffa* and *Momordica* – are likewise planted separately and with the dibbling stick, in places particularly suited

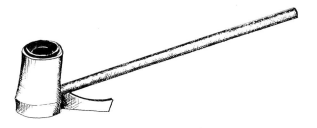

A boy is digging out the inside of a stem of a modern pipe. The bowl and the short, bent stem are carved from one piece of wood; the mouthpiece is then attached. A closeable opening on the top of the bent stem serves to facilitate cleaning. An aluminium ring, which is placed inside the bowl, keeps the wood from catching fire.

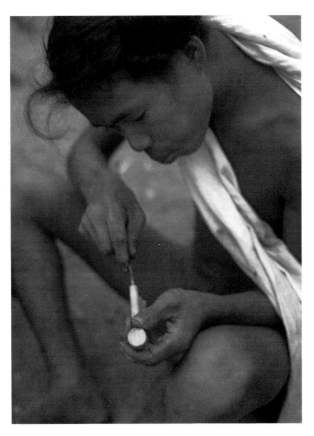

to them. After several rains have softened the ground, clippings of tubers come next. These include taro, yams, and sweet potatoes, as well as ginger and turmeric. Seeds of millet *(Panicum)*, eggplant, colorful flowers, and plants with fragrant leaves are simply strewn over the field and along the edges of the paths.

Chili peppers and tobacco require special treatment. At the beginning of May small gardens are planted next to the houses or perhaps just outside the village, depending on space available. The ground is broken up with a hoe and then fertilized with the ashes of wood which is burned directly on it. Peppercorns which have been loosed from the pods are then scattered over the earth, and the ground is watered. As soon as the seedlings emerge, they are watered twice daily until the rains come; the amount of water they are given is gradually decreased. In June the plants are dug up with the hewing knife and transplanted into the field, generally about one meter (3 ft.) apart. They are planted in between the paddy, which in the meantime is sprouting, only if the soil is very good; normally, however, they are planted separately in a special part of the field. In August one can pick the first pods; in October, November, and December one harvests them about every ten days. Where the ground is fertile, the harvest can yield up to 2 lb. per plant; in general, however, less than 100 lb. can be expected from 0.1 of an acre.

In the hills, tobacco is planted in July; it is sown under the fieldhouse so that no rain may fall on it. By October the plants are about 10 cm. (4 in.) tall; they are then transplanted with a dibbling stick into the field where the paddy has in the meantime been harvested and the ground fertilized with a layer of decaying rice straw. From March on the tobacco leaves may be plucked. Near rivers, on the other hand, tobacco is sown in the open, but only at the end of the rainy season (October, November). The small plants are then transplanted in January into small, fenced-in plots along the edge of the river — plots which have been specially prepared for that purpose. The leaves from these tobacco plants may also be picked from March on. The preparation of the small, fenced-in plots is extremely troublesome because, if there is any *Imperata* grass growing on the plots, the entire root system of the grass must be completely dug up. In return for this trouble, though, one obtains considerably higher yields from these plots than from the mountain fields. The tobacco from the special, river-side plots also has a better taste — valued above all are the upper leaves, which grow especially long when one breaks off the points of the plants before they bloom. After the leaves have been harvested, they are strung on a long bamboo rope and hung up under the roof of the house to dry. In order to use a leaf, one removes the middle rib and then fills the rib, as well as the tips and edges of the leaf, into the better half of the leaf, which serves as a covering. The whole thing is finally held together by a small cotton string tied close to the thicker

Fire saw

As the bamboo thong is pulled up and down in a notch of the split bamboo cane, sawdust falls into the small hole and, due to the heat of the friction, eventually catches fire.

end — the end which is then placed into the mouth. Old and young alike enjoy such a cigar. More often than not, however, there is not enough tobacco to smoke even one cigar a day; a person must therefore occasionally make do with a pipe. Quite often a small piece of tobacco is used as quid. Cigarettes are available on the market, but in the long run they are too expensive even if one buys the worst quality. Most people cannot even afford matches — during the rainy season they become useless anyway unless one keeps them constantly drying over the fireplace. A smouldering stick or embers from the fireplace are, therefore, generally used to light a cigar or a pipe.

To arrange an occasional cigarette-break while working in the fields, then, is impossible; however, even without matches and during the rainy season the Mru know how to light a fire in the field. The only thing they need is half of a split bamboo cane in which a small notch is cut and a long, thin, but strong, cord cut out of bamboo bark. The halved bamboo is held down by the feet with the opening face up; the cord, which passes through the notch, is pulled up vigorously with the hands, alternating right and left. The fine sawdust which is thereby rubbed off collects in the inside of the bamboo cane close to the notch; it becomes hot and finally catches fire — that is, if one can hold out with the pulling, which becomes more and more vigorous, and stir up the smoulder by blowing lightly just at the right time. Since during the rainy season there is almost always a small brook close to the lower end of a swidden field, a person can also cook himself a meal while out in the field.

Since the Mru do not live in the fields during the monsoon season, they need not hasten to erect a field house. Some of them put it up as early as the end of April; others wait until August. Its main function is to serve as a temporary storehouse during harvesttime, but during the weeding time it also serves as a refuge in case of heavy showers. A field house consists of a single small room with an open platform built on the front; and, as is normally the case, everything is built on stilts. If the owner of the field has no sons to help him, he will need a few days to put it up. It is not very reasonable to

Below:
The monsoon rains have come in full strength.

Above:
The root system which was left in the ground (in this case, primarily bamboo) comes out more quickly than the new paddy seeds. By harvesttime one will have had to weed three times.

begin this work in June or July because at that time all available workers are needed for the weeding. This work is done primarily with a small hoe, but the hewing knife is also used. The easiest areas to weed are those which were once covered with bamboo; the more the ground has been invaded with *Imperata* weeds, the more difficult the task. During the weeding period it is not customary for families to help each other; so if a worker from one of the families has to drop out — for example, due to illness — the resulting lag in weeding can, in fact, mean the loss of entire parts of the field, since the earlier vegetation sprouts again and quickly overruns the rice plants. If the way between village and field is long and if a family cannot keep up with the weeding in any other way, family members may occasionally sleep overnight in the field.

Between May and the end of August, all swidden fields must be weeded three times (if anything grows up later, it cannot influence the harvest greatly). During the months of weeding it rains almost every day; however, most people go to the fields unless it pours and storms excessively. The paths are slippery, and many places crawl with leeches. Everything is wet; and when one is weeding, he or she must walk into the middle of wet vegetation and catch hold of it, with no surety that in spite of all precautions one will not in fact catch hold of one of the leaf-green vipers whose bite can be deadly. Even the most zealous weeding cannot prevent the paddy plants from occasionally being attacked by insects which devour the insides of the grains (the danger is less among the less-tasty varieties); nor can one prevent the plants from turning brown and the grains remaining hollow. Neither cause nor remedy is known for this latter calamity. When rats swarm over the entire countryside, stripping the fields bare, an inescapable and total crop failure may well result. This happens, however, only about once every fifty years, when the bamboo blooms and then dies.

During this precarious and difficult time of weeding, when the food supplies of most families are already low, a second sacrifice is held in the field. When the rice blooms at the end of July or the beginning of August, a miniature platform (about

20 cm. [8 in.] high) is put up in the lower part of the field next to the brook; the platform is covered with a piece of banana leaf and decorated at the four corners with bamboo tassels. Upon this small altar one then places some earth from the field, a few roasted grains of sticky rice, and some cooked (sticky) rice which has been pressed into small pancakes. After the altar has been so prepared, one beseeches the river-spirit to send a good harvest as one sacrifices a chicken. The chicken has been brought from home for this purpose; its throat is cut; and, as water is sprinkled over its neck six times, the chicken's blood is dripped over the rice. The same sacrifice is then repeated on the *tur-tut*, the central ritual spot in the field; this time, however, one uses a taro leaf — rather than a banana leaf — from one of the plants planted in that area. This sacrifice is made to the rice-spirit. A bamboo tube, into whose bark a special pattern has been scraped, is stuck into the ground next to the miniature platform. This tube serves as a container for a mixture of water, lemon and lime leaves, and chicken blood. Using a small bamboo tassel, one sprinkles the mixture over the field, to the right and left, as one returns home. The sacrificed chickens are taken home again and consumed there. The entrance to the field is symbolically barred by a piece of split bamboo which has been bowed into a half-circle. The Mru themselves know, however, that this symbolic barricading of the field entrance is but an expression of their desire to keep out unwanted intruders: they hope that the crops now growing in the field will not be excessively plundered by insects, birds, and animals.

Hunting and Trapping

The Mru can do little or nothing else to ward off insects; however, to further protect their crops against birds and animals they use hunting weapons and traps — and not only because these intruders are rivals for the food, but because they themselves are valued food. Domestic animals are undoubtedly the main source of meat; however, they are slaughtered only on special occasions, primarily for sacrifice. Game meat, then, offers a highly welcomed dietary supplement; and virtually

every man in the Hill Tracts would like to be a good hunter. Guns, however, are owned by only a very few persons. The restrictive licensing system of the government, which makes the acquisition of a license generally more expensive than the purchase of the gun itself, renders the possession of a gun unattainable for most people. (In a few rare cases even old muzzle-loaders are still in use.) Furthermore, apart from jungle fowl, wood pigeons, and an occasional magnificient hornbill, whose meat is greatly valued, there is not much to use a gun on — unless one is keen on shooting monkeys. (Though monkeys are in fact eaten, they are regarded by some as being too similar to human beings.)

Both the small and large specimens of red deer have become rare; on the paths frequented by this deer, the Mru sometimes set up spear traps in which they also occasionally catch wild pigs and large cats, or even leopards. Because spear traps can also kill humans — whoever overlooks the specially-erected warning sign and inadvertently sets off the trap runs at least the risk of being badly

When the paddy blooms, a second sacrifice takes place in the field. On the *tur-tut*, which can be recognized by the taro leaves in among the paddy plants, a small altar is set up. Over the altar, which has been decorated with bamboo tassels, one sprinkles the blood of a chicken.

On the edge of a swidden field a spear trap is being set.

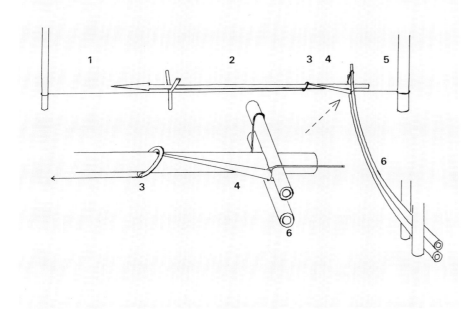

Spear-throwing trap

Over a trail used by wild animals (left, in front), a thin creeper (1) is stretched taut. The creeper runs alongside a spear placed horizontally (2) and is tied to a ring on the spear shaft. This ring (3), made of twisted bamboo lashes, holds down the point of a peg (4), the thicker (right) end of which has been tied with a string to a tree (5). The peg serves to lock a strong, double-bamboo spring (6) into place; the spring itself is attached to the end of the spear. A slight pull on the creeper (1) causes the point of the peg (4) to slip out of the ring (3); the spring (6) is thereby released and the spear (2) hurled to the left. Since the end of the spear is wedged between the double-bamboo of the spring, the speared animal cannot escape with the weapon.

wounded — most people shy away from using them. Spring-pole traps, which are not dangerous to human beings, are more frequently utilized. Found in different sizes, this type of trap is used primarily for rodents, although fish can also be caught with it. If an animal attempts to pass through the noose of the trap, a trigger releases the rope holding down a thin tree or bamboo cane (the spring-pole); when this happens, the spring-pole flies up, closing the noose of the rope attached to it. The chances that a rodent will in fact walk into the noose are substantially increased when the areas to the left and right are rendered impassable. Such is the case, for example, when the trap is attached to a tree trunk bridging a water course. One can, however, also fence in an entire field, leaving only a few openings laid with traps. This strategy helps little against rodents, though, since they can climb over or squeeze through the fence; still, running birds, especially jungle fowl, can easily be caught in this manner. During the mating season, jungle fowl can also be caught with simple snares, that is, with noose-traps which have no triggering device. Out

◄ A mouse has been caught in a spring pole trap tied to one of the diagonal braces of a house.

Spring pole trap

A rope (1) with a noose (2) on one end is tied to a bamboo pole (3). The pole is bent and held in place by a peg (4) fastened to the rope; the upper end of the peg is wedged under the top of a bamboo triangle (5). This triangle is tied to a small tree or bamboo cane (6) over which rodents pass. The lower point of the peg is prevented from snapping backwards by a cross-stick (7) resting against the sides of the triangle; a very thin string (8) runs from this cross-stick to the base of the triangle. A mouse attempting to pass through the triangle sets off the tripping device; a pull on the thin string (8) lowers the cross-stick (7). The peg (4) is released and the spring pole (3) flies backwards, pulling up the noose (2); and as the noose slides upward over the lateral sides of the trap (5), the animal is strangled under the top of the triangle.

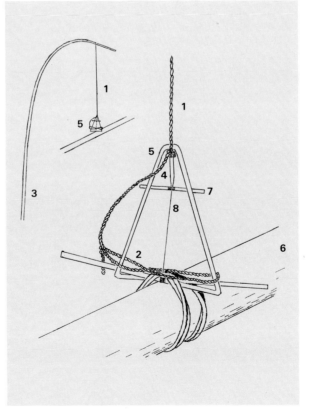

120

in the jungle one ties up a domestic cock as bait and places twenty or more snares all around it; the remaining space is then blocked off with bushes and split bamboo. The cock's crowing entices not only the annoyed jungle cocks to fight, but also the jungle hens. The animals run headlong into the nooses which, being narrower than their bodies, contract instead of allowing the animals to pass.

In lieu of noose traps, one may also place deadfalls in the openings of a fence. Jungle fowl, as well as rodents and iguanas, can be caught in these traps. Above each opening one suspends a log some three meters (10 ft.) long and 20 cm. (8 in.) in diameter. The front end of this log, which serves as a striking beam, is suspended from a piece of bamboo which serves as a balance beam; a string leads from the other end of the balance beam to a small peg, and the peg is kept in place by a bar. A second string, which hangs down from this bar, is suspended just above the ground of the passage way and is covered by a lightweight ramp made of small bamboo slats. If an animal steps onto this ramp, it pushes the suspended string down to the ground and thus

▶ The young man has captured an iguana. He now brings it home tied to a bamboo thong.

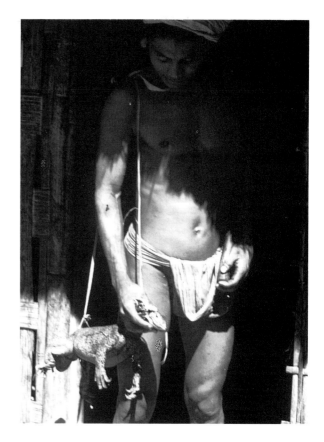

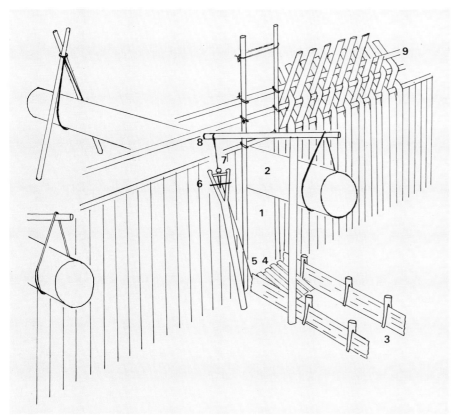

Deadfall

The several passages (1) left in the wall (protecting a field) are hardly wider than the striking beam (2) and approximately 30 cm. (12 in.) high; the narrow corridor (3), some 5 cm. (2 in.) high, should prevent the animal from evading the bamboo slats (4) in the middle of the corridor. These slats are placed from both sides over a string (5) which crosses the passage an inch or so above the ground and leads to the cross-stick (6) of the tripping device. An animal stepping on the slats will force down the string and, together with it, the cross-stick. This releases the peg (7), connected by another string to the balance beam (8), and allows the striking beam (2) to fall. The vertical slats of the some one-meter high wall are spread apart on top by horizontal bamboo segments (9), in order to make it difficult for an animal to climb over.

◄◄
A young man prepares a lime-twig.

◄
In order to catch birds with a lime-twig, insects are used as bait. They are skewered onto two bamboo points at the upper end of the twig (below).

releases the peg; the balance beam subsequently loses balance and lets the striking beam fall from its loop onto the animal. It takes a tremendous amount of work to put up this type of fencing and lay this kind of trap — and one also needs a good feel for the proper adjustment of the traps; if, however, the traps have been well set, something can be caught every day. Pit falls, which were formerly used to capture wild elephants, are hardly dug anymore, since today only cattle are found rambling through the bush. During the season of cultivation, however, the paths to the fields are closed off to cattle.

Small birds are often driven from the fields by bamboo rattles, but birds may also be trapped with lime-twigs. The lime, or glue, is made out of the juice of the Indian *Ficus* tree cooked with some sap of a species of *Dipterocarpus* tree. After the sticky mass has been pulled into strings, it is wound around bamboo twigs; these twigs are then either bound at an angle to branches of fruit-bearing trees or stuck into the ground near watering holes. One also hunts birds with blow guns made from bamboo shafts more than two meters (7 ft.) long. The knotted joints are removed from the outside of a bamboo cane, and the resulting openings are then closed again with wax. Thin bamboo sticks, some 70 cm. (2 ft.) in length, are used as arrows; these sticks are rounded, sharpened, and equipped with small chicken feathers. The feathers are fastened by means of a spirally-wrapped bamboo strip to the lower half of the arrow, so that the arrow is given a spin when blown and experienced hunters can take quite accurate aim. Arrows tipped with poison are not used. Even the bow and arrow is not used as a hunting weapon. Yet there is a kind of bow with which small stones and pellets of dried clay can be hurled. The capability of this "pellet-bow" to hit a given target leaves much to be desired, but boys do use them for hunting birds.

Harvesting

From the middle of August the first ears of paddy are ripe; and although the proper harvesting of paddy begins but a month later, the first fruits can now be taken from the fields. Among other things, one gathers tender cobs of corn, which may be roasted in the hull, as well as the first squash. It is time for a celebration. A chicken must be sacrificed, and also a very large pig if one is available. This sacrifice, however, is not made in the field, but rather in the *kim-tom,* that is, the large room of the house. On the evening prior to the sacrifice, one brings home several items from the field: a few ears of paddy, some taro leaves, a little ginger and some sweetcane (not sugarcane, but rather a kind of sorghum). Some of each of these four fruits is put into a small basket (*klai-puk*); then a sickle and a hoe are added — the sickle being the instrument of harvest, and the hoe, the instrument of weeding. In front of the basket one places a bottle gourd filled with water and a small pot with a drinking reed. The latter has the form of the large, round beer pot; however, instead of beer, it is filled only with a mixture of water and cooked rice, the so-called *hom-noi.* As is the custom, one plucks the neck feathers of the chicken and slashes its throat with the hewing knife. The head of the house bites off a piece of ginger, sucks a mouthful of *hom-noi* from the small pot, and, while invoking the spirits, spits six times on the chicken. With a few drops of the chicken blood, which in the meantime has been caught in a small dish, one smears all objects in the house which are of ceremonial importance: the drum, the three-piece set of plate-shaped gongs, the spears, a few pebbles which are believed to bring prosperity, and also the previously-mentioned basket containing the first fruits.

If one also sacrifices a pig, the pig is killed with a spear just next to this basket; and some of the pig's blood is likewise distributed. Then both animals are cut up, and bits from each part of the animals' bodies — head, ribs, stomach, legs, internal organs — are cooked separately in two banana leaves. Fresh paddy is roasted over the fire and hulled in the mortar. At a later time, every family member will receive some of this rice to eat; first, however, small portions of the rice and tiny bits of the specially-prepared meat are filled into small pieces of taro leaf and folded into small parcels. The household head offers a special prayer for the paddy; and after spitting some *hom-noi* upon one of these so-called *köm-pot* parcels, he places it into the basket. Others are then deposited for the cotton and the taro, for the ginger, and for the sickle and the hoe in the basket. Additional parcels are also distributed to all places in the *kim-tom* and the *kimma* where an object is standing or is being preserved; this includes all types of baskets and mats. This sacrifice is made to all benign spirits who watch over the harvest and the house. Two parcels con-

Hornbills are shot with a gun. Their meat is highly valued.

tain only new rice and some sweetcane: one is thrown from the door down to the ground; the other, from the open platform up to the roof. Only after all of these things have been accomplished may the people eat of the fresh rice and nibble on the sweetcane.

The paddy will be ripe in September. Before it is harvested, large woven mats are brought into the field house and spread out over the floor and all lower parts of the side walls and the back wall; on these mats the paddy ears will be piled up. For the harvesting itself, several families again join together in mutual-aid groups; each participant carries one of the large harvesting baskets. As usual, work begins at the lower end of the plot which is to be harvested. With the left hand, one catches hold of a cluster of ears; the right hand then places the sickle at a point about half way up the stalk and pulls upward, cutting off the cluster. The cluster is then thrown by the left hand into the basket. When a basket is full, it is carried to the field house and emptied onto the mats. The worker returns to the field and begins anew; this process is repeated until the plot is harvested or until so much has been gathered into the field house that only the front part of the floor is still free. Now a bamboo rod is put up diagonally across the room about waist high; facing the interior of the house, the men hold fast to this rod as they work the ears of paddy with their feet — ears which, with the help of a sickle, they have pulled off from the pile heaped before them. With their feet the men lift up a bunch of ears from the side, roll it over, and step down on it, all the time shoving it slowly backwards; then the ears are brought forward again, tumbled again, and shoved backward toward the women, who are fully occupied with the task of shaking the bunches up and down, sifting them for remaining grains. The residue is thrown out the door onto the platform and is from time to time simply pushed over the edge of the platform onto the ground. If the inside of the room becomes too full, one can also do the threshing on a mat spread out on the outside platform (in front of the door). Paddy need not be threshed out in the same manner as wheat or rye, since the small stems of the panicle on which the grains hang dry up when the paddy is ripe and

The ears of the paddy are cut with a sickle.

therefore break easily when bent. Grains which are still green, however, remain on the stalks — as they should, because later they would mold. The loss must simply be taken into account because if one were to wait until all grains were fully ripe, some of the stalks might well die and break off, causing the grains to fall out. The loss would be even greater then.

As soon as the pile of ears has been worked through, the yield from the threshing is sieved with the hands in order to remove any remaining stalks; the cleaned grains are then scooped into baskets. A mat is spread out on the open platform, and two persons, with shovel-shaped winnowing trays in hand, set themselves up on either side of the mat. As the trays are swung back and forth like fans, a third person shovels up rice out of the basket with both hands and — in rhythm with the fanning — throws it onto the mat. After the grains have in this manner been cleaned of all residual chaff, they are spread out on mats in the field house to dry. Occasionally the tumbling mats get damaged; but if some of the grains escape through the holes, they can still be retrieved from the floor of the field house. If, however, the paddy is worked on the open platform and too many grains fall through to the ground, one tries to gather them up by hand as efficiently as possible. Then the next time one comes to the field, one brings along a chicken to pick up the rest.

Anyone who wishes may sacrifice a chicken or a pig during the tumbling; but the sacrifice of a chicken is mandatory only after the last paddy has been cut, worked, dried, and made ready to carry home from the field. The chicken is killed in the field house in front of the paddy. For the invocation, the beer substitute is again used, that is, the so-called *hom-noi* – it would be yet better, though, to bring genuine rice beer from home. Some of each part of the chicken is mixed with a bit of ginger and rice, both of which have been brought along, and wrapped into *köm-pot* parcels. The parcels are then placed about on the paddy, the bamboo mats, and the baskets; a last parcel is thrown outside onto the field on behalf of the cotton which will be harvested later. After all of the paddy and all of the instruments have been taken home – the paddy is carried in the same baskets used for harvesting – the same ceremony is held again. This time the chicken is killed near the storage bin which holds the paddy. Anyone having a pig sacrifices it, too. A pig alone, however, is not enough; not only are chickens more highly valued by the Mru (when they must be purchased, they are also relatively more expensive), but then again some spirits do not eat pork. As was the case with the festival of the first fruits, chicken and pork are cooked separately but packed together into the *köm-pot* parcels which are then placed on the paddy and on all important possessions. As always, the greater portion of the meat is consumed by the people. Yet only after the ceremony is one allowed to eat any kind of side dish along with the new rice – until that time the small red deer, several types of crab, and fish are forbidden. (Newly-married couples are also not allowed to eat these foods.) Likewise, only after the ceremony is one permitted to distill liquor from the new rice, although the brewing of beer is always permitted. Since liquor is always necessary for big celebrations, only from this point on may the larger celebrations (like marriages or cattle feasts) be properly held again. Even now, however, after the rice has been processed and carried home, one still provides for the paddy-spirits. At the appearance of each new moon, or perhaps a little later, the paddy should receive a *köm-pot* from a slaughtered chicken, so that the rice supply will dwindle away as slowly as possible.

Food

The concern for the paddy is well-founded; for all too often a household begins to run low on food supplies before the next harvest. Buying food at such times is quite expensive. After the harvest the prices go down and creditors press for the payment of debts. One must therefore sell one's own rice – and sell it cheaply. This, of course, only increases the prospects of again having an empty storage bin prior to the next harvest. Rice is the main staple food; the Mru eat it morning, noon, and night. Everything else, such as meat and vegetables, is regarded as a side dish, which one values

Tiny portions of rice are being spread on small pieces of taro leaves. After these *köm-pot* have been folded together, they will be distributed, as food for the good spirits, to all ritually-important places in the house. In the background, a small porcelain bowl with rice beer.

but which one can also do without. The amount of paddy needed for each person is correspondingly high. If a family has 800 lb. of paddy per family member in storage, its members can look confidently towards the coming year; for not only will each person have enough to eat, but the family will also be able to entertain guests, brew beer and distill liquor, and keep a few chickens. The family may, in addition, be able to sell some paddy, so that it will have money for occasional shopping. With such a reserve, one can even manage an unexpected illness which necessitates large expenses in connection with a sacrifice, without having to dip into the reserved seed grains. If the only concern is one's own consumption, one can also make do with 550 lb. of paddy per person. In such a case, however, there is no room to maneuver — no reserve for pleasant or unpleasant events. For the Mru, paddy is a staple food, not a cash crop. The latter purpose is rather served by cotton. Should then the cotton harvest fail, most families have little other than paddy which could be converted into money. Only a small part of the paddy which goes from the hands of the Mru into the hands of the Bangali merchants actually enables the Mru to buy something; the larger part serves to cover debts with their exorbitant interest rates — debts which were incurred prior to the previous harvest during some emergency situation.

In Bangladesh official statistics reckon with 200 kg. (440 lb.) of paddy per head per year. Before paddy can be used as food, it must be hulled; this removes the husk and at least part of the silver skin. After it has been hulled, 1 lb. of paddy gives about 0.6 lb. of rice — the amount varies somewhat depending on the type. 440 lb. of paddy per person for one year means, therefore, a daily ration of about 12 oz. of rice. The nutritional value of this amount corresponds to about 1200 kcal.; with 250 kg. (550 lb.) per year, the Mru may have 1470 kcal per day. If we add a maximum of 250 g. of vegetables (= 50 kcal.) and an average of 30 g. of meat (= 80 kcal.) — there is normally nothing else available — we have a total of 1600 kcal. per person per day. Since we are dealing here with average figures, the rations for adults would be about one-third higher.

◀◀
A woman spreads out newly-harvested paddy on woven mats on the *tsar*. Drying the paddy in the sun will prevent it from molding.

◀
An everyday task of Mru women: the pounding and cleaning of rice. What man does not eat, domestic animals devour.

▶
Hard work for women: securing the daily firewood
▶▶
A new house has been built. While children take part in the festive meal given for the workers, the women remain at home. Water serves as a beverage; it is drunk from bottle gourds.

According to the Mru, women eat more than men. As we have seen in relation to the farm work, men take over the most demanding short-term tasks; women, however, must carry water daily (usually two times), and daily they must pound the rice. Additionally, almost every day during the cold season women must carry a load of firewood. Men are not obliged to do such hard work day in and day out, which may well explain why women — as is claimed — do indeed have a higher consumption of calories. The version offered by Mru men, however, is somewhat different. They say that when women are hungry, they put more rice into the cooking pot; but when men are hungry, they go visiting. If this is true, men may well eat less at home, but they do not eat less in general — in the household budget, though, the extra amount consumed by the men is charged to the "visitors' account," not the men's. The men's point of view, then, reflects once again the unequal division of labor; for while the women are working — the women must do the daily cooking — the men take a stroll. (All men do know how to cook, but except for just helping out, they cook only for celebrations).

Mru women get up earlier than the men in order to hull the daily ration of rice (the men, however, cannot sleep any longer). During the cold season, the women pound the rice in front of the house; during the rainy season, inside the house (*kim-tom*). The only thing the men contribute to this activity is the manufacture of the heavy, wooden mortars and pestles and the trays used for winnowing. The paddy is put into the mortar and pounded with the round end of the pestle, in order to remove the husks; then it is winnowed over an old basket in which husks and bran are collected. After this initial process, the paddy is skinned by a second round of pounding; this time the pounding is done with the flatter end of the pestle. A second winnowing finally removes the bran.

At this point, the women rekindle the fire which has been kept alive overnight in the fireplace by means of a thick log. The fireplace is situated on one of the side walls of the *kim-tom*; it consists of a mud square framed with bamboo boards, in the middle of which three conical-shaped stones have been placed. The stones serve as a pot stand; occasionally, however, an iron tripod is used in their stead. The everyday metal pots, which the Mru purchase at the market, have a round belly and a neck; with such shape they rest firmly on the stones and can be taken from the fire with bamboo tongs. After the rice has been washed in a special basket, it is placed with a little more than double its amount of water into one of these pots; it is then brought to a boil, while one stirs occasionally. When the water has been absorbed, the pot is removed from the fire, covered, and placed next to the embers. It will then be turned from time to time. The secret to successful rice cooking lies precisely in this art of turning the pot: the pot must be rotated just at the right time, so that the rice swells up evenly and becomes dry, not pasty. When the rice is done, it is dumped out onto a clean banana leaf which serves as a platter for the entire family. The women eat kneeling, the men squatting. Water is drunk directly from the gourd bottles; as a condiment, there is salt and, perhaps, a green chili pod. At lunchtime one eats the leftover rice which was cooked in the morning; this time it is eaten cold. The evening meal may be a little more varied, but here again rice is the main dish.

Between August and January, that is, about half of the year, fresh vegetables can be brought home from the field; a few types of squash can also be preserved at home over an extended period of time. The rest of the time, however, one must make do with the leaves of wild plants. At the beginning of the rainy season, there are young bamboo sprouts. Banana stalks are also edible, after one has peeled off the outside and stirred up the inside pulp with a small stick in order to remove the hair-like strings. This pulp is cooked with oil, in order to make it more tasty; most vegetables and leaves, however, are cooked with water and salt only. More extravagant ways of food preparation are known; but as soon as oil and spices are called for — things which must be bought — they become financially unviable for everyday cooking.

The availability of fruits is even more seasonally determined than that of vegetables. Most frequently available are bananas — every village has a small banana grove. Papaya are found primarily in the valley villages. Mango and lichi are rare, but in many villages there is a jackfruit tree. Pomelos are part of an old cultural heritage; in contemporary villages, however, it is rare to find more than one or two such trees. In contrast to the land, these trees are the private possessions of the persons who planted or inherited them. Rarely, however, can one harvest much from them, since the fruits are usually looted prematurely by children. If an owner protests such looting, he finds little sympathy, for the fruits are considered to be children's food, rather than food for adults. Mandarin oranges have only recently become common, as whole plantations of the fruit have been planted. They are sold to Bangali peddlers who take them to the urban agglomerations of the plains, where affluent Bangalis buy the fruits by the piece for a price many times higher than they brought in the mountains. Because of this middleman's profit, the Mru would very much like to carry their fruits down to the plains themselves and sell them themselves; yet they fear — and rightly so — that they would imme-

Instead of pots, bamboo tubes are sometimes used for cooking certain foods, for example, sticky-rice, small fish, and shrimp. For the preparation of the small pieces of meat offered to the spirits, the use of these tubes is ritually prescribed.

diately be surrounded and robbed of their goods or money. As mentioned, it has long been customary to consider these fruit trees the property of the person who plants them. He who plants a grove of mandarin oranges, however, incites the anger of the other villagers who do not have the money for such a project; for the villagers see that such an undertaking permanently reduces the land area which traditionally was at the disposal of everyone and that the yields of the field now benefit one individual family only.

Whereas mandarins were brought to the Hill Tracts by Lushai missionaries, limes have been growing wild in the jungle for a long time. Since limes, however, are available for only a short time each year, they cannot serve as a standard ingredient of indigenous cookery. Tea, which must be bought at the market and which on the plains is served with a lot of milk and sugar, is usually spiced with salt only — sugar would be too expensive. Only a few persons know how to use limes to prepare a tasty condiment: a kind of pickled-cucumber chutney. Very common as a condiment are green chilis — but they too are available only part of the year — and a popular fish paste called *ngapi*. *Ngapi* must be bought, but it is relatively cheap; and although the paste is prepared by Bangalis, who also call it *ngapi*, the name is of Burmese origin and would literally translate "rotten fish." Fish caught in the ocean are spread out on seaweed and mud and left in the sun to dry. As the fish decompose, they are pounded from time to time until they have formed, together with the seaweed and mud, one pasty mass. This mass is then formed into large, light grey or dark grey balls, depending on the quality; and after it has been transported in this form into the interior of the country, the fish paste is sold by the piece in the markets. One needs only a little of this paste to conjure up a fish dish in the mouth, but the condiment smells strongly of fish and does not suit the taste of every Mru. Dried fish is much more popular, although it consists of little more than skin and bones even after it has been cooked; in addition to that, it also must be purchased.

It is cheaper for a person to go fishing himself. Traps are very common and are sometimes used in conjunction with the diking and barricading of a waterway. The earlier practice of fishing with plant poison is now forbidden; today men try their luck with bought hooks or casting nets. An old method is still preserved by the women, though: they wade — often in groups — through shallow brooks, lifting up the stones, and catch in baskets the tiny fish and shrimps that try to swim away. Since most of the Mru do not live close to the large waterways, this traditional way of catching fish is perhaps the one most often utilized. The size of the catch, however, is quantitatively small; so although the Mru like to eat fish, it does not make up a meaningful part of their diet.

As mentioned, meat is eaten almost exclusively on festival days, unless one is forced by an emergency to slaughter an animal, or unless hunting or trapping provides a catch. Faced with such scarcity, the Mru are not choosey. Even insects, such as tasty beetles and maggots, are not scorned. Meat is always roasted or boiled. Cattle and deer are skinned, and goats likewise — although goats are very seldom kept up by the Mru themselves because of the damage they might cause. Pigs are singed; dogs as well, in the few instances when a dog is needed as a sacrifice. Chickens are plucked and singed. After an animal has been carved up and gutted, the intestines are cleaned and cut up; everything else — except the skull, the hooves, and similar unedible parts — is also chopped or cut up into small cubes. (Even with larger fish one proceeds in this manner, paying no attention whatsoever to the bones — an indication that larger fish are only seldom available.) Together with some spices (at least some chili pods) which have been freshly crushed in a bamboo quiver, the meat is then cooked in a pot.

With a calabash ladle, some of this "curry" is spooned up for every person and placed next to his rice. Each one may then mix the proportion he desires, but always with enough rice to form a small ball. This ball is shaped with the first three fingers of the right hand — never with the left — and then popped into the mouth. No one is entitled to receive "the best parts." (We may recall that the spirits, too, receive little bits of each part of the animal. Their food, however, should never contain

For crushing chilis and other spices, one may use the internode of a bamboo cane, closed by the node on one side.

Small bottle gourds, cut open on one side, serve as ladles.

any spices; it is therefore cooked separately.) Whatever is chewable is gladly eaten by all who have teeth; whatever is impossible to eat is left for the dogs, who are generally already waiting behind the eaters. If the dogs venture forward on their own initiative, though, they will receive a blow on the nose until they learn to control their hunger.

Domestic Animals

Dogs are always hungry, since they are practically never fed. To be sure, in every house one finds a dog, or even several; but no one really knows why it is there. Once in a while a dog is regarded as a good hunting dog because it discovers small animals in the bush and calls attention to them. In the village strangers are also "announced;" they are never bitten, though, because the dogs have learned that if they come too close to people they will either be struck, or some hard object will be thrown at them. Dogs can also ward off evil spirits; in this capacity, they may in special cases be needed as sacrifices. Generally speaking, however, dogs are useful around the house only if there is a small child in the family who has not yet learned to use the designated places when taking care of his natural needs. Dogs lick up the excrement; and since water runs down through the woven floor of the platform, one need only rinse quickly with water in order to have everything clean again. Dogs also go along to the field; there they again take over the role as consumer of excrement — at least as long as they are that hungry.

Cats are useful inasmuch as they catch mice interested in the paddy in the storage bin. It would never occur to a Mru to feed a cat, and he would not eat one either. Since cats have nothing good to look forward to and, unlike dogs, will not allow themselves to be used as patient toys by the smaller children, they stay out of sight most of the time. Cats are therefore hardly looked upon as domestic animals.

Another partially domesticated animal, which comes occasionally to the village in order to lick salt, is the gayal *(Bos frontalis)*. The gayal is a type of cattle indigenous to the mountainous area of Assam; it has a black coat, a white spot on its forehead, and white stockings. The gayal's wild relative, the gaur, has been almost exterminated in the Hill Tracts. Gayal grow to be substantially larger than the domestic cattle, both the breeds with humps and those without, found all over India. They are never yoked to the plow nor milked, but serve only as sacrificial animals. Since the mountains are their home, gayal, in contrast to normal domestic cattle, are not deterred by thick jungle and steep slopes, especially when it comes to reaching the fields when the harvest is ripening. Relatively simple barricades at easily passable points are enough to keep domestic cattle away from the fields; if gayal are to be kept away, however, one must go to considerably more trouble. The more cultivated fields there may be scattered about, then, the more costly the keeping of gayal becomes. So even if the inhabitants of a village do not directly outlaw the keeping of gayal, a rich man will usually think twice before taking the risk of making himself accountable for all the damages his gayal might do to the fields. That gayal are still kept at all is to be explained by the fact that, as the animals become rarer and more expensive to keep, their price correspondingly goes up. If someone plans a very big feast and wishes to make a name for himself, he must, however, be able to afford the purchase of one of these luxury animals. Only a very few persons can afford such an expense, even once in a lifetime. The Christian Bawm, who live in settlements made up of several dozen households, have found another way to show their reverence for this traditional sacrificial animal: during a good year, people pool their resources in order to purchase a gayal, and the animal is then consumed by the entire village at Christmastime.

Domestic cattle are also not kept by the Mru for field work or for milking; they serve exclusively as animals of sacrifice. Their care is less problematic than that of the gayal; and since cattle can more easily find something to eat in the jungle than on the plains, the Bangalis also like to bring their cattle to Mru villages to be tended. (On the plains, cattle are obliged to be content with the sparse stems and blades of grass along the pathways and on the field dikes; they should, however, stay away from the dikes during the cultivating season, unless

A gayal yearling receives a handful of salt from its owner – that is the only reason it comes into the village.

someone is keeping a close eye on them.) Even in the Mru villages, though, the cattle do not really become fat. It is true that during the planting season their range in the hills is somewhat limited; yet the greenery which is still available to them is more than enough to satisfy their hunger. But the animals are at the same time heavily bled by leeches — so heavily, in fact, that they return home at night covered with blood. They are not spared other vermin either, the most common being worms which eat through the body cavities and larvae which bury finger-deep encasements for themselves in the soft tissue. The Mru can do nothing more than attempt to remove these parasites by hand.

Whoever agrees to look after the cattle of another person must compensate for their loss, should something happen to them, or for any damages the cattle may incur. Consequently, one takes on this job only against payment — the normal monthly rate being about 1/100 of the total worth of the cattle. In the case of cows, the caretaker has the right either to one-half of the calves born during his period of supervision or to a corresponding compensation. From a cow with calf he may also receive some milk; if the cow has no calf, it is useless to try to milk the animal, though, since it gives no milk. In light of the general emaciated state of these cattle, this may seem understandable; but more important may be the fact that the Mru are not particularly interested in drinking milk. Since they have not been accustomed to it since infancy, milk causes them intestinal difficulties even when boiled. Cow dung is indispensable for the clay needed to build the fireplace. That manure which turns up in the village is also occasionally used to fertilize the small garden near the house, but no one goes to the trouble of carrying manure to the field. There are no stalls; so in the evening, when the cattle return on their own to the village, they settle down together wherever they please. Every person knows which head of cattle belongs to him. If the Mru feel particularly close to any domestic animal, it is the cow; of all animals, only the cow may receive a name which is otherwise reserved for humans.

Pigs and dogs may also receive names, but never those used for human beings. Not every household owns a cow or an ox, but there is certainly a pig and a few chickens, unless the last animal has just been needed for a sacrifice. Cattle sacrifices are optional; pig and chicken sacrifices are a must. Just as the most important rites related to the life cycle can hardly be carried out without pigs, so it is too with the annual field ceremonials; and serious illnesses almost always require the sacrifice of a pig. Since such ritual demands constantly reduce the pig supply, very few households are prepared to sell pigs. For all eventualities, in fact, one should always have a pig in the stall, preferably a sow who provides offspring. The pigs kept by the Mru are the black, Southeast-Asian, potbellied variety, although the animals are not exclusively black but occasionally sport white bristles, especially on the belly. These pigs can weigh up to more than 100 lbs.; usually, however, the animals are slaughtered long before they have had time to put on the fat which is otherwise highly valued. Male piglets are castrated at the age of one to two months. No one intentionally leaves an animal uncastrated, since a small uncastrated boar would not become fat and its meat would not taste good. Additionally, uncastrated animals may not be used for sacrifice. It does occasionally happen, however, that an animal escapes the normal castration procedure; should it then at four or five months be too old to castrate, it is immediately slaughtered. Castration as generally practiced causes no problems regarding further litters, since the boars are sexually mature soon after birth and not only suck from the prostrate mother sow, but also copulate with her.

During the daytime pigs run free; only old animals are kept closed in at all times. This is often done only because old pigs could be dangerous for children at the latrine. All pigs are fed. On the platform (*tsar*) of every house there is a tub in which food remains, as well as chaff and bran from the morning's rice pounding, are collected and soaked. In the afternoon this mixture is boiled; then the housewife calls loudly to the pigs, who immediately come running. After pouring the slop into the pig trough, the woman stands guard with a stick, in order to make sure that no strange animal pushes in to eat the food and that the larger pigs do not drive away the smaller ones.

The Bangalis, who as Muslim do not keep pigs, use the rice chaff and bran as food for cattle and chickens. For the Mru, however, chickens cause an additional drain on the rice supply: one reckons 10 kg. per chicken per year. Since a goshawk may occasionally take a chicken or the chicken pest wipe out an entire flock, keeping up chickens is risky business. It is therefore cheaper for the Mru to trade chickens from the Bangalis for rice. During the rainy season when the paths become overgrown, trade is, however, stilled; and since the rituals of the planting cycle, as we have seen, require several chickens, one is nevertheless obliged to keep up a few oneself. Eggs are not eaten: chickens lay so few eggs that one prefers chicks.

At night pigs and chickens are closed up in the shelter under the front part of the *kimma*. It is true that the odor of the pigs waffs up from below, but the bamboo construction provides good ventilation; in addition to that, the sleeping quarters are rather situated above that part of the *kimma* where the chickens are accommodated. With this arrangement, one can at least notice any disturbance in the shed; and this is important because, if one of the wild cats or small leopards found in the Hill Tracts makes a nighttime visit, one must be able to sound the alarm immediately, before the cat can break into the shelter through some hole in the bamboo-cane siding. The alarm is hardly sounded in one house before there is a clamor in all other houses. The entire village gets very stirred up; but only next

Harvesting cotton. The yield is often low and hardly enough for one's own needs. From the returns of a good harvest, however, one can finance a cattle feast.

◀

Pigs are important sacrificial animals. Every day they are slopped with cooked bran and food scraps. Moreover they are free to roam about the village and the bush and devour garbage and excrement.

morning can one look for possible tracks and ascertain whether or not it was in fact just a false alarm. Doves are rarely kept. Ducks are found only in villages near the waterways; at night they also take shelter in the chicken coop. They are fed only soaked, but uncooked, bran. Geese may be kept only by *karbari* and headmen; the animals are considered too dangerous to be put into the hands of everybody. The *mema* would be a very good domestic animal; for without causing any harm to the live animal, one can slice pieces of meat from its body — pieces which will soon grow back again. Unfortunately, this animal has become extinct.

Cotton, Textiles, and Jewelry

Let us return again to the field; for following the paddy harvest there are here still things to be done. In October that part of the field which was planted with cotton is weeded again; in November comes the cotton harvest, which is done in three rounds. The white bolls of fibre are picked by hand, and the same baskets that were used for the paddy are now used to gather and carry home the cotton. In contrast to the paddy harvest, no special ceremonies are necessary this time. Cotton, therefore, is not given the same meaning as paddy. It is, nevertheless, an old cultigen which is still valued today by the Mru. They need it to produce much of their clothing, their blankets, and their covers, which, as far as the traditional types are concerned, are not available on the market. For this reason, even the Mru villages situated at higher elevations cultivate cotton, although the harvest there is generally scant. This is due to the fact that the climate on the ridges is a few degrees cooler than in the valleys; and in order to grow more profusely the cotton would need just those few degrees of warmer weather. There are also other factors, likewise outside the control of the Mru, which may render the harvest less than that which was sown; under very favorable conditions, however, one acre may yield 6 cwt. of cotton. The best bolls are sorted and worked separately, and the seeds are preserved for future planting. In spite of this selection process, the quality and quantity of the fibre, which at one time served to produce the famous Dacca muslin material, lags behind the modern varieties. If the government had really been interested in bettering the income of the swidden farmers, the cultivation of newer varieties could long have been promoted; until now Bangladesh has had to import cotton from Pakistan.

The cotton gin is the only machine utilized by the Mru. The type they use, normally produced by Bangali carpenters, is common all over the Hill Tracts. This contraption consists of a wooden frame with two rollers geared to revolve in opposite directions, the lower part of which is set into motion by a hand crank. The rollers allow only the fibre to pass; the seeds are kept behind and caught in a basket placed below the machine. Ginning, which is done by the women, is rather time-consuming. It is, however, worth the trouble because clean fibre fetches twice the price of unginned cotton; and the seeds can be sold separately. When fibre is to be sold, it is packed into large, cylindrical baskets — each holding 19 kg. (41 lb.) — and carried to the closest market or to any place on the main rivers where it is taken over by Bangali peddlers.

On a sunny day the fibre which has been kept back for one's own use is spread out on a mat on the *tsar*. Here it is teased with the vibrating string of a special bow. This string is set into motion by scraping it with a notched piece of wood. This teasing removes debris from the fibre and fluffs it up. The downy soft fibre is then shaped into small sausages and put aside until the women have time to spin. Women prefer to spin during the evenings when there is an opportunity for mutual visits. If several young girls are gathered together in one house, young men usually show up in order to make some music and chat with the girls by the light of the fire. While Chakma, Marma, Tippera, and Bawm women make use of the spinning wheel, which they acquire from the Bangalis, Mru women use only the manual spindle. This instrument consists of a rod, some 25 cm. (10 in.) long, with a small, round disk (the whorl) attached just above its lower end. The newly spun thread is wound up above the whorl.

If the yarn is to be dyed, it is first wound around a simple reel from which it can be taken off in strands. To prevent the strands from becoming tangled, one normally ties a small string around them. Today dyes are generally bought at the market, likewise the fine, colored yarn used in weaving patterns. The Mru, however, still know how to dye red and blue-black (indigo) colors with homemade dyes. When one wishes to dye some yarn red, the root of a certain tree is dug up, cleaned, cut into small pieces, and crushed in a mortar with a bit of water; the resulting solution is then filtered through a piece of cloth and boiled together with the yarn. Indigo is planted in the field, its seeds being mixed in with the paddy seeds. One pulls the small leaves off the indigo plants by hand and soaks them overnight in an earthen pot; bamboo ashes, which contain alkali, are added to the water as a mordant. (The ashes were prepared back in February especially for this purpose and have been preserved until now.) On the following day the yarn is punched down into the solution and boiled together with the leaves and ashes. After the yarn has been dyed in this manner, the strands are hung up between the necks of two gourd bottles to dry. This entire procedure must be repeated two or three times before the strands become completely black. Material made from yarn dyed with natural indigo fades after several washes and takes on the bluish tinge of jeans; yet the Mru women prefer their indigo to the aniline color which may be bought at the market.

Below:
A woman drums indigo-colored skeins of cotton yarn. To the right, one sees the indigo leaves; next to them, the bulbous earthen pot in which they are soaked and boiled. Above the pot, on the bordering fence of the *tsar*, hangs the "end product": a new skirt. In the corner behind the woman is a rain cover; it is made of woven bamboo strips which have been meshed with leaves. This cover may be hung over the head and back.

Above:
A woman winds yarn into a ball; she has placed the skein around the necks of two bottle gourds filled with water. A rice mortar, turned upside down, serves as a stool. On the small fence bordering the *tsar* is a tray holding raw cotton.

Tension loom

Shed (above) and
countershed (below)
BS   back strap
BB   breast beam
S   sword
H   heddle
L   lease rod
AS   additional shedding stick
SS   shedding stick
B^1, B^2 bars of the loom
W   wall mounting

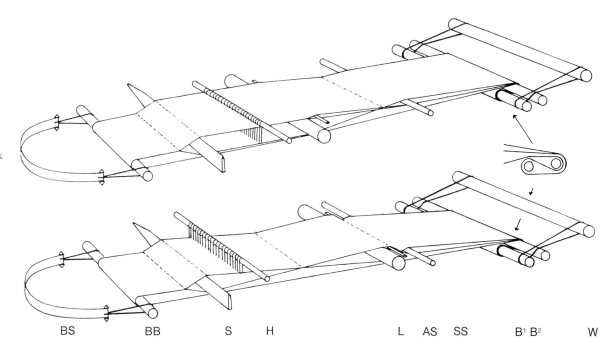

Manual spindle with wooden rod (ca. 25 cm. [10 in.]), whorl, and spun yarn.

Weaving, like spinning and dyeing, is exclusively women's work; however, the men make the looms. While still a young girl, a Mru woman receives her first and prettiest loom from her future husband. The loom, the sticks of which are decorated with ornamental incisions, is given to the girl before the wedding and is considered to be a kind of wedding present. It is not a large machine, but consists of a minimum of six separate bamboo rods and a wooden sword. Two of these rods form the bar of the loom; by means of two strings, the rods are attached to the wall in such a way that the warp, when tightened, does not shift or slip. On the opposite end, a strap runs from the breast beam around the back of the weaver, so that she can regulate the tension of the warp by the movements of her body.

The thickest stick is the lease rod; the warp threads run alternately over and under this stick. A thinner shedding rod with an alternate threading pattern is placed just behind it, so that the lease rod is kept straight and does not slip back in the direction of the bar. Within the space between weaver and lease rod an exchange between the shed and countershed is made possible in that the warp threads running under the lease rod are caught in a continuous heddle thread. This passes over the heddle stick, runs down to catch a warp thread, and up again, from one side to the other. If the weaver pulls the heddle stick up, the warp threads passing under the lease rod are brought up over the upper warp threads. The countershed is thus formed. By placing the sword edgewise, the weaver keeps the countershed open, in order to shoot through the shuttle. Then she loosens the sword and uses it to beat down the weft thread firmly against the previously-woven material. The weaver next pulls the lease rod close to the heddle; this pushes the lower threads, which were pulled up, back into their original position. The shed is now formed again, and the weft can be threaded back through and beaten down again. When the material becomes too long for the weaver to ply the shuttle, the weaver loosens the bar of the warp, passes the woven piece under the breast-beam, readjusts the other rods of the loom, and continues her work. By using threads of different colors for the weft, she can weave horizontal stripes. Longitudinal stripes are more common, however; these result when threads of various colors are used for the warp.

The width of a piece of woven material is restricted by the fact that the rods are generally only about half a meter long (less than 2 ft.). In order to make wider pieces like blankets, three strips of the same

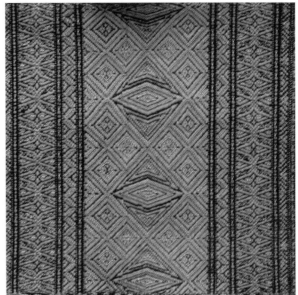

Women's skirts

In the embroidery patterns rhomboid patterns are predominant.

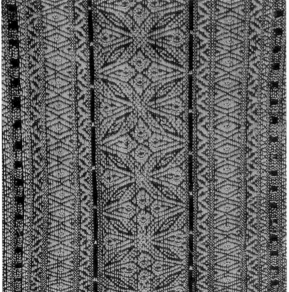

The continouous warp of the indigo-colored *wan-klai* measures 60 × 11 in., the embroidered pattern, 5 × 11 in. The selvedges show red and white threads to which small, cylindrical beads have been sewn.

length are sewn together. For the narrower coverlets in which children are carried, one strip is sufficient. A single strip is also wide enough for a work jacket, the main part of which is woven in one piece from the bottom back. About 5 cm. (2 in.) below the neck the strip divides into two parts; these are then sewn to the back part on the sides under the armholes. The three-quarter-length sleeves are woven in separate strips and then sewn on.

Considerably more skill is needed when a woman weaves herself a skirt (*wan-klai*). A skirt is made of an indigo-colored strip slightly more than 25 cm. (10 in.) wide and 150 cm. (60 in.) long; the ends of the strip are sewn together so that the skirt actually consists of two layers of cloth. This double-layered skirt is wrapped around the hip (the two ends meeting on the left side) and secured by a chain. A multicolored pattern, 10–30 cm. (4–12 in.) wide, decorates the back side of the outer layer of the skirt; however, the pattern is visible only on festival days when a woman wears her skirt right side out. For everyday attire, women wear their skirts wrong side out, so that one sees only the colorful weft threads on the back side of the material, but not the embroidery itself. The pattern design is left up to each weaver. Patterns often consist, however, of rhomboid motifs and meanders, which in a similar form are also woven by the men into some of the baskets and especially into the mats used for a coffin. To embroider a pattern into a skirt, one works colorful threads in between the lease while one is weaving. This is done with the help of a holeless needle which customarily serves as a hairpin. Modern pieces take advantage of the great variety of colored threads which can be bought at the market. Old pieces which were dyed with homemade dyes are easily recognizable: their brownish-red hue clearly contrasts the bright modern red. The edges of the skirts are trimmed with tiny white or red ringlets, depending on the region; formerly, the halved shells of small, pearl-like fruits served this purpose.

Tiny beads, approximately one millimeter in diameter, are also available at the market. These beads are purchased in various colors — primarily red, but also green, white, yellow and black — and fashioned into elaborate chains and belts. The holes of the beads are so small that even the tiniest needles cannot be used for stringing. Mru women must therefore string them by hand; if necessary they use their hairpin to push the thread through the hole. In order to keep the thread from unravelling during this stringing, it is rubbed with beeswax. Such treatment also adds longer life to the chains in general. All thread used to sew blankets and jackets should likewise be rubbed with wax. Beeswax is also necessary for weaving, since all loom rods are waxed with it, so as to slide more smoothly; and the sword is repeatedly waxed even during the weaving itself.

The securing and preparation of beeswax is the responsibility of the men. They smoke out the hives of wild bees, cut up the honeycomb, and press out the honey. (Honey is considered to be medicine for children; mixed with the gallbladder of a lizard, it is thought to be effective against stomach pains.) The remaining comb is then boiled, and the liquid wax which results is poured into water to eliminate impurities. Finally, the wax is reheated and filled into bamboo tubes, where it hardens into round sticks. Beeswax is used exclusively for weaving and sewing. A different type of wax is used to seal over holes, for example, the holes in a blowgun or a mouth organ. This wax,

A woman embroidering her skirt with colorful threads.

Jewelry

1 Earrings: silver disks with a hanging ornament of brightly colored beads and tassels made of red woolen threads; worn by young men (in pierced earlobes) on festive occasions; diameter ca. 3.5 cm. (1.4 in.).

2 Rare fingerring of silver-coated brass: onto the ring itself an Indian quarter-Rupee coin or a simple disk has been soldered; worn on festive occasions by young men and women.

3 Ornamental comb: cut and carved from one piece of wood; spine decorated with aluminium; made and worn by young men; length 20–40 cm. (ca. 8–16 in.).

4 Aluminium bangle with faceted, diamond-shaped pattern: worn by young girls and women (and also occasionally young men) on the lower arm; diameter 5.5 cm. (2.2 in.)

5 Brass bangle with incised pattern: inside hollow; worn by young girls and women on the lower arm.

6 Silver-coated brass bracelet: six-sided; a silver-coated, Persian coin is soldered flat at the point where the bracelet tapers to a narrower width; worn on festive occasions by women and men; diameter (on the outside) 8.8 cm. (3.5 in.).

7 Silver anklet for young girls: six-sided; inside hollow and one side open; points on both ends in the form of a lotus bud.

8 Upper-arm bangle for young girls and women: made of hammered silver foil, with five ridges running lengthwise around the bracelet; the fastener, consisting of three eyelets and a small, silver pin, is found under the engraved decorative plate; diameter (inside) 5.6 cm. (2.2 in.), height 4 cm (1.6 in.).

9 Silver belt: five chainlike strands of interwoven silver wires; the strands are held together at the ends by two silver pieces, each in the form of a figure eight attached to a rectangle; the two ends of the belt are fastened together with a flat, pointed, oval-shaped decorative clasp; worn around the waist by young people of both sexes.

10 Hairpin: iron shaft to which an Indian half-Rupee coin is soldered; worn in the hair-knot by young men; length 11 cm. (4.3 in.).

11 Anklet-rattle for small children: eight ball-shaped brass bells hang from a thick, twisted cotton cord which has been knotted at intervals.

12 Ear plugs: silver, cylindrical shells with engraved pattern; worn daily by women and young girls in the holes of the earlobes; length 3.5 cm. (1.4 in.).

13 Hairpin: iron shaft with hanging ornamental decoration; decoration made of short strands of tiny, colorful beads and tassels of red, woolen threads; worn in the hair-knot by young girls; length 9 cm. (3.5 in.).

14 Anklet-rattle: made of sheet-metal brass bent round; inside hollow, with small, round stones as rattles; worn to dances by young girls; diameter (inside) up to 13 cm. (ca. 5 in.).

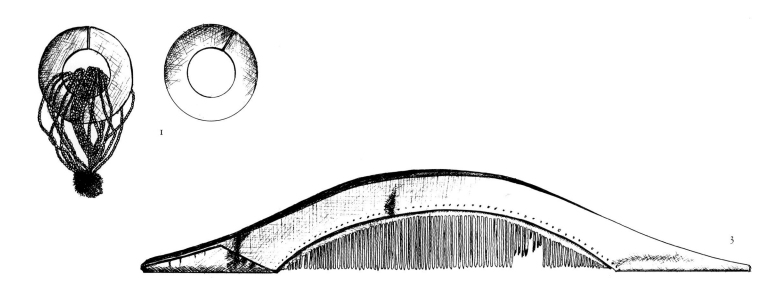

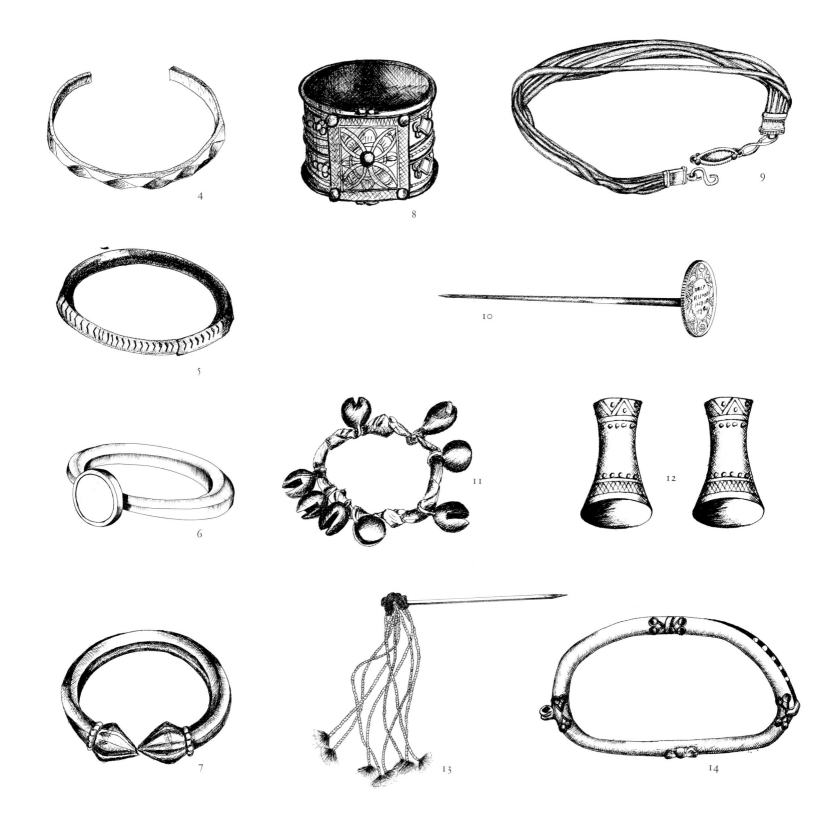

which has the consistency of plasticine, is produced by a type of wasp living underground.

In addition to the small beads, the market also offers Mru women larger beads which are easier to thread. These white and iridescent green beads, however, have the disadvantage of being made of very thin glass; so they break quite easily. Likewise available at the market are old coins to which a small ring has been soldered. Alternated with red beads or hard, red fruits, these coins — formerly made of silver — are fashioned into decorative chains. The longer chains, which are worn only for feasts, are hung from the right shoulder and over the left hip; a shorter type may be wrapped, together with chains of beads, around the hair-knot or slung about the hips. Different types of bangles are also available at the market. Narrow silver bangles and aluminium bracelets are worn around the wrist — the latter are more common; broader silver bangles, which are equipped with a hinge, are worn about the upper arm. Young girls begin wearing the upper-arm bangle as soon as they reach puberty; and since the bangles do not grow along with the girls, they cut considerably into the lower part of the biceps. However, only older women who are no longer so concerned with beauty refrain from wearing them. These bracelets are made expressly for Mru customers by Bangali silversmiths, who also fashion the special type of hourglass-shaped ear plugs worn exclusively by Mru women. Young girls may further adorn these ear plugs with flowers and fragrant herbs.

In contrast to Mru women, Mru men wear little jewelry. Young men do in fact possess bangles and flat, disk-shaped earrings which can be decorated with beaded pendants; but they wear them almost exclusively for festive occasions. A red wooden comb which is decorated on the rounded top with a piece of aluminium belongs, on the other hand, to traditional everyday attire. Yet self-made combs are becoming rarer and rarer, since the colorful plastic ones available at the market represent cheap competition. The hair-knots in which the combs are worn are becoming less fashionable among older men who prefer to cut their hair short. Young men, in contrast, take great pains with the grooming of their hair-knot. The knot is worn on the upper, left side of the head and is often reinforced with strands of the person's own hair which were earlier cut for that purpose. Women never cut their hair short, but rather knot it on the back of the head. In contrast to the men, women always adorn their hair-knot with a hairpin — which is also needed for their needlework. In former times this hairpin was probably a porcupine quill; porcupines, however, have become rare, and the metal needles bought at the market are more durable. For festive occasions, colorful paper rosettes may also be bought at the market; they are used to adorn the hair and are particularly popular among young girls.

Decorative items are not the only things bought at the market; certain kinds of cloth may also be purchased there. Although Mru women wear only self-woven skirts, the men's loin-cloths and turbans are strips of material obtained at the market. There can be no doubt that the women themselves also

◀ On festival days even four-year-old girls wear jewelry: around the neck, the young child sports a two-stranded necklace made of olive-green glass beads, a medallion pendant, and a longer strand of white and red beads; around her hips, she wears a multistranded chain of green beads, as well as a chain of coins; the edges of her skirt are also trimmed with small red beads. Three aluminium bracelets and a cotton string adorn the child's arm. The girl's father is just arranging her hair-knot.

once wove this material and decorated it on the ends with red or black embroidery — among the Mrung this is still the case today. Women's cloaks also come from the market. Modern cloaks are generally green or blue; older ones have red and yellow designs, but were likewise imported. Whether cloaks were formerly made by the Mru themselves remains an open question. The blankets which are still produced cannot be used as cloaks, since they would be far too heavy. These blankets are more than two yards long and, like the women's skirts, of double thickness (i.e. the strip of material has a total length of more than four yards). Where the ends of the strip meet, the warp threads are twisted together into cords. Since the blankets, which are made only of cotton, must be warm even on cold nights, they are woven of thick threads.

Yet technique also plays a role. Marma blankets are considerably thinner; it may therefore be necessary to use several blankets in order to keep warm. The fabrics the Marma women weave for their ankle-length, wraparound skirts are also thinner than those woven by the Mru. If Mru women wanted to produce such thin threads and fabrics, they would be obliged to spend much more time on their spinning and weaving, or they would have to take over the spinning wheel and loom of the Marma. Since daughters, however, learn by observing and imitating their mothers, rather than by verbal instruction as such, the dissemination of such knowledge is extremely limited — not to mention the fact that every ethnic group has its own style of which it is quite proud. (The Marma cannot spin and weave like the Mru either.) Under the circumstances, therefore, it makes more sense for Mru women to sell raw cotton and buy finer cloth with the profits, rather than try with disproportionately more energy to produce such cloth themselves. Their own type of blankets or skirts, however, the Mru cannot buy. Other items, like work-jackets and shoulder bags, could be bought, but are not. Mru women make their bags themselves, although bags are available in the same form and a more attractive style on the market — in the meantime, even on the Western market. Shoulder bags, however, are seldom used; a portable basket serves the same purpose.

Drum
◀
The barrel-shaped body of hollowed wood (50 cm. [20 in.] in length) is on both ends (24 cm. [9 in.] in diameter), covered with barking-deer hide. The drumheads are stretched taut by long, thin leather straps, running up and down between two bamboo hoops. The drum is carried with a string over the shoulder and beaten with both hands.

Harvest Festival

After the paddy and the cotton have been brought from the fields, and after a few ears of corn, some millet, indigo leaves, sweetcane, beans, squash, gourds, taro and yams have intermittently been harvested, a few tubers and late-appearing gourds are still available on into January. Whoever wishes may also help himself to the flowers and fragrant leaves which were planted along the edges of the field paths. It is December, climatically one of the most pleasant months, and time for the harvest festival. The sizes of the celebrations vary, depending upon what can be afforded following the harvest; and those ceremonies considered necessary at this time likewise vary from region to region. At the very least, one must sacrifice a chicken; most households, however, sacrifice a pig — one still small enough to be carried easily to the field. The three plate-shaped gongs and the drum may also be taken to the field. Four people are needed to play the musical instruments; as we shall see, others are soon added. This means that it is not a single household which sets out for such a "field dance" (*üa-plai*), but rather an entire group. The group consists primarily of the men who mutually assisted each other during the field work. The women normally remain at home, since sacrificing is a man's job. This, however, does not keep young boys and girls from tagging along.

One of the men should be a *sra* (a "master") who can lead the ceremony, since no ordinary man could possibly know all of the things which must be done. One begins, first of all, with the various types of ornamental bamboo and their special accessories. The most important piece of bamboo is placed on the broad side of the *tsar*, the open platform of the field house. This bamboo object is equipped with a small piece of matting upon which two shrimps and the head of a small rodent are placed. The rodent should have been caught beforehand; however, these tasty animals — called "bamboo rats," although they are not rats — have become quite rare. They are therefore often replaced with small pieces of ginger cut in the shape of the rodent. No less symbolic is a bamboo slat which hangs at the site; it represents the scabbard of the one-edged ceremonial sword with which the *sra* should dance, if it were available. Then there is a silver hip chain and a bracelet like the ones women wear. A spear is tied up nearby, and a miniature rice bin put into place. The bin is only 20 cm. (8 in.) tall, but large enough to accommodate about 2 lb. of rice and some cotton seeds. (The rice is placed upon a bed of straw; then come the seeds.) On this day water is fetched in bamboo tubes which have special patterns scraped into the bark.

Rituals are held at four places: 1) the middle of the *tsar*, where the pig is sacrificed; 2) the spot next to the "rice bin" on the edge of the *tsar*; 3) the area inside the field house where the assistants of the *sra* are elected; and, finally, 4) the special place in the field, called the *tur-tut*, where the chicken is sacrificed. At each of the places of ritual a small pot of *hom-noi* (cooked rice mixed with water) is deposited; at the third, a jug of genuine rice beer will be preferred. Paddy, bamboo leaves, and flowers are also deposited at the four places of ritual. Seven persons are needed to assist the master. The election of these assistants takes place inside the field house; as a sign of election, the forehead of each person is touched with the tip of a sickle on which a few grains of rice have been placed. One of the assistants must slaughter the pig; another, the chicken; one must call up the earth-spirit; another must pluck out the feathers of the chicken; the last three must be sons-in-law of the host's clan. All other persons present at the ceremony also receive a special mixture dabbed onto the forehead. This mixture consists of shrimp and small crayfish, which have been cooked in a bamboo tube, and the mashed, sour, red fruits of the rozelle. (The rozelle, which is generally planted along the field path, is also a very popular vegetable.) Then earth – if possible, earth from a termite hill – is mixed with ginger, cooked rice, and water and wrapped in the leaves of a wild plant. These small parcels are next distributed as *köm-pot* to all important spots in the field house, as well as to the places of sacrifice.

After all of these preparations have been completed, the piglet, which was brought from home in a loosely-woven basket, is stabbed to death with a sharp piece of bamboo. This is done in the middle of the *tsar* on the special place of sacrifice. The piglet, which is called "the pig of the fragrant odor of the food", is then cut up and prepared for eating. At the same time, other helpers cut up a gourd, chop green pepper pods into small pieces, and crush ginger and tumeric in a bamboo tube. Some of the food is placed on small pieces of woven bamboo matting and presented to the spirits. With a loud "hü" the *sra* calls the spirits to eat. Then a second and larger pig, which was brought along wrapped in narrow bamboo strips, is placed in the middle of the *tsar*. Four men take the musical instruments (gongs and drum), which are decorated with fronds of the fishtail palm, and begin to beat them. As the music is sounded the musicians move in a circle around the pig. An additional man carries three mouth organs, each having a single transverse mouthpipe (the so-called *tu*); but they are not played upon. Still another carries a basket with the chicken. The group then moves to the *tur-tut*; this spot is likewise encircled. One of the assistants severs the throat of the chicken with a sickle and gathers up rice straw, cotton, and taro leaves; then everyone returns to the *tsar*. Here, the group moves again in a circle around the pig, three times to the right and three times to the left, until an assistant "shoots" the animal with a bow and arrow, that is, stabs it to death with the sharp bamboo spike which serves as an arrow. (We may recall that the bow and arrow is never used for hunting.) One of the assistants next takes the chicken and holds it up to the right ear of the pig; seizing also the other ear of the pig, the assistant then moves it around in a circle, again three times to the right and three times to the left. All of this is done as the musicians play and the *sra* dances. Finally, the animals are prepared for eating, and new parcels (*köm-pot*) are made for the spirits.

If someone became critically ill during the period of cultivation, it would be assumed that the illness was related to an angry spirit or to one of the animals which met its death on the field. The bringer of illness would have been promised a sacrifice during the harvest festival. If the promise helped, it must now be honored. Accompanied by the striking of the flat gongs and the beating of the drum, the people move to a "bad" spot of the field. Here one makes a hole with the hoe, lines it with

Harvest festival

Playing three plate-shaped gongs and a drum, four men dance around the decorated bamboo masts at the open platform *(tsar)* of the field house. To the right – the *karbari* of Menyong-Para who here acts as *sra*, master of ceremonies (left). On the *tsar* a pig is stabbed to death with a bamboo spike which is shot with a bow like an arrow (right). Returning from the field, the men play their instruments until they reach the house of the feast-giver (below).

leaves from a special tree, and covers it with a small basket. Into this basket the *sra* has filled a variety of items, namely, some cooked rice, a bit of water, an egg, and some blood and raw meat from the pig. (The raw meat includes pieces from the tongue, the tail, the feet, and the intestines of the pig.) Since one does not know exactly with whom one is dealing, the spirit also receives various types of *köm-pot*. The hoe is left amidst the offerings — as long as the iron of its blade endures the spirit can harm no one else. Finally, as in the case of death, a puppy is killed and left on the spot. The formerly sick person takes part in this sacrifice. Squatting in front of the spot where the pig has been killed, he holds two leaves in each hand, his arms crossed right over left; upon these leaves rice and cooked meat are placed. The *sra* purifies the formerly sick person by spraying him with ginger water. The person must then take the food from the leaves with his mouth, mix it with a mouthful of water, and then spit everything out again. After this ritual has been repeated three times, the person kneels, puts the left arm over the right, and again takes the food and water in his mouth and then spits them out. (We may recall that while eating the men squat and the women kneel.) While all of this is being done, the flat gongs and the drum are again sounded.

The power of the illness has now been broken, and everyone may partake of the feast which has in the meantime been prepared. Leftover food should not be thrown onto the field, but rather deposited near the spot where the pig was sacrificed; the bow and arrow, with the arrow pointing slightly upwards, are placed above the food. Those items of value which were used for the ceremony — for example, the women's jewelry and the spear — are collected and packed up again. The group then returns home, the musicians playing all the while. Before they enter the house of the festival's host, they take another sip of *hom-noi* from a small pot placed at the top of the tree-ladder. After they have spit this out, the musicians cease their playing.

In the house the host has set up two pots of beer. Anyone can drink from one of the pots; the other serves primarily ritual purposes. First, the *sra* draws a drink from the small pot standing on the landing and spews it out over the gongs and the drum; the instruments are now sounded again. Then, as water is being poured over their necks, the assistants draw a drink from the special beer pot. While this is going on, the household head goes into the house and distributes the *köm-pot* which were brought from the field. He then performs the *kom bong*, i.e., he ties a string around the right wrist of each family member. Next, the earth-spirit receives rice and pork. The *sra* carries the rice and pork to the front of the house; and he also takes along some of the ritual beer, some liquor and a sickle. He pours the beer into a small bowl, bites off a piece of ginger, and then spews this mixture over the rice and pork as he invokes the spirits. The *sra* next bites the sickle, spits again, and pours the remainder of the beer out. Now he pours the liquor into the bowl, bites off some ginger, and repeats the whole process. Finally, he places his foot on the sickle, and all those who are watching must walk away to the right. On the following day, the fronds of the musical instruments are likewise spat upon and discarded. This ends the festival.

▶ In their best new skirts, cloaks, and jewelry, young girls wait in a house on the occasion of a wedding.

A red spot should decorate the forehead rather than the cheek.

In contrast to young girls, young men never wear beaded jewelry around the head or neck. Yet they, too, value very thick, long hair, which they tie into a knot on the front, left side of the head. In addition to ornamental combs and hairpins decorated with coins, flowers also serve as decoration; they can even be worn along with the rings in the hole of the earlobe. Neither of the sexes lags behind the other when it comes to new ideas for personal adornment; for festive occasions girls also decorate themselves with ornamental combs, hairpins and flowers.

Red lips and black teeth heighten one's attractiveness.

Left:
During the evenings of the dry season, when the field work no longer demands all of one's daily energy, the girls come together in one house to spin. Young men come by to visit, chat, sing love songs and play upon the eight-pipe mouth organ which is used as a solo instrument.

The groom – with two striking ornamental combs in the oiled shock of hair which is tied into a fine knot.

Left:
At the time of the wedding, a girl must leave her parents' house and move in with the man. Together with the two bridesmaids who accompany her during this difficult hour, this bride waits selfconsciously on the open platform of her future father-in-law's house until he invites her in with a welcoming drink.

Next page:
While the mother feeds her baby soft rice, the dogs wait patiently for the scraps.

What grown-ups do, children are not forbidden.

Even for an old man, a bald head is rare. Only young men sometimes wear silver rings in their pierced earlobes. To wear a safety pin instead is quite unusual.

Children splash boisterously in the water of the brook located below the village.

Women, girls, and a young boy curiously watch the photographer.

Children devise their own toys. Here, a young boy has dug up a so-called bamboo rat and tied it by the tail to a bamboo string. When it is dead, he will give it to his mother to cook – its meat tastes delicious.

In the *kimma* of their house, the front wall of which has been removed, a husband and his son mourn the death of their wife and mother.

The sacrifice of a dog is rare, but occasionally necessary for warding off evil spirits. A dog is not stabbed, but rather clubbed to death; then, however, unless it is to accompany the dead, it is prepared in the same manner as pigs. Its hair is singed off and it is cut up and cooked. The elders are ritually obliged to eat its meat; young people may refuse it.

Right:
It is above all the young men who frequently blacken their teeth with the soot of iron. The black coating disappears gradually whenever one stops retouching it.

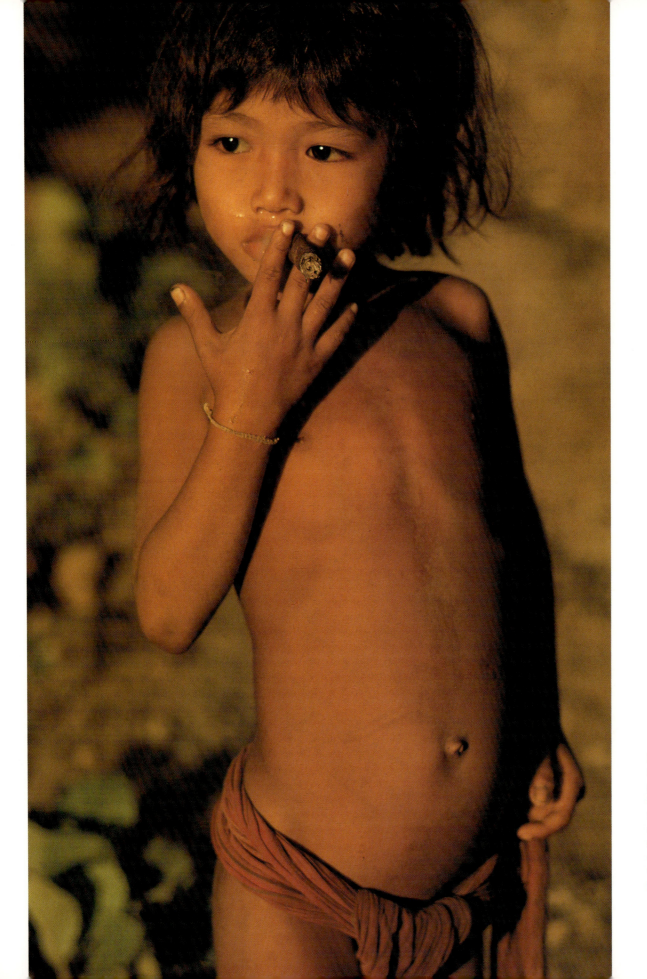

Even a six-year-old may sometimes crave a good cigar. Around his right wrist, the boy wears the string of a *bong-kom*: at the end of sacrificial ceremonies, the oldest family member ties a cotton string around the wrist of each of the other family members.

In order to make the hair-knot appear larger, one may reinforce one's own hair with an additional hairpiece. On a band around his right upper arm, the young man wears an amulet. Oblong capsules such as this one, which contain a tiny piece of paper with a magic formula, may be bought at the bazaar.

Kinship and Life Stages

Like every other settlement in the Hill Tracts, each Mru settlement has its *karbari*, its "manager." This post, as mentioned, goes back to the organization set up by the colonial administration, although the word *karbari* itself comes from the Bangla language. Some *karbari* still use the title of *ruatsa*, a Burmese word literally meaning "village-eater;" *ruatsa* originally referred to a man to whom the king gave the right to live off the earnings of the village. Both terms then imply a dependency upon a higher power. Before the time of the British, the *ruatsa* may have functioned somewhat like the later headmen; in such a case, they may have "eaten" more than one settlement. This era, however, lies more than a hundred years in the past; and it is questionable whether all Mru villages were already at that time subordinated to a *ruatsa* — and whether the *ruatsa* themselves were in fact dependent upon a Marma ruler or whether they simply adopted the title. It is quite possible that the individual settlements had no leader. Even today all concerns are discussed communally, and the *karbari* has no more say in a matter than any other household head.

Nevertheless, an old Mru song does tell the story of a village "big man" who pronounced judgment in matters of marriage. (Part of the story takes place in Arakan and the "big man" is also given a Burmese title.) As we shall presently see, according to Mru custom there is a whole series of marriage relationships which are forbidden; today, it is the sole concern of a pair's relatives to prevent an inadmissable relationship. If the Bohmong learns about such a relationship — the Bohmong is the Marma Chief who was empowered by the colonial government to pass sentence in minor disputes in accordance with customary law — he will collect a fine, even if the relationship would be completely acceptable according to Marma marriage regulations. The Mru interpret the Bohmong's intervention in their own way: in their opinion he sells the permission to marry in defiance of their marriage rules. In the song, the old village head prevents the marriage.

Clans and Marriage Rules

The Mru recall nothing further about village heads, but they do remember something about clan rulers. These men were likewise sometimes called *ruatsa*, although there is also a Mru word for these persons *(tshai-ria)*. Only a few clans, in fact, had such a "big man," and smaller clans were possibly required to pay him tribute. As previously mentioned, some hamlets are called by the name of the predominant clan of the settlement; however, one cannot therefore presume that as a general rule settlements were formerly inhabited by one clan only, or that a clan lived all together in one village. Clan leaders may well have ruled over several settlements and even over the members of other clans who might also have been living in those settlements; but a clan leader would have ruled over members of other clans only if those persons had had no clan leader of their own. Some of the headmen like to point out with pride that their forefathers were *ruatsa*, but the function of contemporary headmen has become something entirely different from that of the older *ruatsa*. Today the headmen are middlemen acting on behalf of the government; within their clan, however, they have no claim to leadership whatsoever.

Today, in addition, clans are no longer political units; yet clan membership is still more important for every Mru than his or her hamlet or village membership. Mru can change their place of residence, but not their clan. The clan name is passed down through the father's line; women retain their clan name after they marry, but cannot pass it on to their children. Children belong always to the clan of the husband, whether he is the biological father or not, even when a wife brings children born prior

◀ Between December and February the nights can become noticeably cool. In the evenings when the temperatures range between 10 and 15° C., it is nice to warm oneself around a blazing fire. Once in a while sparks fly: an internode of a bamboo cane explodes with a loud pop.

to wedlock into a marriage. If one disregards the fact that the woman does not change her clan name at marriage and that the children she bore before marriage do not have to be adopted by the husband, then Mru clans resemble the groups in our society which carry a common family name. Yet not all of those persons in our societies who have the same family name are believed to be related; among the Mru, however, they are. Whoever has the same clan name is in every case considered to be a close relative. Those of approximately the same age are "older or younger siblings"; if the age difference is more considerable, they are "father's brothers or sisters," or (brother's) "sons and daughters"; if the difference in age is still greater, they are "grandparents and grandchildren." None of these persons may intermarry; i.e., the clan is exogamous.

Not only within the clan are there restrictions regarding intermarriage. A Mru man is also not allowed to take a woman from clans which have married women of his own clan. Every clan is related to every other as either a wife-giver or a wife-taker. The clans which give women are the *tutma* clans, that is, the clans from which a father and his brothers, a father's father and his brothers, etc., have already taken wives. The clans taking women are the *pen* clans, that is, the clans into which father's sisters and father's father's sisters have already married and into which sisters and daughters will marry. A clan may also have a *tai-nau* relationship with another clan or several other clans. This is a sibling relationship, and in such a case intermarriage is completely forbidden. *Tai* stands for the older brother, and *nau* for the younger brother; and in some cases such a relationship is traced back to the old martial times when a stronger and a weaker clan made a pact obliging their members to assist each other as brothers. Yet even today two men from two different clans can make a brothers' pact; and this too will result in a prohibition of intermarriage between the two clans. Such an undertaking presupposes, though, that all clan members are in agreement and that no one remembers a time when the two clans stood in *pen-tutma* relationship; and this is very seldom the case.

The traditional marriage relationships between the clans also set the frame for one's behavior toward members of other clans. In principle, one should approach *tutma* men as one approaches a mother's brother or a father-in-law; the *pen* men are approached as sister's sons or sons-in-law. This means that, as wife-takers, the *pen* must show respect to the *tutma*, who are wife-givers. Consequently, when a man goes on a trip he prefers to stay with a *pen* relative rather than visit the home of a *tutma*: in the former case, he should be favorably regarded as a *tutma*; but in the latter, he should behave subordinately as a *pen*. Unmarried men, however, prefer to stay with the *tutma*, since the daughters of the *tutma* are for them potential marriage partners. Only when a Mru man visits villages far from home and meets members of clans of which he had never heard does he become aware of the fact that clans exist to which his clan has no prescribed marriage relationship. Such ignorance, if it is mutual, causes uneasiness, since neither side knows how to behave.

Marriage disagreements or divorces can have no influence on established clan relationships. This advantage of clan rules can, however, be disastrous for those young people who, in contradiction to the prescribed regulations, think that they are made for each other. Two young people can, neverthe-

Kin terms

Symbols used in the kinship diagrams: ∆ male, ○ female, ⌐⌐ siblings, ─── spouses. Lines marked by an arrow are to be read in this direction only, otherwise in any direction, so that, e. g., wife's father = mother's brother. The terms for husbands and children of *tutma* und *pen* women depend on the husbands' clan relation with Ego.

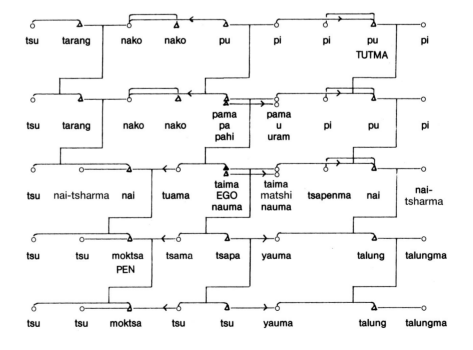

Terms entered above and below those for the central relative are those used for his or her older and younger siblings of the same sex.

For lateral relatives (other than siblings) and their descendants, girls use the same terminology as their brothers; married women follow their husbands' terminology.

(*) : no term, except for
brother's wife: *taima/nauma*
husband's sister: *tuama*
children's spouses' mother: *naitsharma*

Not in the diagram:
a woman's sister's husband: *nai*.

less, hope to have their own way if the relationship between their two clans is a strictly formal one, that is, if there are no existing marriages between the two clans and if there is no one alive who remembers such a marriage. If the father of the young man agrees to the marriage, the primary obstacle is in fact already overcome; the father of the young girl, as we shall see, has less say-so and will eventually have to give in. Precisely for this reason, the consent of the bride's father alone is of little importance. All other household heads of the bride's father's clan also have a say in the matter; and the payment, which they may demand for consenting to a reversal of clan relationships, may in fact be so arbitrarily high that it effectively prohibits the reversal. In spite of their objection, however, an irregular marriage is still possible if the relatives at least agree to accept an appeasement money sent to them by the groom's father through the bride's father. In such a case, the relationship between the two clans which had existed up to that time remains unchanged; and the relationship will remain unchanged for the children of the irregularly married couple. The couple themselves, however, must reckon with the fact that they will be shunned by other people.

Things are quite different if a regular marriage already exists between the clans. In such a case, it would be very difficult for the young couple to obtain permission to marry in the direction opposite to the one prescribed by the marriage rules. If the two clans gave in to the pressure of the lovers, not only would the parents of the two young people have to fear for their moral reputation, but also all members of both clans. Parents, however, must also fear the loss of their children; for as a last resort the lovers might flee over the border into Arakan, accepting a totally insecure future, or they might choose to meet death together. (Parents who held firm to their "no" were responsible for the only cases of suicide known to the Mru.)

Theoretically, all Mru clans stand in a given marriage relationship (*tutma*, *pen*, or *tai-nau*) to all others. If a man is asked about his *tutma*, however, he will usually name only one clan: the clan of his mother's brother. Likewise, if he is asked about his *pen*, he will possibly say that he has none because he does not yet have a married daughter—the *pen* is the clan of a son-in-law. But this is true only from a male point of view. A man marries a *tutma* relative, and his children belong to his own clan. A woman, on the other hand, marries a *pen* relative; and her children, like her husband, belong to a *pen* clan. The children of a woman are her *pen*; their mother is their *tutma*. *Pen* (Khumi: *theo'*) means "those born" or descendants; *tutma* (Khumi: *pakiüng*) are "those below, those behind," that is, the ancestors. Due to their relationship to the clan marriage regulations, the terms '*tutma*' and '*pen*' do in fact take on a different meaning from the man's perspective; however, the kinship terminology likewise equates these in-laws, or affinals, with ancestors and descendants. A Mru, for example, uses the same term for his mother's brothers and his father-in-law (both his *tutma*) as he uses for his grandfathers; and he uses the same term for his sisters' sons and his sons-in-law (both his *pen*) as he uses for his grandsons. Since the *tutma*, as wife-givers ("ancestors"), are superordinate to the *pen*, who are wife-takers ("descendants"), men marry "upwards" and women "downwards." This ranking is evident in the ritualized kinship relationships between the men of the two clans—for example, in the ritual exchange of gifts. It does not mean, however, that wives are ranked above their husbands.

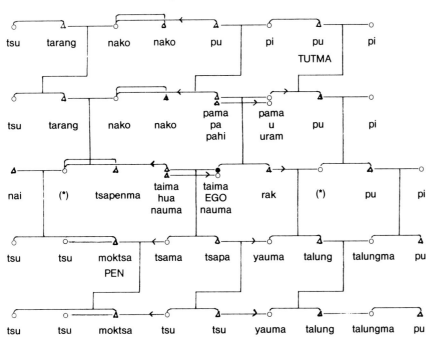

There is no marriage preference with respect to certain relatives. The order is sufficiently maintained when men do not marry a *pen*, that is, a daughter of the women of their father's clan; and when women do not marry a *tutma*, that is, a son of the men of their mother's clan. Children of the men of one's father's clan are *tai-nau* — "siblings" — and, therefore, not proper marriage partners. How do things stand, though, with children of the women of one's mother's clan? Among the Khumi, who for the most part have the same kinship system as the Mru, such children are also considered siblings; so a man is likewise not permitted to marry the daughter of his mother's sister. Among the Mru, however, the man's perspective predominates: a Mru man can marry any cousin on his mother's side provided that her father is a *tutma* man. According to the same principle, a Mru man could also marry his half-sister if her father is a *tutma* man, since she then belongs to a wife-giving clan. But the mother and her sisters are also *tutma* women; in this case, however, the Mru say "no" — that is going too far. The female (uterine) line is therefore respected, but only in the narrowest circle; it is the male (agnatic) line as represented by its clans which is the primary determinant of the marriage rules.

Does this then also mean that the women are at a disadvantage? Women are certainly not at a disadvantage with respect to possible marriage partners, since the restrictions equally apply to both sexes. They are, however, at a certain disadvantage regarding the wedding arrangements and the marriage itself; furthermore, a woman is clearly at a disadvantage with respect to her relationship to her own children, who do not belong to her clan. In some ways women have no formal rights. Yet, as we shall see, that does not benefit the men at all: being less accountable, women have more freedom than men to make their own decisions.

If I have begun this chapter with a short description of a political order which in the meantime has become obsolete and of a social order based on clan relationships which is still operative, it is with good reason: among the Mru everyday life was and is played out against the background, and within the framework, of this male-dominated clan order. We have seen that where there are no regulations which enable the clan system to neutralize a norm violation without threatening its own principles, a man — as much as a woman — risks his life if he attempts to go against the rules inherent in this order. The traditional system of political leadership was also bound to the order of clan relationships, and in retrospect one sees that even a clan head — as a wife-taker — was obliged to show respect to men of other clans because of his mother and his wife. At the same time, though, he could expect loyalty from the husbands of his sisters and daughters. These ties, however, were not dependent upon the fate of individual marriages; they rather confirmed the independently existing clan relationships which guaranteed that all Mru were related to each other in a given manner.

Not the political leadership system, but rather the clan system, connected — and connects — all Mru to each other. It made possible a social order without a state, even if it was not strong enough to prevent the superimposition of a state upon its own organization. This state has taken over the political function of the clan system and, with it, much of the

Married women remain members of their natal group; children are members of their father's group. This becomes most clearly visible in the (rare) cases of interethnic marriage. The picture shows a Lushai mother and her Mru daughter, each wearing her tribal skirt. Girls have to learn weaving; but they must learn it from another female relative, if their mother belongs to a different culture.

role once played by the men. Officially, the right to administer justice has been taken from them; yet, notwithstanding the Bohmong's sanctioning of irregular marriages with fines, the Mru still maintain the clan order — if only ritually. This may well have been little different in the past, since it is indeed not men who determine what must be done, but rather the rules. He who does not live up to the rules does not challenge a claim to power, but instead only proves himself to be a dishonorable person. If he suffers some misfortune, no one will be surprised; and no one will come sympathetically to his aid. Violations of ritually-sanctioned norms always have negative consequences because they offend the spirits. What exactly will happen, the Mru do not know; but experience teaches them that it can be nothing good.

It is beneficial to have rules, since rules provide a necessary orientation. Yet this does not mean that everything is regimented; rather, just the opposite. Rules supply the Mru with a basic framework within which each person is free to make his or her own choices. This we have already seen in relation to the annual cycle of farming activities. It becomes even clearer when one looks at the marriage rules; these rules do indeed prescribe whom one may not marry, but they do not stipulate a certain marriage partner for any person. They also permit a person to marry outside his or her own ethnic group. If such inter-ethnic marriages are rare, this, according to the Mru, has rather to do with incompatible cultures, that is, with the differences in the rules related to married life which persons of different cultures are obliged to follow. Additionally, since women retain membership in their own clan, no one would expect them to change their ethnic identity. Inter-ethnic marriages are, therefore, easiest when the cultures of the two partners are relatively similar. Mru culture is most similar to the Khumi or even the Bawm. The Marma and the Chakma, however, have completely different kinship and religious systems, although they do at least still know how to cultivate a swidden field. The Bangalis, on the other hand, do not even know how to do that! The Mru not only have nothing in common with the Bangalis, but they also do not wish to have anything in common with them; for, unlike the Mru, Bangalis are a people who do not tolerate customs different from their own. I know of only one case where a Mru man married a Bangali girl; but when the man came to realize that the girl knew nothing about all those things which Mru women should know, he sent her back home. The man had already forfeited his good reputation among his own people, however, when he made the mistake of marrying the girl; for Mru believe that whoever does such a thing must be exceptionally stupid or completely degenerate morally. A married couple addicted to opium was also considered to be morally degenerate because, as settlement for their debts, they agreed to give their daughter in marriage to a Bangali. The relatives of the girl pooled their resources and prevented the marriage, but still no Mru wanted to marry the ransomed girl, since she could have refused to allow herself to be sold. Parents cannot force a girl to marry against her own will.

Premarital Life

One of the standard formulations in Mru love songs reflects, in fact, the role played by the girl in the acceptance or rejection of a prospective suitor. The young man laments that the girl's parents have chosen another man for her, but his lament is always accompanied by a plea that the girl not allow herself to be blinded by the prospective — and what appears to be a good — match. Such a plea makes sense only if the girl has something to say in the matter; and in fact she does. The girl has even more to say than the young man — not because daughters have more rights than sons, but because the rules stipulate that a wife moves in with a husband. Neither the parents of a young man nor those of a young girl can force their children into a certain marriage. The parents of the man, however, have a better chance to block an undesirable match; for if they refuse to accept the daughter-in-law, she cannot move into the house. If, on the other hand, the parents of the girl refuse to accept the young man, she just runs away from home. If a young man affronts his father, he also risks being disinherited; he would then have difficulty securing the ceremonial weapons necessary for his role in the exchange system between clans. A young girl does not have to worry about such things.

Be that as it may, as long as the wishes of the children do not violate clan regulations, the parents will somehow have to give in if the two lovers are truly serious. The resistance of the parents can have one purpose only: to put this seriousness to the test in order not to run the risk of having the young marriage immediately break up again. If Mru parents really wanted to decide the fate of their children, they could follow the example of the Bangalis and try to marry off their daughters as early as possible, so that the girls could not have any sexual relations before wedlock; but it is precisely this custom which is cited by the Mru as proof of the moral degeneracy of the Bangalis. Mru girls may wait to marry until they think they have found the right person; until that time, they are free to gain whatever experience is necessary in this regard.

And whatever the daughters may do, the sons are also allowed. Yet the situations are not identical. A Mru girl can flirt with someone, but, as a general rule, it is the young men who make the advances. Young girls are shy; young men are, too, but it is expected of the girls. It is considered improper for a young girl to be seen alone in the company of a young man; this is true even in one's own hamlet where the young people have known each other for many years. For this reason, young girls feel more secure going around in groups. When girls in groups cover their mouths with a half-open fist, hardly hiding their giggles, one never knows whether they are just self-conscious or whether they are making fun of someone. If a young man wishes to speak with a young girl without having her withdraw from him, he must choose the evening hours; at that time he will find her and her girlfriends spinning together in one of the houses—the girls always expect a few young men to drop by to entertain them.

Most of the time the young men who drop in to visit a group of girls are the young men of that particular hamlet. After the harvest, though, when there is less work to do and when one can also afford to stay away from home for a day, young men may also go visiting in the neighboring vil-

Blackening the teeth

Shiny black teeth are considered beautiful by young people. An old hewing knife is whetted clean, and a burning piece of bamboo is pressed onto the clean spot. After the evening meal, the iron soot is rubbed on the teeth with the finger, so that it can set overnight. After one or two weeks the teeth are lacquered black. The coating must be retouched every few days, otherwise the deep black color gradually fades and finally disappears.

Mouth organ
▶

8 – 10 bamboo pipes, arranged in two rows, are stuck into the side of a bottle gourd; they are then glued to the calabash with the dark brown wasp wax. The neck of the gourd is extended by means of a bamboo blowing-piece. Into the lower end of each pipe, which has been inserted into the gourd windbag, a single reed (R) is fixed; each pipe is also equipped with a finger hole. The single pipes sound only when their finger hole is covered.

Bamboo zither
▶

The resonating body of the bamboo instrument (sound hole visible in the center) is bordered left and right by knotted joints which have been perforated. The strings consist of four strips of the outer rind which are held away from the body of the instrument by small sticks acting as bridges; the strings are secured at both ends by a ring so that they will not become loose. Length: ca. 50 cm. (20 in.).

lages — on such occasions they look very impressive, with flowers in the hair and black lacquered teeth. When young men visit a neighboring village, it is proper for a colleague in that village to show them where the girls are. If the visitors are given any trouble in this regard, they will not behave in a friendlier manner when the visit is returned; and, in solidarity, the girls in their hamlet will also appear sullen. The hamlets are so small and the occasions of meeting so few that one only hurts oneself in defying the principle of reciprocity. Tensions are nevertheless noticeable and such visits fairly rare. Once in a while a young man may accompany a relative on a visit to a neighboring village, or he may even have some errand to accomplish there himself; he would, however, be very shy about going alone to a "spinning circle" in another hamlet, unless he had already been introduced to the people there, that is, unless he were visiting "old acquaintances." Girls would have less difficulties in joining in, but they are able to visit other settlements even less often than the boys. Cattle feasts and the dances associated with the feasts offer the major opportunities for girls' groups to visit other hamlets. It is quite true that in most hamlets only one of these large feasts takes place every few years; yet the more hamlets there are in the neighborhood with which one is on good terms, the greater the chances that one will be able to take part in one, or even several, feasts each year. Feasts offer the opportunity to meet many other young people and to initiate new friendships; however, the only possibility one then has to strengthen a new friendship and become better acquainted with another young person is, again, within the context of the spinning circle.

In the spinning circle the girls are occupied with spinning and can devote their attention to that activity. The abilities which the young men may attempt to prove are of a completely different nature. The day's news is soon exhausted; inexhaustible, however, are the possibilities of poetic and musical performances. Some musical instruments — such as the bamboo zither, the two-stringed violin, and, above all, the eight-pipe mouth organ — serve to entertain almost exclusively within the context of the spinning circle. If girls

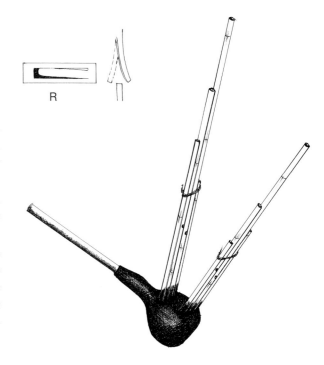

also make music, they play the bamboo flute. All of these instruments are normally played as solo instruments; for the orchestra which accompanies festival dances, a different type of mouth organ is utilized. An even more important contribution to an evening's entertainment than the playing of an instrument is the composing of a song. Through song young men can attempt to give expression to their feelings. The songs consist of standardized phrases and forms which can always be combined or supplemented in a new way. There is also a whole series of ancient narrative accounts in song

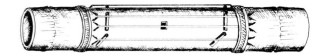

form, but only a very few young people learn them. What every young man tries to master, instead, is the technique of composing new love songs. Not to be able to sing properly is a terrible strain on a young man's self-confidence. A good composer and singer, on the other hand, can easily make himself popular among the young girls. To marry a good singer, however, means in fact to render him silent, since these evenings of entertainment, in which a man may give expression to the pain of his love, are the prerogative of the unmarried.

Mentshing Atuang, the composer and singer of the *Plong Rau Meng* (Love Song), is notching a bamboo cane.

Plong Rau Meng

Tshong leng ö
tsi tshang long ba, tsi tshang long a
hom prek prai li, hom prek prai wöi döi ö
apre tarua, tan dong öi lang
hom tan döi le, u ö ba
tshong wang tö ang, tö kung thi klai
ang plong i rui döi kabö, rau rök ö

U ko ö le
kling tshia tshek hai, kar ko pom wöi katse
phung ram wui en, wui tum dong lu
kau phom tsün yung, kön tse dönök nöm, u öi

U rau ö
yang bong tong teng, tong rö hung kada
kliu re ram min, re ram bön lön
manong wang ni, dang de la ram
ni nong e da

U rau ö
lung ko plong mon, palai döm tson, pawa kom rui
kar ko plong mon, palai döm tson, pawa kom rui yong da
tshong om plong mon, khin wang li len
khin wang li len khök u ö, rau rök ö
en wang tö ang, tö kung thi klai
hom tan döi le

Pai a ö
pröt tsong tui tang, pröng mom tson hön
la ko wang rung, ni nong khan ka
la ko wang tshot, tshot thum phai phia
ni nong e ka, tsi prö lö mani

Love Song

O, beloved,
we two, ah, we two,
harmony rent asunder, separated, not together,
divided in villages, in different rows of houses,
in loneliness, ah, you,
beloved, you abandon me, leave me behind empty,
sorrow in my heart – o, young morning!

O, bright darling,
with the rod of the iron arrow in the chicken basket
a man pulls you down – you flower, down the staircase,
in order to bind you like bamboo canes bound together into a post, o you.

O, morning you,
on the mountains of the Yangbong, on the chain of mountains,
the leaves turn yellow, drop the leaves of the silk-cotton trees,
after those rainy days, the leaves of the cotton plants,
one day.

O, morning you,
as the cattle on the low plains all together are pensive,
the chickens on the low plains all together are pensive,
so will you become, beloved, pensive, when the time comes,
when the time has come, o you, o, young morning,
you abandon me, leave me behind empty
in loneliness.

Look there,
in the east, as clear as water, from the edge of the horizon,
the moon climbed up, on that day,
moonbeams fell upon the matting of the floor,
that day, at that time when we spoke to each other:

kang ding wöi löi, rong nöm tsatöm tse dia *rau rök a* *en wang tö ang, tö kung thi klai* *ang plong i riu dönöm, rau rök ö*	we two shall follow the rule, in the proper place, ah, young morning, you abandon me, leave me behind empty, sorrow in my heart – o, young morning!
U ö le, u rau ö *en plong thüm rau, pangö e ka* *lai döm tsing yöng, tsing mung krung yong* *ang tse tanöm, u ö ba* *ang ria tsin daku, taklep pöng köi* *ang ko tsin tai rau, tut tse tang tang* *en wang tö ang, tö kung thi klai da* *ang plong i rui döi, u ö*	Ah, you – o, morning you, when the pain of your love overpowered you, like a lowland bean, like an entwining tendril, surely I held you, o yes, deep in my insides, in all the folds and coils, in my innermost self I am aching, you abandon me, leave me behind empty, sorrow in my heart – o, you.
Dam li ö, dam li ö *tshak klam ya ö, ang rui bong tanga* *ang kri bu tang leng, ang bong tshong tang töm* *u tse dia le*	O, refreshing wind – o, refreshing wind, you who can cool the heart, for the fingers of my searching hand the brass vessel which I cover, which I embrace, this should be you.
U rau ö *phung ram tuk lung, padöi mi tse* *paklik döng rui, tsang klik döng na* *hom tan döi le, u ö ba* *phung ram tsang en, rui bang langa* *tsa tsi tsakang mi klai döm töm* *hom tan döi nöm, u ö ba*	O, morning you, a man who knows not how to hold you, seeks your embrace, presses you to his bosom, without harmony, ah you! a man forms you, with the fingers of a searching hand, into a basket, to empty in the rice of the dried paddy, without any harmony, ah, you!
U rau ö ba *en tum tshinglong alö mi da* *nöm u rui en, rui rong nöm töm* *ang yan khök nöm le, u öi*	O, morning you, you flowering tree, which you are, your mother seeks for you, seeks a proper place, I was rejected, ah, you!
U rau ö le *rang lö mi da, en kung thi rong köi* *rang tsam tsöng a, pia tui nöm kar wa* *kön tse dönök le* *tur tsam ui nguk, ui pia run run* *da tse yong da, en kung thi köi* *rang tsam ui nguk, ui pia run run* *rang tse dönök nöm, tshang ngan a*	O, morning you, I, here at the place you left behind, I shall turn into a chicken which pines for water, into nothing else, as a dove which sobs for berries, coos longingly for berries, abandoned by you in this way, I shall sob for berries, coo longingly for berries, nothing else, remembering the beloved.
U rau ö *tsi kling paing pyo dia tshik ba ö* *en nöm u tang, nöm u rui en* *rui rong nöm töm, tse le ngan po* *kar ki tsau pün, pün kri bia pa* *arong nöm töm döi lö ngan po* *plong krek kröi ngön, tsi keng tong rui daba* *mi phung köi le, tsi keng tong rui tshik* *mi phung köi ba öi*	O, morning you, let us yet be happy! Your honorable mother, your mother seeks for you, seeks a proper place – yet remember where the fat chickens are piled up, piled up on the plate of the brass dish, is not the proper place, remember also what the heart longs for – is it not that we two come together, and in this world we should come together, yes, in this world.
U rau ö le *tsi lai thi wan, tsi plong ko rau dale* *u rau ö le, u rau ö ba* *marüm klau poi, klau döng tsahap* *wang dang dia le, wang dang böt*	O, morning you, the content of our words, the pain of our love, ah, oh, morning you, o you, morning you, in the forest the leaves of the *klau*, with the smooth top and the rough underside, go and look for them, go and look.

When a young girl and her friends gather together in the *kim-tom* of her parents' home for an evening of spinning and entertainment, her parents retire to the *kimma*. The gatherings can last long into the night, and the parents may not always be happy about having their night's rest disturbed; but most of the time they do not object because the more frequently the young people meet in their house, the more renowned becomes their house and their daughter. Furthermore, parents can take for granted that young people will behave themselves properly — indecent language and behavior are disapproved of. Apart from a sip of water for a dry throat, there is nothing to drink. A quid of tobacco, and also an occasional piece of areca nut, may serve as a stimulant — the latter tastes particularly good when wrapped in a betel leaf upon which a little hydrated lime has been spread. The exchange of such small items between the two sexes is limited, however; for if a young girl accepts a small betel nut parcel from a young man, she knows that he will consider it a sign of her willingness to meet him. The boy may also have invested the parcel with magic properties which would cause her to fall in love with him. There are less risky methods to indicate one's interest. A young man may throw a girl a few small balls of rouge wrapped in some paper; by sticking them into her hair-knot, the girl signals her readiness to meet his advances. Such "love letters" may also come in the form of a small piece of material which the boy has torn from his loin-cloth. In lieu of the material, a girl may use her hairpin, which she casually leaves lying so close to the young man that he can pocket it.

The above-mentioned rouge — it is actually potassium permanganate, which is bought at the market

In contrast to the Bawm and the Lushai, the Mru have no tradition claiming that the young men of the village formerly had their own house. In a few places, however, a house without walls stands in the village square. Here, the men congregate in order to discuss common concerns or weave their baskets in the airy shade of its roof. Such houses are also to be found among the Marma.

—is a necessary ingredient for the beauty care of young people. Both sexes use it to color their lips red; and a large, shiny red-green spot on the forehead is considered most attractive. Girls can also put smaller spots on their cheeks; but these spots must be well placed and made with the right amount of color. Since mirrors are rare and since the color does not wash off quickly once it has been applied, it is good to have someone help you paint your face. If such a person, however, plays a joke by putting an unsightly spot in the wrong place, one may take revenge; so the application of color, which takes place during the evenings when young people entertain themselves, can deteriorate into a true color-battle—a battle which, of course, ends quickly due to the exhaustion of the weapon. Such battles, however, give a young person the opportunity to touch with his or her hands someone of the opposite sex. Apart from such moments of tomfoolery, this is considered bad manners; to show in public that one is fond of another person violates a proper sense of decency.

After an evening get-together, the girls go home to sleep. The young men occasionally sleep in the house of a friend, even in their own hamlet. Among the Mru, there are no houses in which the young men of a village could lead their own life and to which they could once in a while invite a girl. The jungle, likewise, offers no cozy, secluded corner; so the field houses remain the only places of rendezvous. Yet it is hardly possible to meet unnoticed in the field house during the day. One's absence at home would soon be conspicuous; and when one is outside the settlement, everyone asks where you are coming from and where you are going—the normal way of greeting another person. So only the nighttime remains. Without lanterns, however, a nighttime rendezvous is a daring undertaking because of snakes and other imaginary dangers. A young man in love will nevertheless engage in such activities, but a girl will not easily agree to nocturnal meetings.

The only possibility still open to a young man, then, is to try to sneak into the house of the young girl at night—unnoticed. If he is not extremely familiar with her house, he will hardly succeed. He must know exactly which places in the floor creak loudly and where he will find his girlfriend, otherwise he might awaken one of her siblings or someone else sleeping in the same room. In contrast to the men, who use the sleeping blankets as a kind of mattress, women tie the blankets high on the sides into a kind of hammock which touches the floor. Still, the lovers must be very careful not to draw the attention of someone nearby—someone who would then sound the alarm immediately. If an alarm is sounded, only a quick exit can keep the visitor from being recognized. It is true that the father has no legal grounds for taking action against the uninvited lover of his daughter; yet it is most humiliating for the young man if he is caught, and he may even be beaten by the father and brothers of the young girl. The father, however, should spare himself the trouble of rebuking his daughter excessively: first of all, the villagers would laugh at him because he cannot accept the inevitable; and, secondly, he would only cause his daughter to brave the dangers and slip away at night in order to meet her friend in a field house.

It is obvious that neither the circumstances themselves nor the rules of proper behavior make it exactly easy for young people to spend a few undisturbed hours together. Nevertheless, it can happen that a girl becomes pregnant before her wedding. A child born out of wedlock has no legal disadvantages; for it will later be fully accepted by the husband of its mother and integrated into the husband's clan. Yet pregnant women prefer to marry before the child is born and before the question of the child's father is raised. There is a special reason for this: premarital sex does not always abide by the clan regulations, and bearing the child of a man whom one cannot marry reveals something which should rather remain hidden. Abortions are performed; but without previous medical knowledge or experience, they endanger the life—or at least the future child-bearing capability—of the woman. Barren women must expect to be sent back to their parents; inversely, pregnant women can count on someone marrying them. The begetter of a child born out of wedlock can claim no rights if he does not marry the girl; however, such sexual escapades can be costly for the young man's father. First of all, the girl's father can demand compensation from him, since from this point on only the small, but no longer the big honorable, wedding ceremony can be held for his daughter. Secondly, the villagers can insist that he sacrifice a pig on their behalf, so that the harvest does not ruin in the fields or the paddy vanish from the storage bins.

If a girl becomes pregnant by a man who will not wed her — no matter what the reason may be — her chances to marry are not reduced, though perhaps her possible choices. Only girls with severe physical or mental handicaps find no husband at all, but not every man finds a wife. There are young men who can be particular about whom they marry and others who must be happy if they finally find a young woman who is willing to marry them; this essentially depends upon the wealth of their fathers. The previously-mentioned pleas in the love songs — that the beloved should not allow herself to be blinded by riches — have good reason. Not only is it less enticing to have to slave away in a poor household, but, since everyone can cultivate his own field, one may wonder how these people came to be so poor. There may well be unfortunate circumstances, but are not the persons themselves to be blamed? The only thing that a young man from a poor home can offer as counterevidence is unflagging hard work and good management — evidence which is important in any case, since being the son of a wealthy family helps a young man little if he is a ne'er-do-well whose modest wealth will soon be spent. To get married is particularly difficult for young men whose mothers have died and whose fathers can no longer work properly, and even more so for those who have only brothers to care for and no sisters to assist them. In such cases, a wife is badly needed. Precisely for this reason, however, the situation is unattractive; for a girl it is far more pleasant to be able to found a new household with the husband alone. It can happen that an older brother must care for younger siblings and, in place of his father, also finance the siblings' weddings. Such a man may one day find himself old and alone, and still without a wife. His only hope then is to find a widow who is willing to spend her last years with him.

As far as prospective wives are concerned, a young man should understandably be careful to marry an industrious woman — "industrious" means above all strong and hardworking. In contrast to what has just been stated about a young man's family, the wealth of a girl's family is of little importance as long as her reputation is good. In fact, for a girl other criteria are more important; these include above all her beauty. The most important criterion for beauty is fair skin; whereas other aspects of a girl's charm may be ephemeral, fair skin is lasting and can even be passed on — it is hoped — to the children. Nothing is worse than having skin as dark as the Bangalis — who, incidentally, value fair skin no less than the Mru, since those of fairer skin claim to be descended from more distinguished ancestors. The Mru make no such claims; even the dark-skinned daughter of a headman, whose great-greatgrandfather was a *ruatsa*, must reckon with the fact that not everyone will want to marry her. A light skin color often goes along with a broad face and a sturdily-built body — darker types are narrower and more slender; and since sturdy women are particularly valued, due to their ability to work hard, it should not be surprising that in the love songs one repeatedly sings the praises of the young beauty who is like the dawn, whose face is like the sun, like the moon. But: beauty is of little value if it does not go hand in hand with moral integrity. Beautiful girls, therefore, cannot put off marrying too long unless they want to arouse suspicions. It can happen that girls with very dark skin do not marry until they are around thirty, unless they are willing to marry a man living in less desirable circumstances. The choice is in any case not very broad; for in addition to the restrictions imposed by the clan system, one also has spacial limitations. Marriages within the same small settlement are in fact rare; but if people live more than half a day's journey apart, they hardly have an opportunity to meet. Wide age differences between marriage partners is not considered desirable, but a span of ten years is tolerated. It is also considered acceptable for the woman to be older than the man, yet one does not like to talk about this later because it usually suggests that both man and woman were simply grateful to find a partner.

Wedding and Marriage

▶ Chickens are expensive, but a necessary gift for the *tutma* (wife-givers).

Weapons used as gifts move in the same direction as the chickens. Spears may be made completely of iron, or they may consist of iron points (1) and ends (3) fixed to a wooden shaft (2). Spears and iron arrows (4) are also needed for the cattle feasts. Ceremonial knives equipped with a metal handle (5) have become very rare.

As far as the young people themselves are concerned, affection and love play a large role in the choosing of a partner. Parents are, however, more concerned with practical matters. Parents and close relatives of young people deliberate about proper and desirable marriage partners, and they occasionally make noncommittal inquiries here and there. These initial contacts are made primarily by the fathers; how far they go in securing the consent of their children in such matters is their own affair. In the final analysis, however, it is the young people who make the decision: they may decide not to marry, in spite of the encouragement of their parents, or to insist upon a marriage, in spite of their parents' disapproval. If an agreement is in fact reached at some point, it is the duty of the young man's father (or a member of his clan) to make a visit to the father of the young woman, in order to secure the latter's consent. As a rule, the young woman's father seems to discountenance the match, giving a long list of his daughter's weaknesses and faults. (These deficiencies need not be true, but if the groom's side insists on going ahead with the marriage, they cannot later complain if some of the negative points turn out to indeed be true.) The same procedure is repeated when this first official visit is soon followed by a second, at which time the groom's father is accompanied by two or three other household heads who act as witnesses to the fact that the groom's side accepts the bride with all her faults. Formerly, a head of cattle had to be taken along and sacrificed on this second visit; today it is enough to bring some smaller items: five to seven chickens, an iron spear, an iron arrow, a ceremonial knife, and three bottles of liquor. On this occasion, the bride's father is also obliged to slaughter a pig and have fish ready to feed his guests.

All of these gifts reflect and reinforce the existing clan relationships. Just as women can only be given to the *pen* by the *tutma*, so chickens and weapons can only be given to the *tutma* by the *pen*. Fish and cloth go once again from the *tutma* to the *pen*; pigs are neutral — that is, both partners may eat of their meat. The *tutma* have the privilege of being supplied with chickens by their *pen*, but no *pen* may eat from one of the chickens of his *tutma*, since that would be the same as reversing the relationships between the clans and would have to be corrected by a special ceremony. Weapons and chickens are the "male" goods which the wife-takers must deliver to the wife-givers; lengths of material and fish are "female" goods which the wife-takers receive from the wife-givers. Woven material enters into the picture only later during the wedding ceremony; but as a down payment toward the final sum of wedding gifts, the groom's father must already at this point bring along approximately one-third of the total price.

After the gifts have been handed over and payment has been made, the two young people are considered to be engaged, although they need not appear at this point. Should the young woman then marry a man other than her betrothed, the first groom's father may claim full recompense for all gifts presented up to that point. If, on the other hand, the groom looks around for someone else, the bride's father keeps everything. If the young woman becomes pregnant by a man other than her prospective groom, it is now the groom's father, rather than the bride's, whom the progenitor will have to compensate for the dishonoring fact that under these circumstances only the small wedding ceremony—and not the big one—may be performed. Seeing that the big ceremony would exceed their means, most fathers in fact agree anyway to carry out the small ceremony. If this is done, fathers can even spare themselves the expense of the engagement. Ultimately, the small ceremony can even be performed without the consent of the bride's father, provided that there are good grounds for believing that he will ultimately reconcile himself to a fait accompli. Formerly, such a situation was the primary reason for performing the small ceremony. The fact that this ceremony has become customary today may be related above all to the general economic deterioration. It may, however, also reflect greater independence on the part of young people.

The first thing a young man must do when he is ready to marry is reach an understanding with his bride. After having agreed on a date and time of day, he sets out with a friend and "kidnaps" the girl—normally at night. The girl herself takes a few friends along as company. Since the father of the young man is aware of what is happening, everything has already been prepared at home. While it is still morning, a pig is sacrificed; at the end of the ceremony, a string is tied around the right wrist of each family member. The new daughter-in-law also receives a string and is thereby officially received into the family. If the bride's father has in fact not realized what has been enacted, he may in his anger proceed to bring his daughter back home; but he must reckon with the fact that she will shortly be abducted again. It is therefore much better for him to grin and bear it and agree with the young man's father on a time for the presentation ceremony. Until this ceremony has taken place, he may either take his daughter back home again or leave her with her husband. The whole affair is particularly problematic if the abduction takes place during the rainy season, when all workers are needed for the weeding. Better wait then until after the harvest, when the storage bins are full.

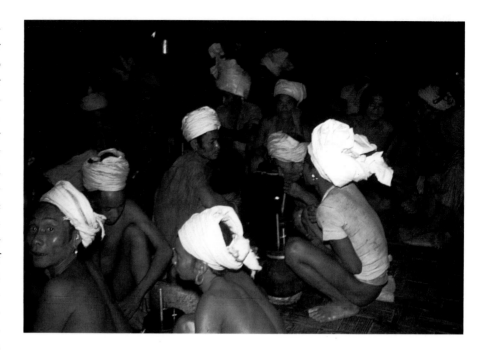

A few weeks later the bride's father, along with people of his clan and his *tutma*, goes to the house of the young man's father for the presentation ceremony; he takes along a large pig which has already been slaughtered. The young man's father should have already slaughtered chickens and prepared two large beer pots. Next morning the presentation of the bride price takes place. In the afternoon, the bride's father distributes spears to his *tutma* — spears which he himself, as *tutma*, received from the groom's father and members of the groom's clan. The beer for these ceremonies must be supplied by the groom's father. The distribution is no easy matter because everyone repeatedly rejects the goods offered: either the spear is not large enough or the price is too high. One must negotiate the demands of those receiving spears, since the bride's father will later receive back from these persons textiles of equal value. On a visit to the groom's father, the bride's father will have the fabric distributed in turn to members of the groom's father's clan—from whom the spears originated. In the end, therefore, members of three clans have exchanged spears and fabric; but the circle is not closed, since each of the partners in this transaction has again other *pen* and *tutma* to whom he will pass on the goods on the occasion of other ceremonies. One cannot make a profit from such dealings;

The *pen* (wife-takers) have gathered in the house of the bride's father to drink beer (he can be seen in the back to the right); as a gift from him, they received new, shiny-white turbans.

The belly of the pig which is to accompany the bride has been filled with gourds and stones, and its skin has been smeared with blood. Young *pen* men must carry it on an unusually short pole, the ends of which have been anointed with fat, soot, and pepper; and they should do this without allowing one of the tassels to fall off.

sooner or later each person gets back the value — in either material or spears — of what he has paid out. The more ceremonial goods a person has in his possession, however, the more exchange transactions he may participate in, that is, the more obligations he may incur and meet again. When a person exchanges such goods, he is at the same time strengthening symbolically the existing clan relationships. That marriages offer a special opportunity for such exchanges is obvious; it is likewise clear that no wedding celebration, however small, is a purely personal affair between two young people. It rather, in each and every case, places several clans under certain obligations.

In the big wedding ceremony even the wife-takers (*pen*) of the groom's clan play a role. They accompany the father of the groom and his people when the groom's relatives go to fetch the bride and bring her to their village. Chickens and ceremonial weapons are taken along for the bride's father, and he must have enough pork and fish on hand to feed the slew of guests five meals. The bride's father's clan and his *tutma*, who are likewise present, may not eat from these foods; instead, they receive the chickens which the visitors have brought along. Right on the first evening, the bride's father presents lengths of material to the people of his future son-in-law, that is, he invites these men to take their places at one of the beer pots which have been set up and to allow one of the long, white fabrics to be wrapped about their heads. Instead of turbans, women receive cloaks. The visitors can put the bride's father in an embarrassing situation by demanding more and more lengths of material; this is actually a demonstration of their own wealth, since at one point they will be obliged to return the value in spears. However, according to the rules of the festivities, the visitors in their own turn will also be given a hard time. For example, not only is the food the visitors receive on the following day too highly spiced, but pepper pods by the pound are also poured into the fire in the dining room. The doors to the room are closed, and the guests must endure burning eyes and irritated throats until they are let outside again.

In the meantime, preparations begin for another exciting event which is actually the main amusement of the entire celebration. An extremely large pig is killed, gutted, and cleaned; then it is smeared with its own blood and red coloring and studded with small, tasseled arrows made from bamboo. Its belly is filled not only with gourds and ginger roots, but also with large stones — it should be as heavy as possible. The legs are tied together, and the animal is suspended from a bamboo pole which is kept as short as possible. The ends of the pole are then rubbed with lard, soot, and pepper; and on top of it all comes a scaffolding with more tasseled sticks. When the preparations are complete, the pig is hung, by means of a joint effort, from the uppermost railing of the outdoor platform (*tsar*). Two pigs should actually be prepared in this manner, so that one may be carried in front, and the other in back, of the bride — normally, however, one is kind enough to cut up the second pig in portions which are easier to transport. Moreover, two special six-pipe mouth organs are prepared; they will be played by young men of the bride's own clan from the moment the bride leaves the house of her parents until she arrives at the house of her groom. The special pig, on the other hand, must be carried by two or four young men from the clan of the groom. From the time the pig is hauled down from its place on the platform railing until it reaches the village exit, it should not touch the ground, and none of the small tassels should fall off. If this does happen, though, each time it costs the groom's father one rupee. (Formerly, the rupee was a silver coin. Ten Indian rupees were equal to one British pound sterling, and Lewin estimated in 1869 that the value of a family's annual paddy harvest was around 30 rupees. In the meantime, however, inflation has reduced the value of the rupee considerably; in 1960 a Bangali rupee, which is called *taka*, roughly corresponded to a German mark — not in terms of the actual exchange rate, but in accordance with the Bangali standard of living.)

Before the men carrying the pig can leave the platform, they are given a glass full of liquor to drink. The person handing them the glasses first takes a sip himself, mixes it with ginger — and, if he really wants to be mean, with some tobacco juice — and spits the stinging mixture into their faces. As the only renumeration for their trouble, the carriers then receive a turban from the bride's father. The turban is bound around their heads as they drink from a beer pot standing on the ground. All of this is done while the men hold high their heavy burden — by its greasy, soot-covered, peppered, and stubby ends! — so that it does not touch the ground. In the meantime, the bride is fetched. If she has lived in her own small room within the *kim-tom*, this is forced open by the groom's people while her people resist. In the end, the groom's people will take hold of her; and, accompanied by some of her girlfriends who act as bridesmaids she will follow along behind the pig, down the steps to the village exit. If the line of houses is long, this walk may take quite a long time because the villagers block the way. In the meantime, there is more drinking, during which the carriers are not forgotten. Only after the "kidnappers" of the bride have fought their way free to the end of the hamlet are they finally permitted to pass unimpeded. The pig may now be set down and rescued; after that, the group hurries home. Everyone may come along; *tai-nau* and *pen* are especially invited.

In addition to the bride's father and his clansmen, their also come along. This includes particularly the mother's brother and the mother of the bride. The mother's brother receives at least five rupees and a spear; the mother, ten rupees, a chicken, and a hewing knife. The ten rupees are called "breast-milk-cow" and probably stand for a cow which the mother in former times received in acknowledgement for nursing the daughter. Then gifts are presented to the *tai-nau* of the bride's father, that is, to his blood brothers, his clan brothers, and a representative of each of his brother clans. As *tutma* of the groom's clan, each of these men receives a pot of beer and a spear; being guests, they are also

served chickens. On the morning of the second day, one of these chickens is placed together with a spear, a hewing knife, and a ceremonial sword next to a special beer pot; then the bride's father positions himself behind these items and receives from the groom's father one hundred silver rupees — the actual bride price, which is a fixed sum not dependent upon personal wealth. He who no longer possesses silver coins must pay their equivalent value in the present currency. As a small return gift, the groom's father receives two bolts of cloth, each about 20 yards long.

After the meal, the bride must sit behind the beer pot where her father received the bride price; across from her, at another pot, sits the groom, who now for the first time must officially appear before the bride's father. The bride's father — and he alone — gives a speech. He addresses first his

During the night the bride was "abducted" and brought to the bridegroom's house. The groom's father has killed a pig and is now conducting the *bong-kom* ceremony by which the bride is symbolically tied to her new family.

Old Indian silver rupees serve as bride price. The two sides of the coin are called "flower" (number) and "monkey" (head).

daughter and then the son-in-law, admonishing them to be good married partners, faithful to each other. The groom's father then leads the *bong-kom* ceremony in which the young wife is received into his family and tied to it (symbolically) by a string around the wrist. Following the ceremony, the young wife may, if she wishes, go home again with her parents for a few days. Without further ceremony, she is thereafter fetched by her husband—unless he actually accompanied her. Likewise without any attendant ceremonials, the young wife's wealth is escorted to her husband's house a month or two following the wedding. (Prior to that time, she had only the bare necessities.) The wealth, however, which consists of blankets, skirts, jewelry and, according to agreement, weapons and gongs, is not given to the young woman as a dowry; it must rather be paid for by her husband's father. Accordingly, her wealth becomes the property of her husband's family, even if—as is the case with skirts and blankets—the young wife may have woven them herself prior to the wedding. In case of divorce, the wife can take these things with her only in the event that they are not yet paid for—people prefer to take some time in these matters—or that they are bought back. (In the case of skirts and other non-commercial items, it is particularly advisable to buy back the articles, since they are transferred at a conventional price far below the present cost of both materials and labor).

It is different with regard to the bride price, that is, the 100 silver rupees. Decisive for its fate is the question of who caused the final break-up of the marriage. If the two partners separate by mutual agreement, the husband gets back the bride price, as well as the gifts given to the wife's mother and the wife's mother's brother. The same is true if the wife leaves the husband, and in such a case the wife's father must also pay the husband an additional thirty-rupee separation fee. If, on the other hand, a man sends his wife away, he loses all claims to the bride price and must, in addition, pay a separation fee of forty rupees. If the family of a divorced wife should be unable to pay back the husband that which is due, their obligations may be transferred to a new husband if the woman remarries. Then, instead of paying the bride price to the woman's father, the new husband would pay it to her divorced husband.

Settling the question of guilt on the basis of one criterion alone, namely, who sent whom away, or who deserted whom, has definite repercussions in everyday married life. For example, if a wife does not fulfill her duties, the husband would be in the wrong and would forfeit the bride price if he sent her back to her relatives. And how could he possibly complain to her father, who had already warned the groom's people that his daughter was not perfect. If, on the other hand, a husband is little inclined to work, a wife cannot simply leave him, unless her father is willing to pay for the fact that he did not prevent his daughter from marrying such a husband. The father will pay, however, only if his daughter has not married against his will. Here we can see that a girl also does well not to defy her father.

The fate of the marriage is in fact dependent upon both partners; and in keeping with the dictates of the traditional division of labor, both persons are also dependent upon each other. It is true that men and women can, if need be, live without partners as bachelors and widows. Men can, for example, fetch the daily water, pound the rice, and do the cooking; women can also slash and burn, clear, cultivate, and harvest a field. (Occasionally young girls do this on a small scale. From the yields, they make liquor which they sell; and with the money, they buy jewelry, which then actually belongs to them.) Living alone, however, is not considered an ideal state by anyone. Without the help of neighbors and relatives, illnesses can put a single person into a desperate situation. Who should care for the field and do the cooking while one is sick? And who should care for an elderly person who is weak and without children? It would simply be better for such a person to die quickly, unless the person still harbors the hope of finding someone who, in spite of having children, would be grateful to have a partner with whom he or she could share the daily workload. Single adults are incomplete beings who, according to the rules, are also incapable of giving a feast—even if they had the means to do such, which is hardly ever the case. A young man having his own family will also have more to say in the circle of household heads than an older person who is single — from society's point of view, the young man is one of the elders, and the older person, still a youth.

To be father of a family not only means to be prepared to accept the responsibility for running one's own household, but also to maintain reciprocal relationships with neighbors. During the cultivation period, everyone in the mutual-aid groups is soon cognizant of each other's abilities and attitudes no matter what sex the person may be. After a woman marries, she moves to a new place, unless, of course, she marries a man in her own hamlet. Due to the kinship relations mediated by the clan rules, wherever she goes, she will find herself already related in a given manner to all other persons; yet she must still establish personal relationships with most of the people. On the basis of the clan rules her mother-in-law is related to her as a father's sister, that is, a person whom she must neither serve nor even be subservient to. It is true that the wife initially lives with her husband in the house of his parents, but within a few days a new house may be built and the young couple becomes independent. Only when the youngest son marries may a new house be deemed unnecessary, and this is always the case when but one of the parents is still living. The young husband would then, however, become the head of the household and move with his wife into the *kimma* of his parents, while the parents would move out into the *kim-tom*. The woman in the *kimma* is mistress of the house — in such a case, therefore, this would be the daughter-in-law, and not her mother-in-law.

Yet the term "mistress of the house" does not in fact do justice to Mru relationships. Among adults, no person is subordinate to another, neither children to their parents, nor a wife to her husband. There is only partnership. Everyone knows what his jobs are and what he must do, so no one needs to give instructions. Mutual agreement is sufficient. We have already seen that parents cannot force their children into a particular marriage — the rules that must be adhered to are not subject to their arbitrary wishes; the only way they can influence children tending to go against their wishes is by threatening to reciprocate, that is, by threatening to turn a deaf ear to the children as well. Whoever does not meet another person halfway need not expect the latter to meet him halfway. Most Mru have already learnt this lesson as children or as young adults. If parents are lax, however, allowing their children to get away with shirking their work responsibilities, they ultimately do the children a disservice, since such habits adversely effect not only the harmony of a young couple *per se*, but also the willingness of neighbors to cooperate with the couple.

As has been stated, a diligent husband cannot send a lazy wife away — nor can an industrious wife run away from an idle husband — without being considered the guilty partner. The best way to guard against such disappointments is to make a careful check, prior to the wedding, regarding a person's reputation in his or her own hamlet. He who does not believe what he hears, however, relying instead on love to transform a partner's character after marriage, may ultimately be let down by the partner. Should such be the case, there is only one possible means of persuading the spoiled partner to change his or her ways: in conjunction with relatives and neighbors, one can stop cooperating with or helping the partner. If the partner then cannot tolerate this situation, he (or she) must either agree to change his (or her) ways; or he (or she) must — by sending the wife home or by deserting the husband — openly declare his (or her) unwillingness to continue the marriage. Because of the loss of the bride price, however, a declaration of guilt is more expensive for a man than for a woman. A woman also has more of a chance to force her husband to relent: she may repeatedly go home to her parents for a few days at a time until it is more than her husband can stand. That she is able to do this, even when she in fact is the one who does not want to fulfill her duties, is a form of leverage the man must accept as long as the wife's parents play along. Such a course of action is, however, a double-edged sword, since a woman's reputation can be damaged by such behavior.

Loud and constant quarreling, which because of the permeable nature of the house walls can be overheard by the entire hamlet, is as strongly disapproved of as the use of physical violence. Furthermore, the outcome of a physical bout cannot necessarily be predicted — because of the daily rice pounding and water carrying, the muscular strength of the women is also considerable. Men in a drunken state may once in a while get into a fight, but I never saw an intoxicated man who would have thought of harassing a woman. Mru men are not gentlemen; without a moment's thought, they leave heavy work to the women. But then they are neither domestic tyrants nor patriarchs either — they have no ways or means to be either. Mru men are simply the heads of their households — and if a husband should die, the wife can also take over this function. Being the head of the house does not mean, however, that the men give orders. They rather carry out certain rites and, in cooperation with others, maintain the rules which guarantee the continued existence of the established order.

This equality between the sexes in the private sphere, which contrasts the special responsibilities of males in legal and religious matters, is clearly evident in cases of adultery. While premarital sex is tolerated by society, extramarital sex is disapproved of. Still, although adultery may demonstrate dissatisfaction with one's spouse, it is not recognized as legitimate grounds for divorce, neither from the man's nor the woman's side. A wife may become furious with an unfaithful husband, or a husband with an unfaithful wife — and, depending on temperament, this may express itself in various ways, but apart from such domestic frustrations and a damaged reputation among the neighbors, the guilty marriage partner, particularly the wife, has to fear no further punishment. For the husband, though, this is true only as long as he becomes involved with an unmarried girl. A man is called to account if he interferes with the marriage of another man — the woman's behavior plays no role in the matter. A lover caught with a married woman should pay the deceived husband approximately one-third of the bride price; he should also sacrifice two pigs at the husband's homestead, in order to placate the angry household- and village-spirits. Finally, he should pledge that he will not do such things again and will restore normal relationships.

Children resulting from extramarital relationships always become members of their mother's husband's clan, that is, their social father's clan, no matter who the biological father may be. The same rule applies to children born out of wedlock, once their mother marries; however, if a woman brings a child with her into a marriage, and if the marriage ends in divorce, the child may choose to go with the mother. The child would, in fact, still retain its membership in the clan of its former stepfather, but only until the mother remarries. At such a time the child would have to choose whether to return to its former (step-) father, go again with the mother, or remain with the parents of the mother. If the child chooses to go with its mother, it will become a member of the new stepfather's clan; if it stays with the mother's parents, it will become a member of the mother's father's clan. The opportunity to change clan membership is terminated only when the child itself marries. If a couple divorces, those children born within wedlock may also go with the mother, but in this case the father — or brother — of the woman must give a kind of security deposit to her divorced husband. If the child eventually goes back to its father's family, this security deposit, as well as a reimbursement for food and clothing for the child, is returned to the woman's father. If the child does not return to its father, though, nothing will be paid back. Yet a child always remains a member of its father's clan. This example is a definite discrimination against the woman, since a woman cannot pass on her own clan membership to her child; it is a discrimination reinforced by the fact that the father can always demand the return of the child. Parents are therefore placed on equal footing only insofar as a child may decide for itself with whom it wishes to live.

Birth and Childhood

When a child is born, nature itself decrees that its parents will fulfill different roles. The mother-to-be performs as many of her daily chores as possible until the very last moment; but during the last months and weeks of her pregnancy she spends more and more of her time in the hamlet or house. Arrangements are made with three or four experienced women in the neighborhood who should assist in the birth; as soon as the labor pains begin, these women are informed. The mother gives birth in a squatting position in the extreme back part of the *kimma*. The father may be present and, in difficult cases, may even try to help; most of the time, however, he stays close by in the *kim-tom*. Prior to the birth, the man takes his hewing knife and cuts out a sharp-edged sliver from a bamboo pole in the *kimma*. This pole, which reaches up to the roof ridge, has been placed in the *kimma* precisely for this purpose, since the sharp-edged piece of bamboo will serve to cut the umbilical cord. The afterbirth is placed into a small, portable basket which the father must hang from a tree far away from the house. The child's first bed is a blanket or a matting of banana leaves. In the fireplace of the *kimma* a hot fire is kindled for the mother; and for five or six days and nights she must sit with her back close to this constantly stoked fire, so that her body "dries out". She must also sleep sitting upright, resting her head in her hands; and from time to time she is bathed with warm water, in order to offer her some relief. The Mru believe that unless the new mother is treated in this manner the blood will rush to her head and cause her to go mad. As sustenance, she receives only rice and warm water — no salt, no spices, no vegetables, etc. Only at the end of nine days may she leave the *kimma*, and until that time no sacrifice may take place in the house. When a child is born, not only are there restrictions which apply to the house, there are also restrictions which apply to the entire village as a whole. On the day following a birth field work must be stopped; otherwise, the paddy would spoil. (The prohibition to work is linked to the blood emitted at birth — which, by the way, is called by the same name as menstrual blood. Menstruation, however, is not associated with dangers or special regulations for anyone and is also not treated as something shameful.) There is another day of rest when the remains of the umbilical cord fall off. No supernatural perils are linked to a stillborn child or to the death of a baby who dies during or after birth, but it is very dangerous should a mother die in childbirth. In such a case, all members of her clan must adhere to the special diet followed by a woman in childbed until the dead woman has been cremated. The woman's relatives should come to see her a last time, but they have to take special precautions; and strangers are warned not to enter the particular house or the hamlet. The death of a woman in childbed is considered to be an "evil death," and the woman's spirit becomes dangerous for the living.

Twins are undesirable. According to the Mru, there is a danger that the father or the mother, or at least one of the twins themselves, will die; this is then usually the case. The belief is so strong that the Mru consider it futile to try to save one of the twins if it in fact becomes ill. The offspring of forbidden marriages, particularly of marriages between two persons whose clans stand in sibling relationship, are also thought to be incapable of surviving. This belief also proves to be valid, even though the parents, who live together in spite of the prohibition, may reject it. No one will come to their aid when the spirits punish them.

Not only in such cases, however, is the death of a child relatively common. Generally speaking, for

As they themselves eat, the mothers also feed their children. Provided there is no younger sibling, children may feed at their mother's breast up to four years of age.

the Mru the death of newborn babies or small children is nothing out of the ordinary. Death may already strike at birth: if a child does not begin to breathe, nobody knows what to do. Prematurely deceased children are omitted when a couple responds to inquiries about the number of children they have. According to the data I have on a few families, however, the mortality rate for newborns does not exceed 10 percent; in most of the families not one single child died. In view of the fact that the Mru have neither modern medicine nor medical knowledge at their disposal, this would seem to indicate relatively sound hygienic practices. Yet people die at all ages (women earlier than men), and it may well be that nearly half of them die before reaching the age of eighteen.

On the morning after a birth, the father kills a very small chicken; then he plucks it, dresses it, and cooks it in a bamboo tube. In contrast to usual practice, the chicken is not eaten; rather the midwives wash their hands with its broth and leaves like those which are placed into the small basket with the afterbirth. Without this ritual, the midwives would be unable from this time forward to do their work properly. The father then cuts a piece of turmeric into two parts, calls out a name, and throws down the two halves. If both pieces fall with the cut side up or down, the name is regarded as rejected; if they fall on different sides, the name is approved. Both parents can suggest names; and if they are rejected, one need perhaps change only a syllable in order to gain approval. Instead of the turmeric halves, one may also use two cowrie shells for the omen. (These shells are bought at the market. Formerly, they served as the smallest unit of currency; today, besides being utilized for the naming ceremony, they are only used in combination with red beads for the arm bracelets of small children.) The omen, however, does not guarantee that the chosen name is in fact the correct one. If a child falls ill, cries a lot, and refuses to eat, one seeks the aid of a woman who knows how to identify the right name; she does this by reading the movement of the bow which is normally used for teasing cotton. Apart from such cases where a name is believed rejected, once a name has been given it cannot arbitrarily be changed; however, many children soon receive a nickname — not always a pleasant one — which supplants their true name. Adults may also sometimes be given a new name. Perhaps the nickname used up to that point no longer seems appropriate, or perhaps only now have similarities become apparent which would identify the person with an ancestor. Should physical characteristics already present at birth give the impression that an ancestor has indeed been reborn in a child, the child receives the ancestor's name immediately, provided that the omen confirms this initial impression.

A child is nursed as long as it likes or until its mother becomes pregnant again. After the third month it is given additional food in the form of rice, which the mother chews up and passes to it by mouth. Later unchewed rice is also put into its mouth at every meal; if it becomes hungry between meals, the mother puts it to her breast. Carried in a shawl draped over the right shoulder and the left hip of its mother, the child spends its time in constant bodily contact with her. As soon as it can sit in the carrying-shawl and go long enough between

Small children are often taken care of by their fathers; even when men go about their work in the village or celebrate a feast, they take the youngest child with them in a shawl on the back.

Insects may serve as toys.

◀◀
A young boy plays with a lizard he has caught.

◀
A boy takes a puppy for a walk – dogs are not always handled so affectionately.

mealtimes, an older sister, or very often the father, may also carry it around. If no one is free – and especially at night – the shawl is used as a hammock. As soon as a baby can sit up and crawl, it may move around the house by itself and try out whatever it pleases. There is nothing valuable standing around which it could break or tear up. Since it wears no clothing and since the floor can easily be cleaned with water, there is no need to give a young child any special toilet training – that dogs make themselves useful in this regard has already been mentioned. Without any problem, the child learns after a while to do its business in the corner of the *tsar* designated for that purpose. If it dirties itself, it is washed. If, however, it does not wish to be washed, then it is simply not washed; for even the smallest children are not forced to do anything they do not want to do.

As soon as a child has made its first attempt to stand and walk, it awakens general interest. One encourages it, speaks to it, and furthers its understanding of the language, without resorting to baby talk. When a child is able to understand more of the language, one likewise tells it no fairy tales – to tell a child something which one does not believe oneself would be like lying. In a crucial situation, the Mru may lie when they are afraid, but they are ashamed of it. To tell a child something false intentionally would be even worse. If children say or do something wrong, it is due to a lack of knowledge or ability; in such cases, therefore, punishment is useless. As time goes on, children simply gain certain knowledge and abilities as they listen, observe, and imitate. Nothing can be achieved by force. The only thing one can do is warn the children of the consequences of bad actions; and, as a general rule, such consequences are related to the reaction of the spirits *(tshüng-nam)* – even if the nature of the spirits is often as indefinable for the Mru as the "psychosomatic effects of social mechanisms" are for us.

This tolerant attitude of the parents over and against childish "stupidity" and even antisocial behavior is rooted in a conception of the child as a human being who is only in the process of becoming. The behavior which might well result from such tolerance is, however, balanced or corrected in the children's play groups. In the play groups children learn with and from each other how they must get along with other people. Occasionally, the goings-on in such groups may become quite rowdy; yet there is a strict distinction made between high-spirited teasing and malevolence. He who becomes abusive or even violent must reckon with the fact that he will be forced to stand on the periphery and watch for a few days. Parents do not interfere in such activities in order to defend their children; they know that children must learn and that unpleasant experiences are part of the learning process – such experiences only confirm the exhortations of the parents. Children are not forced to learn. On their own initiative they must observe and appropriate for themselves those abilities and that knowledge they wish to possess. Parents do not instruct, they do not explain how one should do things; rarely do they correct mistakes. It is left up to the children to observe and imitate; and most children's games involve the imitation of adult activities. There are, to be sure, specialists *(sra)* among the adults who have served a special "ap-

▶ An older sister has to take care of her younger siblings. Here she carries her small brother on her back; he is adorned with a beaded necklace and an anklet.

Drawing pictures

◀◀ If children want to draw, they customarily use their finger and the cleared-off ground of the village square.

◀ Here the ethnographer has given a young boy a piece of paper and pencil. The drawing shows two spirits with many heads (the multiple circles); on the sides of the heads are eyes and ears (with slits); below that is the mouth.

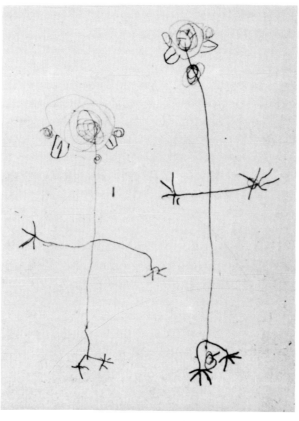

Playful competition

◀◀ Two boys play cows; two others hold them by the tails of their loin-cloths.

◀ One of the old sports of the Mru, the Khumi, and the Bawm is a kind of inverted tug-of-war: two persons or parties place themselves on each end and each side of a bamboo pole and try to force the competitor backwards. Here, the two bigger boys have won over the four smaller ones.

Developing skills

▶▶ Two young boys, using long bamboo reeds as mouth organs, and three girls organize the dance of a cattle feast. Next to the sacrificial posts located in the village square, the children have put up their own posts. Two large stones represent the bound cattle.

▶ Without untying the cord, the hollow bamboo segments on each side of the longer bamboo tube must both be brought to one side. Even adults have much trouble solving this puzzle.

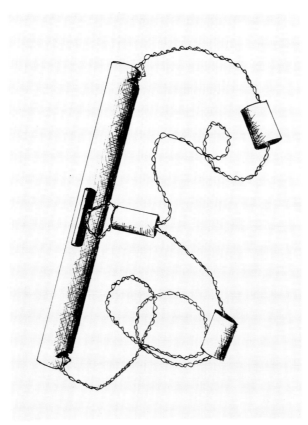

Formation of groups

Even before young children begin to wear clothing regularly, they join in the play groups of their respective sexes. The boys' groups occupy more space and are more active than those of the girls; girls stick more closely together and often only watch.

prenticeship;" but such training takes place in like manner — there is no esoteric knowledge. A young person, who follows around a master of religious ceremonies, taking note of everything he hears and sees, will one day — as soon as he is grown and married — simply be familiar with the rules and able to lead the corresponding ceremonies himself. He needs no one's blessings in order to do this, but others must recognize that he knows the rules better than they.

In the first, third, fifth, or any other odd-numbered year of life before puberty, the earlobes of both girls and boys are pierced. For such an occasion, a cow or bull is sacrificed, and a special feast is held. When the wound around the small, inserted piece of wood is healed, the hole is stretched by a small roll of leaves until it is large enough to accommodate ear decorations. No further ceremony is held at this time. The first wearing of clothing — at four or six years — and the beginning of puberty likewise mark no occasion for any special celebration or ceremony. In spite of this, children and young people are conscious of their new status. From six years of age onward, they can move about in a seemly fashion in their clothing. From fourteen, they place much emphasis on an expressive appearance; and they deck themselves out in a specific way. In their relations with members of the opposite sex, young boys vacillate between boastfulness and magnanimity; girls are giggly, or coquettish, and "feel shy." The playful imitation of adults is something of the past; young people now work alongside their parents. For those who must replace a father or a mother, the serious side of life begins two or three years earlier than for others; for many, however, the mood of the moment may still determine their participation in the family's work. In principle, though, everyone would like to distinguish him- or herself in the eyes of the other sex; and the mutual-aid groups, which take turns working the fields of their members, offer one of the best opportunities for doing this. Girls can also demonstrate their special abilities in the area of textile production, even if they must wait until the next big feast to wear the decorated sides of their skirts turned to the outside.

Pig sacrifice

Pigs are almost never slaughtered merely for consumption. They are rather sacrificed for the welfare of the family, that is especially in case of illness. For a big offering a first pig is killed near the staircase in front of the house, where a decorated bamboo pole has been set up. Next to it a miniature platform is erected (left). During the sacrifice, a drum and three plate-shaped gongs are beaten. If a second pig is sacrificed, it is killed on the *tsar*. Again, special bamboo constructions will be erected, on which rice and turmeric will be deposited (above).

The pig is killed on a "hearth", a bamboo mat covered with earth. Later on, a small fire will be lit on this "hearth"; and pieces of the pig's brain will be burned. On the tray lie banana and ginger leaves, as well as the cotton threads, which will later be used in the *bong-kom* ceremony; the pieces of banana leaf will be used for preparing *köm-pot*, gifts for the spirits (right). Small pieces of meat skewered on bamboo thongs serve the same purpose (below).

Illness and Death

Smaller festivities occur more often. Some of them, like the festivals already mentioned in connection with the cultivation cycle, recur annually; others take place irregularly. The irregular occasions necessitating a ceremony are rarely happy ones like a wedding. Much more often, in fact, illnesses require the offering of a small or large sacrifice. Yet no matter how unpleasant the situation may be for those directly concerned — for example, for the sick persons themselves or even for the households which cannot really meet the expenses of such an undertaking — a festivity is always a pleasant experience for everyone. There is meat to eat and beer or liquor to drink, at least for the men. As far as the Mru are concerned, this sacrificial feasting on the occasion of an unpleasant illness is no contradiction; for in each and every case the spirits must be put into a good mood. In the case of illness, the sacrifice anticipates the recovery; often, however, the sacrifice is made only after the recovery has taken place. (He who honestly cannot come up with the means to pay for such a ceremony promises the spirits that the sacrifice will be made later, and they can be sure that the promise will be kept.) Whether or not an illness demands a sacrifice depends ultimately upon how normal — or abnormal — the illness appears. Intestinal difficulties occuring at a time when dysentery is rampant or after one has eaten bad food offer no grounds for special treatment; likewise, if a person has injured himself, he knows the reason for his injury. If a person repeatedly has bad luck, however, or if he, without obvious reason, has a bad pain or fever or does not recover from an illness within a normal period of time, it is presumed that a sacrifice is necessary. Symptoms reveal only partially which spirit is responsible for the illness and which sacrifice must therefore be offered. As a matter of fact, most Mru spirits have very little "personality" — there are no priests who could formulate a doctrine regarding the spirits. In each case, though, there is only a limited number of ceremonies from which to choose. In order to determine which one is required, the Mru utilize different methods of divination, the most common type being the reading of the oscillation of the bow which is normally used for teasing cotton. Fittingly, those persons most well-versed in this particular art of divination are women. The sacrificial ceremonies themselves are, on the other hand, carried out almost exclusively by men, although not every man has a command of the detailed knowledge necessary for such ceremonials. If need be, a specialist from another village may have to be called in.

Prior to the end of the nineteenth century, there was supposedly still a kind of shaman who could send his soul out to make direct contact with the spirits when he was in a state of trance. Today the knowledge related to such abilities is forgotten, and even the knowledge of medicinal plants is only rudimentary. Remedics against pain, malaria, and dysentery can be purchased from Bangali merchants; but one is often ignorant about how to take or apply the medicines. And no matter what Bangali quack doctors may sell at high prices, it hardly ever helps. The Mru are convinced of the effectiveness of injections, although the obligatory inoculations are not without risk since the local medical personnel often use dirty injection needles. Traditionally, there was no remedy against smallpox except taking refuge in the jungle. To gain some protection against cholera — a disease which in former times normally broke out between the months of May and July — one either closed the village to strangers, or abandoned the village altogether and spread out in the field houses in order to lessen the danger of infection. Sacrifices against such epidemics were not only considered to be useless, they were even forbidden. Sacrificial ceremonies aim at holding and binding the community together; epidemics require isolation.

By affirming community, many ceremonies help to ease or overcome suffering. To these ceremonial occasions belongs, finally, the funeral. In order to give all relatives the opportunity to see a dead person one last time, the corpse must be preserved for two or three days. The closest relatives first wash the dead person and dress him or her in fresh clothing. A woman is also dressed in her jewelry, and a man receives a new, white turban. A small basket is then woven; a chicken is killed; and two pounds of rice are cooked. The rice, along with the legs, the

Above:
Before a third pig is killed inside the house, four special musical instruments are sounded. They consist of gourds, into one side of which a single pipe has been inserted. After the meat has been cooked, little pieces of pork are wrapped in pieces of banana leaves as *köm-pot*.

Below:
Humans cannot eat pork until the *bong-kom* ceremony has been performed. In conclusion of the ceremony, the children assemble in a circle, and the eldest member of the family blesses them by moving the tray (used for the ritual objects) in a circle above their heads.

Above:
A woman has died and her body will be kept in the *kim-tom* for a few days. Her jewelry hangs on the coffin; food and drink stand in front of it. In the background, three drummers playing upon two drums beat out the three-tone melody of the death dance.

Below:
Two men carry the coffin on a pole to the place on the other side of the stream where it will be burned. Young boys accompany the dead person for the last time: they play upon the set of three plate-shaped gongs which is used for all sacrificial ceremonies.

stomach, and the head of the chicken, is put into the basket and placed at the head of the dead person. A coffin is next prepared from green and white (or dyed red) bamboo strips which are woven alternately in special patterns. After the coffin has been placed in the middle of the *kim-tom*, with the foot towards the *kimma*, the dead person is put inside and covered with a cloth, leaving only the head visible. A large pig is sacrificed for the funeral meal; at every mealtime, the dead person is also given a serving. The pork, along with a handful of rice, is simply put into the basket. If the family owns a cow of which the dead person was particularly fond, the cow may also be sacrificed; however, one must kill it by cutting its throat, rather than by stabbing it to death with a spear, which is the normal procedure on festive occasions. Such sacrificial meat may not be given to people of other households. In addition to this prohibition, other things must also be done in a way normally forbidden. Water and food scraps, for example, may not be emptied onto the *tsar*; they must rather be poured down the steps.

After the corpse has thus been laid out in state and after the first animals have been slaughtered, the dance of the dead *(wak-plai)* begins. It must be performed three times a day. Those instruments serving to accompany the dance include the following: three mouth organs, each consisting of a single pipe inserted into the side of a bottle gourd *(tu)*; three plate-shaped gongs; and three drums, each sounding a different tone. The succession of tones to be played upon the instruments is fixed by the text of the funeral songs *(wak-long)*. The songs themselves, however, are not sung; the instruments simply reproduce the pitches of the syllables — Mru is a tonal language having three pitch levels. The spirits understand the text, which in part alludes to the origin of death. The poem also speaks of the construction of the coffin and of the sacrifices; it allows the dead person to lament his fate; and it hints at a dance of birds — probably a dance of men as seen from the perspective of the spirits. Among human beings, only a few specialists *(tu-sra)* know the text; and they tell the instrumentalists which succession of tones must be played. In addition to this customary dance of the dead, there is a totally different form of dance which a surviving husband must fear if the members of his dead wife's clan believe that he did not treat his wife well. The husband is obliged to present a spear to every member of the wife's clan who attends the funeral; and, in addition to the normal chicken and rice, he must also supply them with plenty of rice liquor. If these clan members are in a foul mood, they perform a wild dance around the coffin; during this dance, which is done to the beating of the drum, they may tear up all of the household furnishings and hack up the walls. No matter what the attitude of her clan may be, a dead woman's brother is always entitled to a final payment. This "hair burning" money symbolizes the fact that even as a corpse the woman still belongs to her brother's, and not her husband's, clan.

On the evening before a cremation young men near the coffin play a game — something like "heads-or-tails" — for money. The winnings of the "bank" go to the deceased. For the cremation itself, each village household brings a few pieces of wood; next morning, the wood is tied into bundles and carried on carrying poles to the cremation site. There it is piled up. In the case of men, the pyres consist of five layers of wood; in the case of women, six layers — an extra layer in recognition of their daily task of securing the firewood. While some men transport the wood, others carry the coffin and the burial offerings to the cremation site; they are accompanied by the beating of the three plate-shaped gongs. The coffin of a man is placed on the pyre with the head toward the west; that of a woman, toward the east — a woman should look toward the west, and a man toward the east. The stack of wood is then set afire with a torch — first at the head, then at the foot. As soon as the flames are high, one wrings the neck of a chicken and throws it into the fire. A dog is clubbed to death, held for a short time over the fire, and then thrown aside. After the pyre has burned down, the last coals are extinguished with water. The remains of the bones and any jewelry or gold pieces which have survived the fire are then collected and, along with a hewing knife and a hoe, covered with a cloth. In front of these objects, one places a bamboo tube full of rice and the pot in which the funeral bathwater had been prepared. Finally, over all of these things, one constructs a slanted roof.

A little to the side, one also constructs a small bamboo house for the dead, complete with fireplace and staircase. (The house is approximately one meter [3 ft.] high.) A cloth "cradle" is then hung up inside the dwelling. Women receive, in addition, a new skirt which has been shredded, as well as bracelets and strands of beads — or at least the remains of such retrieved from the ashes. Men are given a loin-cloth. Utensils, such as a basket, a drinking bowl, and a bottle with some rice beer or liquor, are also added to the other things. In front of the tiny house a small sacrificial altar is erected. A pig and a chicken are killed and, together with rice, prepared for eating. The dead person receives a little bit of everything; those persons present eat the rest. The dishes used for this meal, as well as a round beer pot, are left behind in front of the small house. All of those who have taken part in the ceremony must take a drink from the pot and spit it out again; as they do this, the ceremonial master touches each on the forehead with a small piece of wild ginger root, so that they will not thereafter suffer headaches. As soon as the participants reenter the village, ashes are thrown over each of them by the wives who remained at home. In the afternoon another pig is slaughtered in the house of the deceased; on the following day, no one is allowed to work in the fields.

The small house of the dead receives no further attention or care. It slowly decays, and its remains can easily be cleared away — for example, on the occasion of the next crematory ritual. Some people are afraid to go too close to the "cemetery," particularly at night; others are not afraid. The soul of the deceased leaves this place and sets out for the other world. The first leg of the journey is dark and sinister; however, the dog which was killed shows the soul the way. And the chicken which was cremated along with the dead person goes ahead and picks up the vermin. At a certain point, the soul comes to a fork in the road. Here, a judge sends bad persons to the place of darkness and no return and good persons to heaven. In heaven, where people arrive rejuvenated, they are reunited with previously-deceased relatives and spend much

Cremation and burial

Above:
A dead body is normally cremated and the remains of its bones are wrapped in a cloth. Along with a fan and food (in a bamboo tube) for the journey of the deceased, the cloth is placed under a slanting roof (left). Meanwhile a little house with two rooms is prepared; its walls being woven in the same special decorative patterns as those used for the coffin (cf. p. 6). In one of its rooms a cloth is suspended as a cradle, the other is furnished with a miniature hearth (right).

Below:
The baskets and pots used in the funeral are left on top, or in front, of the house. Before leaving the place of cremation, each assistant draws a sip of *hom-noi* from the beer pot and then spits it out again (left). In the case of children and very poor persons who have no family, one does not go to the expense of a cremation ceremony. A few strips of bamboo tied together replace the coffin; and the dead person is buried. What little the dead person possessed is left behind on the fenced-in grave (right).

of their time sitting in the shade of a large *Ficus* tree or entertaining themselves with games and by shooting with a bow and arrow. If a soul so desires, it may ultimately even be reborn on earth.

The soul of a person who died an "evil death" also reaches heaven: it climbs up on a rainbow. (It is said, however, that a human being has seven souls; one of these may perhaps be left behind at the cemetery.) Persons who die an evil death are those who drown, those who burn to death, those who fall from a tree, those who are killed by a tiger, those who are caught in a trap, and, above all, those women who die in childbirth. In all the villages hearing of an evil death one must refrain for a day from doing any work which is not vitally necessary; one may also close the villages to strangers. Still, the relatives of the dead person are to be invited to the ceremony. The coffin of a person dying an evil death is woven only in white; the meat of the pig, the first sacrifice, may not be eaten. In fact, until the cremation no relative is permitted to eat meat at all. Relatives may eat only cooked rice and drink only water. Strangers are not permitted to eat anything in the house of the deceased person, and the death dance is omitted. Only after another special pig sacrifice has been made, following the ceremony, are the eating restrictions lifted. An additional pig must also be sacrificed for members of a dead wife's clan if the woman died an evil death; otherwise, they could no longer eat the chickens to which they are entitled in any of the households of the husband's clan.

Children under three months of age may not be cremated; they are buried in the ground. Most of the time, older children up to two years of age are likewise buried. One also resorts to burial in the case of epidemics; not because cremation would be inadmissible, but because there are not enough persons to assist in the cremation ceremonial. Finally, one also buries those adults who no longer have family members who could pay for the funeral festivities. In the case of burial, the corpse is simply wrapped in a piece of cloth; there is no coffin. Likewise, no animal is sacrificed, and no death dance performed. The grave is dug with a hoe; and after it has been filled up again with earth, it is fenced in on all sides. Several things are put on top of the grave for the dead person: a rice pot with a lid; the bottle gourds, tongs for the pot, and the pot used for the preparation of the dead person's bathwater; the clothing and jewelry worn by the deceased; the hewing knife and the hoe which were used to dig and fence in the grave; the basket and straps used to carry the various items to the burial site; and the carrying pole used to transport the corpse to the grave. None of these objects may ever be used again.

▶
At the dance.

Next page:
The reluctant bull is dragged with ropes into the enclosure which has been decorated with bamboo tassels.

Adorned with necklaces, combs, hairpins, flowers, bracelets, anklets, and chains of beads and coins, the girls put on their anklet-rattles in preparation for a dance.

Left side:
For a celebration, everyone puts on his best jewelry. The wooden combs, which are partially covered with aluminium, are selfmade.

◀
"Hey, you with your chain of coins! How much time do you still need to put on your anklet-rattles?"

▶
A Mru belle in festive attire sports a precious, old chain of Persian silver rupees.

The dance begins. In the coolness of the morning, the girls wear their vividly-colored shawls. Now it is becoming hot.

All mouth organs (*plung*) used for dances are equipped with bourdons; the longer the pipes, the lower the pitch.

Left side:
The types and numbers of bamboo decorations over the ceremonial grounds depend on the number and type of animals sacrificed; moreover, decorations vary from region to region.

The larger the feast, the more beer pots the host must set up. After the dance, the young men invite the young girls to drink.

The amount drunk is replenished by water, which is filled into the pot by means of a small bamboo tube. Hence, the pot is always full; but the beer becomes thinner and thinner.

A view of the hamlet's ceremonial ground. The dancers surround the cow which is tied up in the decorated enclosure. At the right, one sees the stand with the large bronze gong; just below that, a small altar covered with a piece of banana leaf, three beer pots, two small pots and several swallow-tailed bamboo tubes filled with rice water. On the wall of the house there is a *tu* pipe decorated with tassels.

One of the assistants, with his child in a shawl on his back, strikes the plate-shaped gong.

Accompanied by dancing girls, young men drag the slain cow to the feast-giver's house, where it will be skinned and cut up.

There is no dancing unless there is a feast. Since festival occasions are so rare, young people dance far into the night.

Unlike beer, liquor may be drunk even when no ceremony is in progress. The first glass or the first cup is always presented to a specially honored guest.

Right side:
After the cow has been skinned and cut up on the open platform of the feast-giver's house, its meat is cut into small cubes. Along with chili peppers and other spices, it is then cooked in big, flat pots on the village square. Women and children watch what is being done – the preparation of meat is strictly a man's affair.

A special invitation to the ceremony is issued to the relatives on both wife-taking and wife-giving sides (*pen* and *tutma*). The *tutma* are given chickens to eat, and they receive their own beer pots in the feast-giver's house. Attached to the stick placed crosswise on the pot is the measuring rod; it indicates the amount each person should drink.

The distillation of rice liquor is a woman's job. The alcolholic vapor rising from the brew in the beer pot is cooled in a section of bamboo cane (wrapped in a damp piece of cloth) and then caught in a small pot which is submerged in a container of water (left). By means of a small test tube placed in the container, the quality of the beverage may be controlled.

Cattle Ceremonies and Feasts of Merit

The most important days in the course of a year are those on which one can attend a feast, and the most important days in the life of a person are those on which he himself can host such an occasion. Men are considered the hosts, the "feast-givers"; however, only after a man is married may he organize a feast where cattle, gayal, or buffalo are sacrificed. Not every man is ambitious enough to work and plan toward a feast, but many are forced to host one without ever having had the intention — in cases of serious illness it may be necessary to sacrifice a bull or a cow. He who has had a particularly good harvest also does well to host a feast, in order not to evoke the anger of the spirits and the envy of other villagers. Thus, feasts prevent evil and safeguard the physical and mental health of the members of the family.

Everything beyond the simple sacrifice of a head of cattle, however, aims primarily at enhancing one's social standing. To be sure, a Mru can also distinguish himself and gain merit by taking over the position as head of the hamlet (*karbari*). For services rendered while fulfilling this post, he will receive no reimbursement; just the opposite, he will have additional expenses since all visitors having no relatives in the hamlet will be housed — and will also expect to be fed — by him. Whoever in agreement with the other villagers takes over such a post must be prepared to work extra for his prestige. Since the same is true of a feast-giver, it is not surprising that the person hosting the most, or largest, feasts in a given hamlet is generally the *karbari* — or, perhaps, someone who would like to qualify as his successor. A *karbari* has no power to command; a feast-giver likewise acquires no power, only prestige. In traditional Mru society, wealth accumulated by a man and his family by means of their own work cannot be translated into power — as long as every household is entitled to farm part of the village land, the only way to force others into permanent dependence is to engage in usurious moneylending. This, however, runs completely counter to traditional kinship obligations. A feast-giver who is suspected of having squeezed his wealth out of others, rather than having worked for it himself, must fear to have his feast shunned. Instead of more prestige, then, his money would rather buy him public humiliation.

Just how much temporary and perishable wealth a Mru feast-giver should transform (by spending it) into lasting renown is not defined; one therefore need not exhaust all of one's resources. Among the Khumi, one can hardly escape such, however, since the guests bring gifts which the host must later return with an added bonus; and the more "credit" they give him on what he will produce in the future, the greater his prestige. These feasts of merit have the effect, therefore, of preventing single families from establishing themselves in an economically dominant position. He who resists the pressure to distribute his wealth must expect to be negatively sanctioned by the spirits (illnesses). Yet he who not only yields to the pressure, but also goes all out to prove himself in such endeavors, does honor to his name and erects a monument which lives on after his death. Among the Khumi, such a monument is concretized in the form of a megalith which is put up on the ceremonial grounds. The Mru, too, put up stones, but mostly of a rather small size. The deterioration of the economy, the diminishing of land resources, and the fall in production yields have meant a decrease in the possibilities of hosting feasts of merit — particularly large ceremonies. Today one very seldom has the means to host such a feast. By the 1950s, only a few old men knew the rules for carrying out

◀ Sunset

the most highly ranking feasts; these men had still been able to participate in such ceremonies at the beginning of this century.

The months of December and January — that is, the period between the cotton harvest and the cultivation of new fields — are considered the best time for giving a feast. The time of the waxing moon is also preferred. As far as larger feasts are concerned, however, the preferred time schedule is largely theoretical. The preparations can in fact drag out so much longer than anticipated that the feasts do not actually take place until sometime between February and April. A small feast can be prepared from one day to the next, as long as rice beer and liquor are either on hand or can be procured from neighbors. In the case of larger feasts, however, a crucial preliminary task must first be completed, namely, the pounding of huge amounts of rice. This pounding stretches over several days and must necessarily precede the preparation of beverages. The sacrificial animals are almost always purchased from outside; for although a feast-giver is not forbidden to slaughter his own cattle, he is normally too fond of them to kill them unless circumstances force him to do so. Those neighbors and relatives participating in the feast likewise do not like to see their cattle slaughtered. Yet it is not the procuring of the larger livestock which proves to be most difficult; it is rather the accumulation of the large number of chickens which must be prepared for the guests from the *tutma* clans. Since Mru households keep only a few chickens due to the risks involved, feast-givers are dependent upon peddlers to supply them with chickens; and peddlers are not absolutely reliable. All important relatives must be invited well in advance of the festivities. Finally, before the ceremonies can begin, two days must be allocated for the preparation of the festive decorations. (Those for smaller feasts may be prepared in a few hours, if all men of the settlement lend a hand.)

Women's Work: Alcoholic Beverages

The pounding of the rice and the production of the beer and liquor is, as always, women's work. Beer is prepared in large earthen pots which are bought at the market. A layer of paddy is first put into the very bottom of the vessel; then comes cooked rice which has been mixed with some brewer's yeast. (The yeast is prepared ahead of time from wild plants and parboiled rice.) Depending on the size of the pot, anywhere from 4 to 40 pounds of cooked rice may be put into any one vessel. The mouth of the pot is covered with a banana leaf and tied shut with a bark string; after about four days

Women hulling rice for a cattle ceremony. Some beer pots have already been lined up.

one can pour off a sweet-tasting, milky beer. Most of the time, however, one adds a little water and leaves the pot well sealed for two to four weeks; the fermented rice which results has a slightly sour taste. This rice is then covered with a layer of fresh banana leaves which is held firmly in place by a woven, hexagonal-shaped bamboo frame; and a long, thin piece of bamboo, which serves as a drinking reed, is placed vertically into the pot so that its lower end reaches all the way down into the layer of paddy. Finally, the pot is filled up with water. After the head of the house has sampled the beer, convincing himself that everything is in order, the guests may be invited to drink by order of rank. The drinking-mark, which varies somewhat according to ceremony, guarantees that all participants drink almost exactly the same amount. As soon as the water level has sunk to the lower end of the mark, the person drinking relinquishes his place to the next one in line; before that person begins to drink, however, the water level is raised again to its previous height. Since the water continually soaks through the banana leaves into the beer, the beverage becomes slightly weaker with every drink; the participants can continue to drink, though, until they find the beer too flat. The water which remains in the pot at the end of the feast is simply poured out, and the rice which remains is fed to the pigs.

If liquor is to be prepared, the layer of paddy is unnecessary, since its purpose is to prevent the drinking reed from becoming clogged. The mash is simply prepared with water and then distilled after two or three days of fermentation. To distill the liquor, the housewife puts the large, round beer pot on the fireplace and covers its mouth with the severed upper half of a bottle gourd. This gourd reaches up to the upper end of a tube which slants diagonally downward and is wrapped in a damp cloth; where gourd and tube come together mash acts as a seal. The lower end of the tube extends into a small pot which stands tipped in a larger container of cooling water. The success of the distillation depends upon a proper regulation of the fire combined with the constant cooling of the tube: if the mash begins to burn toward the end of the distillation process, the whole brew will later taste terrible; and if the tube is not kept constantly cool by a dousing of water, the alcohol will escape as steam. About one bottle of liquor can be obtained from two pounds of rice — admittedly, not one with a very high percentage of alcohol. (The Bangalis know how to produce one bottle of high-proof alcohol from four bottles of normal liquor; this is accomplished by means of an additional distillation. During the last war, when oil for the kerosene lamps was scarce but when there was still sufficient rice, a substitute fuel was obtained in this manner.) In contrast to beer, which is neither bought nor sold, liquor can be bought by the bot-

▶ A young man drinks from one of the beer pots placed at the edge of the ceremonial grounds.

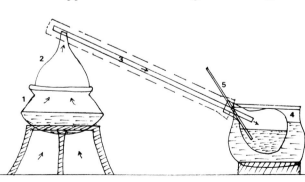

Distilling apparatus

1 wort container over fire
2 bottle gourd without bottom
3 cooling tube wrapped in cloth
4 receptacle in waterbath
5 testing tube

◀◀ A new mouth organ is being constructed.
◀ The tiny bamboo reeds are being glued into a pair of small pipes.

tle; however, no one buys a bottle to drink alone. Among the Mru alcohol is consumed only on social occasions. For example, one should honor a particularly important visitor with a bottle — a bottle which must be full and then drunk to the last drop.

Only a person having a full storage bin can set aside paddy for alcoholic beverages. On the whole, alcohol consumption is low: for the annual budget, one figures 12 lb. of paddy per person per year for beer and liquor together. Whoever does not have this much paddy to spare can do without liquor. A pot of rice beer, however, is a must for some of the seasonal festivals; it is also obligatory for all occasions which include a pig sacrifice and which, like the wedding celebration, end with the *bong-kom*, the ceremonious tying of a string around the wrist of all family members. The *bong-kom* is done to fortify the soul, and the beer is also for the soul. The beer pot has its own string, which is the strap tying it shut; in the course of the ceremony, this strap may be neither damaged nor loosened. Guests may bring beer pots as gifts to the ceremony's host, but never without a strap. A person wishing to give a big feast must have a general supply of alcoholic beverages over and above those beer pots necessary for the ceremony; therefore, during the days and weeks prior to a feast, not only are the women in the feast-giver's household busy, but also the neighboring women, since guests will also turn up at their homes.

Men's Work: Mouth organs and Decorations

During the weeks prior to a feast, the young men are also occupied with something special. Rather than coming together each evening to court the (perennially busy) young girls, they now meet in order to repair and tune their mouth organs *(plung)*. They must also do a lot of practicing. There is a special type of mouth organ which can be played as a solo instrument at any time and another type which is particularly used for weddings, but the playing of mouth organs in orchestra is allowed only at cattle ceremonies. The mouth organs played in orchestra distinguish themselves from other types by having bamboo tubes serving as bourdons placed over the tops of their pipes and by varying in size. Some of these instruments have tiny pipes only a few centimeters long; others have large pipes several meters in length and are so heavy that they must be carried in a shawl hung over the shoulder. Every *plung* consists of a gourd bottle into the round belly of which two rows of bamboo pipes have been vertically inserted — the back row for the right hand, and the front row for

The bourdons on the pipes of the mouth organ (right) are sometimes decorated by their owner with simple red or green drawings (left).

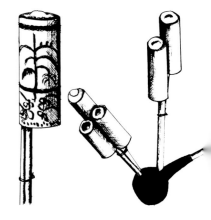

Although mouth organs are not used for small cattle ceremonies, three plate-shaped gongs, a cymbal, and a drum are always necessary. Along with the large gong, they are, in fact, *the* ceremonial instruments. The two stones at the foot of the sacrificial posts were put into place during previous ceremonies.
▶

In order to play the extremely large mouth organs, the players must carry them in shawls knotted over the shoulder.

the left. The musician blows air into the bottle and plays upon the pipes, each of which is equipped with a finger hole. On one side of the bottom end of each pipe — that is, on the end sticking into the gourd — there is a second opening into which the frame of a tiny bamboo reed has been inserted and glued with wasp wax. A small clump of wax on the reed itself makes it possible to modulate the frequency of its vibration and thereby to tune the instrument. If the wax gets out of place, however, it can cause the reed to stick to the framework. In order to prevent this, both are smeared with lime. With regard to the tuning of the *plung*, one must tune not only all of the pipes of one individual instrument (generally in 4ths and 5ths), but also all instruments to each other; for when played together in orchestra, the instruments must harmonize. Since these instruments are played fairly infrequently — perhaps only once a year — , the wax seals and the bamboo pipes, or even the gourds themselves, usually become brittle. The instruments must therefore be repaired and partially reconstructed before each performance. The members of the orchestra also change over time: one by one the young men marry and thereby leave the group. Young boys growing up must therefore be trained, since they will eventually fill the vacated positions. So, night after night the young men tune their instruments and practice, until they feel they can play confidently in public. No prior precautions, however, can prevent the need to repair the mouth organs again during the dance itself. Due to the movements of the dance, the wax seals fixing the pipes to the gourds loosen easily — this is particularly true of the very large pipes. When this happens, air escapes prematurely at these points. From time to time, therefore, a musician drops out briefly in order to re-glue his pipes. If it is a truly successful feast, however, the musicians virtually play day and night, although orchestras from different villages may relieve each other.

Small cattle ceremonies do not require a mouth organ orchestra; but the three plate-shaped gongs, the drum, and the cymbals, which normally accompany the mouth organ orchestra, are always necessary. Unlike the mouth organs, which are played only by unmarried men, these indispensable ceremonial instruments can also be played by older men. Mouth organ players move clockwise in open formation around the sacrificial animal which is tied up in the center. Opposite the men stands a row of girls. The girls hold hands and move backwards as they dance; the rhythm of the dance is accentuated by their anklets and the chains of coins slung about their bodies. The same rhythm and succession of tones are repeated over and over, in several rounds, although they are introduced and repeatedly interrupted by shorter periods of smaller and faster steps done to a quick beat of the gongs and sustained notes of the mouth organs. The sound of a Mru orchestra is anything but monotonous, though nothing at all like a group of European fife or bagpipe players. During the night, one can hear them from miles away, from one mountain to the next; and from a distance the sounds of these orchestras, strangely enough, remind our ears above all of church bells.

Before the feast can begin, the men, as mentioned, have yet another task to perform: the preparation of the festive decorations. For each sacrificed head of cattle, a large bamboo mast, which towers high above the roof, is put up beside the staircase of the feast-giver's house. The lowest four yards of the mast are not decorated in any special way. The next two yards or so are decorated with nine rings made from twisted bamboo strips; mounted on these rings are tasseled sticks. (In order to create such a tassel, the inside of a bamboo stick is scraped toward the node; the two narrow sides are scraped only a little, so that small, frizzy curls appear.) Above this part, over an area of some four to five yards, the branches of the mast are cut off, and tasseled sticks are tied on in their stead. Over this, one secures a herringbone-shaped piece of latticework several meters in length. This latticework towers high over the top of the bamboo mast and, after it has been mounted, bends downward, carrying on its end a crown of large tassels. Finally, on the very top of this backward-bending piece of bamboo, a model of a hornbill, fashioned of split bamboo, may be placed.

Another decorative element used for all kinds of feasts is a four-yard-long bamboo pole decorated with tassels. (Some of the tassels are produced by

Bamboo art

Mru existence is dependent upon bamboo. Bamboo is also the major medium of artistic expression.

◄
Among the Rümma Mru, the crown of the large mast which is set up beside the staircase of a feast-giver's house consists of four bamboo tassels fixed to a ring.

Below:
The lower part of the large mast, which will be set up beside the staircase, is adorned with tassel rings. If there is no bamboo cane long enough for the mast, it must be constructed of two poles put together.

scraping the bark of the pole itself; others are tasseled sticks which are stuck into the pole.) Two poles of this type flank the post in the middle of the ceremonial ground to which the sacrificial animal is tied. One such post must be erected for each head of cattle sacrificed. After the feast the post is simply left stuck into the ground, and occasionally it sprouts again and becomes a tree. Cattle which are to be sacrificed are generally not only tied up, but also fenced in. Rising above and projecting over their enclosure is an open bamboo scaffolding, the size of which is indicative of the magnitude of the feast. The finest specimens are richly decorated with tassels and carved, red, wooden spires.

On one side of the ceremonial grounds, a stand for the big gong is erected; it is likewise partially decorated with tassels. Close to the gong, the beer pots for the dancers are put in place. In some villages, this side is allocated to the males and the opposite side, marked by another group of beer pots, to the female dancers — the idea being that the girls should invite the young men, just as the men invite the girls, to drink from their pots. Customarily, however, only the young men, who do considerably more justice to the alcohol, invite the girls. Near the gong stand, a miniature altar is erected; upon it, rice and wild ginger are placed on a covering of banana leaf. Four small bamboo tubes, the lower ends of which are carved into the shape of swallowtails, are then stuck into the ground next to the altar; these are filled with *hom-noi*, a ritual drink made from water, cooked rice, crushed ginger and turmeric. In addition to these tubes of *hom-noi*, a small, round pot of *hom-noi* is also required (sometimes even two or four pots).

Bamboo sticks the length of two internodes are being fashioned into "flowers". For the long tassels the sticks are scraped toward the two nodes. The areas between the tassels are decorated with small, curly buds. These "flowers", which for the time being have been placed into a bamboo tube, will later be inserted into the shaft of the large ceremonial mast.

▶

A man prepares the herringbone-shaped piece of latticework from which the crown of the ceremonial mast is hung.

The Sacrifice

The first animal to be sacrificed is a small chicken. The ceremony takes place in the feast-giver's house. Only after this sacrifice has been made can the ceremonial instruments be taken out of the house. In addition to the set of plate-shaped gongs and the drum, these musical instruments include — depending on region, type of festival, and general availability — the large gong, a small cymbal and three *tu*. (The *tu* are always decorated with fronds

of the fishtail palm). The sacrificed chicken, which is cooked and then wrapped with some boiled rice in a banana leaf, is also taken to the ceremonial square; there it will later be eaten by children from the host's household. First, however, a wing of the chicken is removed; the host or one of his assistants brushes this wing across the head of the sacrificial animal tied up in the village square and then rubs it against the bamboo mast next to the staircase. Before the musical instruments may be played, they are spit upon with some of the *hom-noi* from the small pot. Then, as the musicians play the "strong rhythm" on their instruments, they circle the sacrificial animal eight times. These eight circumambulations correspond to eight verses of *tu* poetry, even if the *tu* themselves are not played, but are only carried along. (In the majority of cases the *tu* are not even carried along, since they are allowed only at larger cattle feasts.) Following this prelude, the rhythm changes from the "strong rhythm" (continuous beating in two-four time) to the "soft rhythm" (three even beats plus a pause of like duration). The festival dance, which is accompanied by the mouth organs, may now begin.

If the *tu* are to be blown, one needs a master (*sra*) who knows the verses. The *sra* may also be given the task of conducting all ceremonies and selecting the ceremonial assistants. Normally, there are two assistants — or two per sacrificed animal (cow or buffalo). To select the assistants, who must always be men, the *sra* places some hulled rice on a piece of bamboo, holds it over the fire, and asks whether or not the person under consideration is suitable. If the rice stays where it is, the concerned person is approved; if the grains slide or fall off, he is disqualified. As soon as the assistants have been selected, each receives a bottle of liquor from the feast-giver as renumeration for his future work; he must then drink the liquor with members of the host's family. This selection takes place on the evening preceding the feast, that is, before the cattle have been tied up on the ceremonial grounds; and after the special bottle of liquor has been consumed, the assistants may not drink any more alcohol for four days. They are also not permitted to eat oil, spices, or any kind of condiment normally eaten with rice; they may, however, eat the sacrificial meat, salt, and ginger. During their time of service, the assistants must also refrain from engaging in sexual intercourse. To lift the prohibition at

Cattle ceremony of the Rümma Mru. During the first eight times around the sacrificial animal, the three plate-shaped gongs and the drum are joined by three *tu*; the *tu* are decorated with bamboo tassels and palm fronds, but they are not played.

◄◄
Corner piece of the large bamboo scaffolding under which the sacrificial animals are tethered. It is made of long tassels, arches with small curls, and wooden spires mounted on top.

◄
A *tu* consists of a bottle gourd transversed by a single pipe with the reed in its middle. It is blown in a set of three instruments; the differently tuned pipes vary from 3 to 5 feet in length.

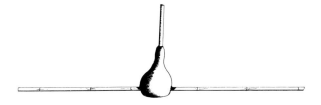

With a hewing knife, two young men scrape the bark of a bamboo cane into tassels. The two younger boys are making thread squares.

▶▶
Squatting next to the small altar and the four swallow-tailed bamboo tubes, the feast-giver's grandsons eat the chicken which was sacrificed to mark the beginning of the festival. Though needed for no special purpose the iron arrow (on top of the upside-down basket) just has to be there.

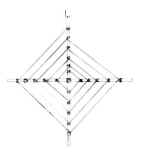

Thread squares made from red and black cotton strings (ca. 10 x 10 cm. [4 x 4 in.]) drive away evil spirits.

the close of the feast, a mixture of sour leaves and one or two shrimp, which have been pounded and cooked in a bamboo tube, are spread on the fingernails and toenails of the assistants.

The primary duties of the assistants include tending to the guests and assisting in the house of the host. For the duration of their office, they may at the request of the host enter the *kimma*, that part of the house which is normally off-limits to non-family members. For example, they may need to fetch spears or pieces of cloth, or distribute small packages of food for the spirits (*köm-pot*). Assistants must also lend a hand in all larger ceremonies; they are normally the ones to kill the animals, although the host himself may also take over this job. If two types of "medicine" are to be prepared and distributed during a ceremony, this again is a job for the assistants. To prepare these medicines, about a dozen types of wild plants are gathered and crushed in two bamboo tubes; the blood of either a dog or pig is then added. The pig's blood, which is dripped into one of the tubes, produces the "clean medicine;" the dog's blood mixed with the plants in the other tube produces the "dirty medicine." A stick with some cotton wrapped around one end serves as a brush; this brush is dipped into the tube as the mixture is distributed. Only the assistants may give out the "medicine." During the first night of dancing, the "clean medicine" is dabbed first of all on the sacrificial cattle (three times); then it is dabbed on the foreheads of all participants and guests, even on those who are sleeping. The "dirty medicine" is needed for several different purposes. Even before the ceremony begins it is used when one fells the trees to which the cattle are to be tied: the trunk of the tree is sprinkled with the blood of a chicken and some of the medicine. After the post is put up on the ceremonial grounds, it is again sprinkled with medicine. Likewise sprinkled are the bamboo mast near the staircase and the small, swallowtailed bamboo containers of *hom-noi* at the drinking place.

This "medicine" is needed for the last time on the third day of the celebration when the assistants fetch stones from the stream — a stone for each head of sacrificed cattle. In return for the stones and on the very spots from which they were taken, the assistants normally deposit some cooked rice, some cow brains, a little draft beer, and some liquor; in some villages, however, cow blood and manure are sufficient. The stones are then buried at the foot of the posts to which the sacrificial cattle were tied and are flanked right and left by the lower jawbone of the animals. The river-spirit is informed before the start of the ceremony; on the afternoon of the first day, before the dance begins, an assistant puts

Buffalo sacrifice

A last drink is poured over the mouth of the stabbed "head-pillow" of the buffalo (top left-hand corner). After it has been towed away, a procession of elderly women circumambulates the bamboo cage. A *pen* of the feast-giver, who earlier played the plate-shaped gong, supplies them with rice liquor (above left). Finally, an assistant thrusts the spear in between the ribs on the right hand side of the buffalo (left). The extracted tongue of the sacrificed animal is being nailed to the sacrificial post (above).

up a tasseled stick at the stream and drips the blood of a chicken over it. During big feasts of merit one may also, at the same time, offer a sacrifice to the mountain-spirit. This sacrifice is offered upon a small bamboo altar erected at the same place; it should be a goat or even one of the feast-giver's own head of cattle. The animals which are sacrificed at the river must be slaughtered by cutting their throats. Those tied up within the ceremonial grounds, on the other hand, may never be slaughtered in this manner; they must be stabbed to death with a spear.

Animals are tied to the sacrificial posts on the ceremonial grounds without ceremony. One lashes them with the top of the head against the post; and in the case of buffalo one ties the hind legs together and places supporting poles crosswise under the body. These supports, however, usually collapse if the animals can no longer hold themselves up on their own legs. Until they are sacrificed, the animals receive nothing to eat, but one allows them to drink and douses them occasionally with water. At night the animals are covered with blankets, although this offer of warmth often lasts only a moment or two; the blanket is quickly wrapped around the post, too. One — or even more than one — buffalo cannot be sacrificed alone; in addition to the larger sacrificial animal(s), such a sacrifice always requires at least one small calf. This calf is called the "head-pillow" of the larger animals and is killed first.

After the animals have been tied up on the first day and then repeatedly danced around during the night, they are sacrificed on the morning of the second day. They are first spit upon with *hom-noi* from the small pot close to the gong stand. Then the drum and plate-shaped gongs are again sounded, and the *tu* is perhaps blown — this time during eighteen circumambulations. All members of the host's family congregate at the place of sacrifice; they draw some *hom-noi* from the small, round pot and then spit it on the sacrificial post. During the eighteen circumambulations, or immediately thereafter, when the young people are again dancing and playing their mouth organs, a few old women also circle the enclosure, slowly feeling their way along. In the meantime, an assistant brings a spear, a banana leaf, and a bit of hulled rice and wild ginger from the feast-giver's house; and as he invokes the spirits, the assistant throws some of this food six times over the sacrificial animal. He finally plunges the spear into the ribs of the animal from the right side; without a sound the beast collapses and dies. An assistant pulls the tongue out of the mouth of the animal and, while another pours water over its snout, cuts off the tip; he then nails this tip to the sacrificial post with a bamboo spike. On the right side of the largest animal sacrificed, a castrated piglet is laid close to the spear wound; and after rice and wild ginger have been thrown over it, the piglet is also stabbed with a spear, again from the right side. The other sacrificial animals are only touched with the piglet; it is thought to be their assistant.

Interpretations

There is a story which explains why the tongue of the sacrificial animal is cut off; unlike *tu* poetry, this story is known to every child. When God created the world, he sent a cow to impart to all peoples the rules for their way of life. The cow went first to the Bangalis and told them everything — among other things, that they should weed once and harvest three times a year. Then the cow ascended the mountain with the scroll for the Mru in its mouth. As midday neared, however, it grew hot, the cow became hungry and thirsty and moved its tongue around in its mouth; and before long it had swallowed the scroll. When the cow finally came to the Mru, it told them that they should weed three times and harvest once. Dissatisfied with these instructions, the Mru went to God and complained. God summoned the cow, and the beast had to admit that it had swallowed the true message and imparted the false one. When God heard this, he became angry and hit the cow in the mouth — this is the reason that, until today, the top front teeth of the cow are missing. God then commanded the Mru to bind the cow to a post, dance around it, and finally kill it. They were then to cut out its tongue — the tongue which had given them the wrong message — and nail the tongue to the post. In the cow's third stomach the Mru were to find the book which God had intended for them. Apart from this, however, there was nothing else that could be done regarding the rule, as it had already been declared and hence stood: weed three times and harvest once.

Similar stories about a lost script — explaining the difference between themselves and the literate peoples of the plains — are also found among other hill tribes of Southeast Asia. The Mru version is, in fact, common knowledge and readily recited, but does not really fit the spirit of the cattle ceremony. There is no feeling of one's taking revenge. The sacrificial animals are not only dabbed with "clean medicine" prior to and together with the people, but they are also kept warm at night and even given a companion to accompany them in death. The water which is poured over the mouth of an animal is a last drink; but before this water is poured over them, old women walk around them solemnly. As young men seize the binding rope and drag the dead animal to the feast-giver's house, where it is to be cut up on the open platform, the animal is escorted by dancing girls. According to the Mru, it should not have grounds for complaint about bad treatment. The cow, which in the simplest case is used as a sacrifice for sick persons, should render the evil spirits well-disposed toward those offering the sacrifice. Finally, while the animal is being towed, the "cattle-tail-pullers" may go into action. These are *tutma* or *pen* people — that is, the feast-giver's clan-based affines — who oppose the animal's being towed away. The "cattle-tail-pullers" either actually take hold of the tail of the animal and pull in the opposite direction, or they sit upon the animal until the host "redeems" it, that is, until he presents his *pen* new turbans and his *tutma* spears and supplies them with liquor.

As already mentioned, a set of three *tu*, which is otherwise reserved for the ceremonies in commemoration of the dead, is blown during the large cattle ceremonies. In the *tu* verses dancing men appear as birds before the spirits, and the sacrificial buffalo appear as fish. The crowns of the large masts on the host's house hang from a herringbone-shaped piece of lattice-work identified as a "fish," and a "hornbill" is often perched on top of

▶
The animal should now be taken to the house of the host where it will be cut up, but a cattle-tail-puller tries to prevent this.
▶▶
Two cattle-tail-pullers have settled themselves on top of the dead animal and are waiting for the host to redeem it. Will he come soon and bring them the material for a new turban, as well as a bottle of liquor?

◀
Little "hornbills" made of plaited strips of bamboo are perched on top of the fish-shaped latticework of the ceremonial mast. The mast towers over the roof of the feast-giver's house.
▶
A big feast of merit of the Anok Mru. Under the large decorative scaffolding, two buffaloes are tied up and fenced in. Dancing girls and musicians playing mouth organs circle clockwise around the animals. If dancing groups come from several villages, they normally take turns dancing. Here, however, three groups dance simultaneously.

them. In a story concerning the origin of the cattle ceremonies — a story known only to a few masters of the old songs — the bird perched upon the bamboo mast is the feast-giver's brother. In a preceding episode of the story, the brother was in fact transformed into a bird. The feast-giver himself acquires his wealth by catching a demon with a fishnet. He slays this "monster ruler," who is a devourer of men, domestic animals, and entire villages; and then he cuts the demon up and distributes its flesh — according to the instructions of the slain one — in the way the *köm-pot* should still be distributed today. After all of this has been done and while the large drum is constantly being beaten, all of those things reappear which had once been consumed by the "monster ruler." Yet, that is not all. Before all of this has taken place, the feast-giver marries the granddaughter (or sister's daughter) of the "monster ruler", so the demon is in fact his *tutma*. From *tutma* ("ancestors") one receives fish; from their *pen* ("descendants") the *tutma* receive birds (in the form of chickens). In our story, those who receive are the birds/men; those who give are the fish/sacrificial cow or buffalo.

Feasting

The most important *tutma* relative, the brother of the host's mother, is not only invited to the feast; he is also fetched by an emissary. At the entrance to the host's hamlet, the guest stops; and the emissary runs through the hamlet announcing the guest. In order to welcome the guest, the feast-giver proceeds to the village entrance carrying at least one bottle of liquor; the welcoming ceremony which follows is possibly done to a rifle or cracker salute. Drinks are passed around, and only after they have been consumed does the party proceed in high spirits to the feast-giver's house. Chicken and rice have in the meantime been prepared at the host's house, and now a large beer pot is put into place and "tapped". After the honored guest has taken a drink, he himself invites the men to whom he feels particularly tied to drink at this jug. Then everyone else is free to drink there.

There are still other close relatives of the host who receive a special invitation to the feast, since on the evening of the day when the sacrifice is made, or perhaps the following day, they should participate in a ceremonial exchange. Whoever comes as a *tai-nau*, that is, a relative from a brother clan, brings the host a pot of beer. In return, on the occasion of the exchange ceremony, the *tai-nau* is invited to partake of the beer from a pot placed in front of him. In addition to the beer, he receives some money, which he is not obliged to pay back until he

himself hosts a feast. In addition to a pot of beer — at least one pot is necessary for every clan — *tutma* relatives taking part in the exchange receive a spear, the worth of which they must later pay back in cloth. After that, both *tai-nau* and *tutma* receive a gift of meat to take home with them; this includes special cuts from the sacrificed cow or buffalo. In addition to the sacrificial meat, the *tutma* must always be served chicken. A part of the chicken is brought to the host by his *pen* relatives; a *pen* relative wishing to indicate a special relationship to the host gives the host a spear, the worth of which the *pen* then receives back in the form of a new turban. As soon as those men preparing the festive decorations have finished their work, they are entitled to receive a large pig slaughtered for them by the feast-giver. The pig, however, is not just a payment for the work; it is also a sacrifice to the spirits on behalf of the decorations. As symbolic protection against evil influences, thread squares are sometimes hung on the staircase of the host's house. They take the form of a small spiderweb and are made from red and black cotton strings. Among the Dopreng Mru, who on the occasion of a feast "renovate" the host's house by inserting and attaching particularly decorative bamboo poles and strips, a dog must also be sacrificed for protection.

Like the pig, the dog is gutted, singed over an open fire, cut up into small pieces, boiled with spices, and finally consumed. A bit of the cooked meat from both the pig and the dog must, however, be wrapped in a banana leaf and deposited at the foot of the sacrificial post. The fireplaces of the feast-giver's house are understandably inadequate for the preparation of the various kinds and large amounts of meat needed for the feast. Within the house, therefore, only the rice is cooked. The meat is cooked outside: whole rows of cooking pits are dug in the ground, and large, flat, iron pots are placed over these pits. In contrast to everyday cooking, which is customarily done by women, the preparation of ceremonial meat is exclusively a man's affair. The task of distributing the meat belongs to the assistants.

The more cattle or buffalo one sacrifices, the more meat there is to cut up and tend to. For this reason, the sacrificial animals are slaughtered at intervals of several hours, rather than all at one time. The ceremonies which accompany the sacrificing must be performed only once; however, the mouth organ dancers are always present. (They even dance around the empty enclosure.) In some regions, the musicians climb up into the feast-giver's house at the close of the celebration. There they find beer pots standing in the middle of the *kim-tom*. The girls form a circle and dance around the pots; the mouth organ players dance either inside or outside the girls' circle. Instead of the normal dance step, the dancers now stomp as hard as possible, so that the whole floor shakes. The floor of a good Mru house must be able to take such hard treatment; if the feast-giver no longer has full confidence in its stability, however, he does well to put up numerous beer pots and bring in many guests, hoping that the young people will soon sit down and drink as well, rather than jump around too wildly.

On the third day the earth-spirit receives an offering. (In some villages this takes place on the second day, before the sacrificial beef can be eaten.) Boiled rice and some of the liver and intestines of the sacrificial animal are placed into a small, round basket; a swallowtailed bamboo tube is filled with beer drawn from one of the pots. All members of the family then gather on the open platform. Each

At the close of the sacrificial ceremony, the oldest man ties a cotton string around the right wrist of all family members. On the round, woven tray one can see a cup of beer, a small piece of ginger, and the small gourd bottle with which the soul is summoned; next to the tray, a small bowl with rice flour.
◀
Outside the house, men cook the meat for the feast.

receives some rice and meat, two servings in the left hand, and one in the right; each takes some beer into his mouth; then each person throws and spits everything onto the ground. Next the remaining beer and some liquor are poured out; finally, the entire basket—along with some raw meat, some cooked meat, and some ashes wrapped in a banana leaf—is thrown down onto the ground. Under the house, the dogs compete for the tidbits of food. The people move into the house in order not to disturb the spirits during the meal.

After the assistants have placed the stones at the foot of the sacrificial post, that ceremony which also closes less significant festivities takes place in the host's house. The *bong-kom*, as it is known, consists of the tying of a string around the right wrist of all family members. The string for a cattle ceremony must be dyed red and black; customarily, these colored strings are distributed by an elderly *tutma* of the feast-giver, or even the *tu-sra*. The family members gather round a beer pot which has been specially prepared for the *bong-kom*, and some beer is drawn from the pot and put into a small bowl. The *sra* takes some of this beer into his mouth and sprays it over the head of the youngest family member. Then he blows six times over a small bottle gourd holding some unhulled rice, shakes the gourd, and says a prayer. After this is done, he ties a string around the wrist of the person concerned and spits some beer on it. Finally, the *sra* dabs a mixture of flour and turmeric on the forehead, the breastbone, and a dorsal vertebra (at about kidney level) of the person. This ritual is then repeated for every other family member. The *sra*'s prayer expresses the wish that nobody become ill and that all be successful in all their endeavors. The string may not be removed at will; however, it does not matter if it becomes loose or even gets lost before the end of the feast.

The benevolent spirits are also remembered at this time. Small pieces from the liver, the intestines, a shoulder and a leg of each of the sacrificed animals were put aside and are now prepared. Having been kept separate according to type (beef, pork, or chicken), the pieces of meat are first cooked in separate bamboo tubes; then they are cut up into tiny bits and wrapped with some rice and ginger in small sections of banana leaf. These *köm-pot* are finally distributed to all important places in the house, as well as to the sacrificial posts, the stones, and the utensils used on the ceremonial grounds. Unlike the Khumi and the Bawm, the Mru pay no special attention to the skulls of sacrificial animals; but particularly nice specimens may be kept as mementos.

On the final day the food and drink restrictions of the assistants are lifted. Then several items are brought to the open platform of the host's house (*tsar*): the musical instruments which were used for the ceremonial processions; the beer pot which was used for the *bong-kom* ceremony (the drinking mark of which is broken off beforehand); and a small chicken which has been boiled without any spices. The assistants take a little bit of the chicken into their hand, sip some of the beer from the pot, and, as the instruments are being played, throw and spit these things on each of the musical instruments in turn. The assistants then take another mouthful of beer and spit it to the left and right of the beer pot. After this has all been done, everything is taken into the house, where the same ritual is repeated. The host closes the ceremony by carrying out the ritual himself a final time; and as the beer is spit out to the left and right of the pot for the last time, water is poured over the head and neck of the host so that no malevolent influences are left behind. The musical instruments are then taken into the *kimma* and may not be played again until the next ceremonial occasion. Particularly honored guests are accompanied home; others have already departed in the meantime. The festive decorations will tell of the feast until they disintegrate during the next rainy season. After that, the only remaining evidence will be the sacrificial post and, at its foot, the stone commemorating the feast-giver's merits. Everyday life goes on.

Epilogue

Everyday life goes on, but it is changing — and not for the better. Not only is the fertility of the land decreasing — land upon which too many people's existence is already dependent — but the hill people's right to the land itself is being disputed. As a result of the building of the Kaptai dam in the Chakma region, the hill people had already been forced to squeeze more closely together; yet because there were still fifteen times more people per square mile on the plains than in the Hill Tracts the government concluded — without taking into consideration the ecological differences of the two areas — that there should still be ample opportunity for landless Bangalis to settle in the hill region. As early as 1960, therefore, the government began to settle additional people in the outer edges of the Tracts. Still, the immigration policy became legalized only in 1964, when the restrictions imposed by the British on non-indigenous peoples were lifted, while at the same time the Hill Tracts were declared off-limits for foreigners. The fact that the population of the Hill Tracts has doubled since that time might appear to support the government's view of ample land reserves. Yet part of the immigrant Bangalis live in the main towns and market areas, being themselves not active agriculturalists, but rather additional consumers of local resources. The indigenous population, then, has had to tighten its belt even tighter in order to feed themselves *and* their "uninvited guests." Wherever Bangali farmers settled, indigenous people had to be expelled. The flat valleys of the central and northern Hill Tracts offer the best example of this process of settlement: Hindu Tippera and Buddhist Chakma by the thousands left their homeland and moved into India; Marma moved to Arakan and lower Burma.

The first large stream of refugees left the northern Hill Tracts in 1971. Along with these people there also fled Hindu Bangalis from the plains area bordering the Tracts. During the Bangladesh struggle for independence, these people had to fear not only the Pakistani army, but also — and above all — their Muslim neighbors. When Pakistani rule in Bangladesh was brought to an end by the intervention of Indian troops, the Bangalis who had fled during the war were invited to return home to what was then a new, secular state; and they were promised the return of their properties. The tribal inhabitants of the Hill Tracts, on the other hand, whose chosen representative, the Chakma Chief, had taken sides with Pakistan, were suspected of collaboration. They were powerless against land-grabbing Muslim Bangalis who, during the turmoil of war, had settled in their villages. The search for hidden collaborators offered paramilitary troops a good excuse to maraud around in the hills. A delegation of the hill people, which wanted to negotiate with the new government the reestablishment of the Hill Tracts' protected status (abrogated in 1964), in order to stop further immigration, were simply told that ethnic identities must disappear. Shortly thereafter, the Bangali army, supported by the air force, invaded the Hill Tracts for the first time. The army wanted to crush the enemies of the new regime; however, by massacring villagers and ransacking and burning down villages, it succeeded in doing just the opposite. The villagers became convinced that they could expect no help from the new government, that they would have to take care of themselves. In order to defend the interests of the indigenous population, an armed resistance movement, the Shanti Bahini ("fighters for peace") was formed, primarily among the Chakma.

The general decay of public order in Bangladesh led to a takeover of power by a new military government — a government which reverted to a decidedly pro-Muslim and anti-Indian stance. Although the government's policy vis-à-vis the wishes of the political representatives of the Hill Tracts remained in fact the same, the resistance movement in the Hill Tracts profited from the anti-

Indian stance of the new military government: it began to receive support from India. Yet the Shanti Bahini did not present a united front; they rather consisted of various groups having different ethnic ties and varying political alignments. Some were prepared to make concessions; others were determined to resist, making no concessions whatsoever. Occasionally, therefore, they even fought among themselves. In addition to these Shanti Bahini, there were Bangali-Muslim groups, also resisting the military government, which had retreated into the Hill Tracts. So even in the Bangali Chittagong area one could denounce unpopular neighbors as "fighters for peace" and count on their leaving the remand prison only as cripples. Finally, the Hill Tracts also became a refuge for members of the Mizo liberation front, a movement which fought against the Indian central government in Assam. As time went on, the Indian government therefore changed its attitude to the Hill Tracts and, as a result, tightened its borders with the region. Officially, the Indians wanted to block the way of guerrilla troops into their country; in fact, however, they primarily blocked the influx of refugees.

Yet time and again whole tribal villages tried to flee; for wherever the guerrillas struck, the Bangali army devastated everything in the surrounding villages. They plundered the houses, raped the women, and tortured, mutilated, and killed all the men they could get their hands on. In 1981 alone, 10,000 members of the hill tribes are believed to have been killed. The purpose of this reign of terror was not only to frighten the inhabitants out of lending any support to the guerrillas, but also to threaten, in a most basic way, their very existence. As far as the new Bangali settlers were concerned, they had to fear that the Shanti Bahini would attack their villages and attempt to drive them back to their original homes. As a response to this threat, the government adopted a measure which has proven itself successful in many a counter-insurgency program: the erection of so-called "strategic villages." Inhabitants of these villages, which were under military control and which were denounced by the guerrillas as concentration camps, could leave the village to do prescribed jobs only after a thorough search and only without rations. Anyone walking about freely, therefore, had to reckon with the fact that all provisions for the road, as well as all paddy, salt, medicine, and money, would be confiscated. In spite of this, the guerrillas knew how to survive. A large proportion of the population may well have been in agreement with the guerrillas' goals, namely, the reestablishment of a society where the indigenous inhabitants may live in freedom and security, the establishment of an indigenous administration, and the winning of autonomy for the Hill Tracts. The situation of the Shanti Bahini, however, might have appeared hopeless; for over and against their some 5,000 men the Bangladesh military government could and did deploy what experience in other countries had shown to be effective in crushing a guerilla movement, viz. an army and police force of at least ten times the number of the guerillas.

In the long run, however, this strategy cost the state a disproportionately large amount of money; and were it not for international development aid, the government would perhaps have been forced to consent to a cheaper solution, that is, to a peaceful arrangement. Development aid money has been used to finance the constantly growing army and to train and equip it for anti-guerilla warfare; it has also been used to construct strategic all-weather roads through the impassable Hill Tracts, making them (and their forest reserves) more easily accessible. For the donor countries it amounted to sheer hypocrisy to deny support to anything obviously serving the purposes of genocide, while allocating at the same time funds for such useful purposes as the development of communication facilities which not only benefited military operations, but also facilitated the harassment, displacement, expropriation and expulsion of the indigenous population. When internationally pressured to comment on the reported violations of human rights in the Chittagong Hill Tracts, the representatives of the government vacillated between a flat denial of the mere existence of an indigenous tribal population, and a formal pledge to protect of the lives and interests of these tribal people. The only credible pledge, however, would have been the re-opening of the Hill Tracts to international humanitarian organizations, to social scientists from other countries, or journalists independent of any government. For more than twenty years, however, only economic and technical development experts under official government contract have been permitted to visit the Hill Tracts, for example, representatives of Shell Oil Company who were searching for oil.

As early as 1964 the government (at that time still Pakistan) requested that an international team of experts study how one could make best use of the land. These experts rightly discovered that the traditional system of slash-and-burn cultivation was perfectly adapted to local conditions; they also found, however, that with this type of cultivation the population would soon no longer be able to maintain itself. The experts therefore made the following proposal: the traditional swidden cultivation should be done away with altogether; the land should subsequently be used primarily for plantations and forest production; and the inhabitants should work in forestry or "other development industries." In one of the first areas to be tested, the people were forbidden to cultivate their traditional fields. Under the instructions of forestry officials, they were instead forced to plant quick-growing timber, bananas, pineapple, cashew nuts, guava, papaya, and citrus fruits. According to official calculations, after a few years the people should have received a good income from these products; but following the first harvest there were in fact no markets for the products. Having grown no paddy and receiving no money to buy it, the people began to starve; so whoever could manage left the controlled area and went in search of a new area in which to make his living. In subsequent years, however, due to the massive immigration of Bangalis, the displaced indigenous inhabitants had practically no other choice than to allow themselves to be "rehabilitated." "Rehabilitation" meant placing together in one village up to sixty families of various ethnic backgrounds (in such a way, cultural peculiarities can most easily be eliminated); each family was given a maximum of five acres of land and placed under obligation to use the new methods of cultivation. With the help of billions of dollars worth of credit from the Asian Development Bank, the new order should be realized over the whole of the Hill Tracts within the next few years. One can already foresee the results: he who has nothing left to eat will pawn his land to a moneylender and will eventually become a landless day laborer.

The wide valleys in the north and the area around the artificial lake are more agreeable to the Bangali settlers than the steep mountains of the south; however, since the Shanti Bahini are active primarily in the north and since the government is interested in Bangalizing all of the Hill Tracts, the southern valleys have also become a settlement area. The Mru have not been spared the developments accompanying this settlement: not only have two strategic roads been constructed through their region, but substantial army units have been stationed in the valleys of the southern rivers, so that life in the surrounding villages is no longer safe. More importantly, Bangali settlement has resulted in the forced eviction of large groups of Mru. In January of 1983, for example, the army forced the Anok Mru in three *mouza* bordering the Chittagong Plains to leave their villages without any compensation whatsoever.

"We want the land and not the people," a high-ranking military official reportedly said. The main concern of the government, however, can be neither the natural resources (such as natural gas and oil) nor the forestry products, since these things could be exploited even *with* "the people." It has rather to do with land for more and more Bangalis. By means of terrorism, resistance to Bangali expansion can be repressed; but it can not be completely eliminated until the entire indigenous population has been either exterminated or driven off. Surely no one believes that this Final Solution for the non-Muslim inhabitants of the Hill Tracts would in fact at the same time solve the problems of Bangladesh. One thing is certain, however: without foreign aid the government of Bangladesh could not flourish. Would it be asking too much to require the Bangladesh government — as a small remuneration for the aid — to allow the inhabitants of the Hill Tracts to survive? Put more concretely: would it be asking too much to require the government to discontinue its military and police terrorism and, in place of the terrorism, to grant the ethnic groups their own administration and allow them to use their own land and their own reserves? Instead of carrying out "development projects" to destroy traditional cultures and ethnic groups, should the government not refrain from hindering — if indeed it will not support — those projects which are in keeping with the interests of the indigenous population and open up for them an acceptable path to the future?

In 1987, despite several previous efforts at repatriation, more than 10% of the population of the Chittagong Hill Tracts were living in Indian refugee camps under miserable conditions. They had been beaten, robbed, tortured, raped, mutilated, or nearly hacked to death by Bangladeshi military forces or armed settlers and now insisted that it would be more humane just to shoot them dead on the spot, rather than send them back to what had once been their homeland. The tribal resistance movement demanded the withdrawal of the settlers and the repatriation of the refugees under the supervision of the UN. The government of Bangladesh then finally ordered the armed forces to stop persecuting of the hill people, even if provoked by the Shanti Bahini; it also appointed a committee to negotiate with representatives of the hill people, in order to come up with a political solution.

In the spring of 1989, just in time for the UN conference on human rights, the parliament of Bangladesh not only repealed the Regulations of 1900, but it also adopted three new bills providing for the constitution of local government councils in the districts of Rangamati, Khagrachori and Banderban. A majority of seats on the councils, as well as the chairmanship of the same, is reserved for the local tribesmen. Each council may draw up its own regulations for running the affairs of the district; each will be responsible for the maintenance of law and order and will, for this purpose, recruit a district police force; each will assess the social and economic needs of the people, levy taxes, and initiate development projects financially supported by the central government. In all of these activities, however, the councils will have to come in for the approval, or to secure the consent, of the government, which reserves for itself the right to dissolve the councils.

The councils will also have to settle land questions. However, they will have no say over the forest reserves nor the area of the Kaptai lake. Nor will they be able to give the land back to the tribesmen who once cultivated it, since under state law swidden cultivators were never recognized as owners of their land. Their land became "unclassified state forest", while they themselves came to be treated as squatters. Bangali businessmen and local officials, on the other hand, managed to buy thousands of acres of swidden land for conversion into rubber plantations; their newly acquired rights to tribal lands were no less officially registered than those of the poor Bangali settlers who, upon government initiative, were provided with five acres.

The district councils will also be entitled to appoint minor officials, although these will still be under the command of the higher officials appointed by the government. And, last but not least, the local councils will have no authority to order the military forces out of their districts — they may well prove to not even be interested in doing this, since the new "political solution" falls far short of the demands of the "fighters for peace". The war will continue, with some of the tribal people having been bought over by the government. Hill people will kill hill people without realizing that they need each other. There would be no local councils, and the councils would have no claims to press for, without the resistance movement; likewise, the resistance movement would achieve nothing but bloodshed were it not for the legalized representatives of the hill people, who, as intermediaries, are willing to collaborate with the government.

Bibliography

Concerning the Mru, very little has been published; publications containing interesting primary data are marked by an asteric. Due to the political situation, reports on the Chittagong Hill Tracts in general were multiplying during the last years; here the bibliography is far from exhaustive; but all important older sources (in European languages) on the ethnography of the hill tribes have been listed.

Abdus Sattar. 1971. In the Sylvan Shadows. Dhaka.
Aggavamsa Mahathera. 1981. Stop Genocide in Chittagong Hill Tracts (Bangladesh). Calcutta.
Ahmad, N. 1958. An Economic Geography of East Pakistan. London.
Ahmad, N./Rizvi, A.I.H. 1951. 'Need for the Development of Chittagong Hill Tracts'. Pakistan Geographic Review 6,2: 19–24.
Amano, Toshitake (ed.) s.a. The Hillmen of the Chittagong Hill Tracts in East Pakistan. (Report of the Scientific Mission of Osaka University to East Pakistan 1964). Osaka.
Amnesty International. 1986. Bangladesh. Unlawful Killings and Torture in the Chittagong Hill Tracts. London
*Ba Myaing, U. 1934. 'The Northern Hills of Ponnagyun Township'. Journal of the Burma Research Society 24: 127–148.
*Ba Thin, U. 1931. 'The Awa Khamis, Ahraing Khamis, and Mros in the Chin Hill Area (Saingdin) Buthidaung Township'. Census of India 1931, vol.11,1: 248–256
Bangladesh Groep Nederland. 1981. Moord op Minderheden in Bangladesh. Chittagong Hill Tracts. Amsterdam
Bangladesh Groep Nederland. 1988. 'Bangladesh: Refugees from an unknown war. Bangladeshi tribals in India.' IWGIA Newsletter 53/54: 33–51
*Belitz, Harry. 1987. 'Im Schatten des Waldes. Naturvölker in Bangladesh.' Delta 1: 32–43. München.
Bernot, D. 1958. 'Rapports phonétiques entre le dialecte marma et le birman'. Bulletin de la Société Linguistique 53: 273–294.
Bernot, D. 1960. 'Deux lettres du vice-roi d'Arakan au sujet du rebelle King-Bering'. T'oung Pao 47: 395–422.
Bernot, D. and L. 1957. 'Chittagong Hill Tribes'. In: S. Maron (ed.), Pakistan Society and Culture, 46–61. New Haven.
Bernot, D. et L. 1958. Les Khyang des collines de Chittagong (Pakistan oriental). Matériaux pour l'étude linguistique des Chins. (L'Homme, n.s.3). Paris.
Bernot, L. 1953. 'In the Chittagong Hill Tracts'. Pakistan Quarterly 3: 17–61
*Bernot, L. 1954. 'Les Mro et leurs orgues à bouche'. Science et Nature: 13–15.
Bernot, L. 1960. 'Ethnic groups of Chittagong Hill Tracts'. In: P. Bessaignet (ed.), Social Research in East Pakistan. (Asiatic Society of Pakistan Publications, 5: 113–140). Dacca.
Bernot, L. 1967. Les Cak, contribution à l'étude ethnologique d'une population de langue loi. Paris.
Bernot, L. 1967. Les Paysans Arakanais du Pakistan Oriental. L'histoire, le monde végétal et l'organisation sociale des réfugiés Marma (Mog). Paris/La Haye.
*Bessaignet, P. 1958. Tribesmen of the Chittagong Hill Tracts. (Asiatic Society of Pakistan Publications 1). Dacca.
*Brauns, C.-D. 1973. 'The Mrus, peaceful hillfolk of Bangladesh'. National Geographic Magazine 143,2: 267–286.
*Brauns, C.-D. 1977. 'Das glückliche Leben der Mru'. GEO-Magazin 3: 58–76.
*Brauns, C.-D. 1983. 'Les stirpe dei uomini fiori'. Airone 23: 86–101.
Burger, J. and Whittacker, A. (ed.). 1984. The Chittagong Hill Tracts – Militarization, Oppression, and the Hill Tribes. (Indigenous Peoples and Development Series 2). London: Anti-Slavery Society.
Census of Pakistan, 1961. District Census Report Chittagong Hill Tracts.
FORESTAL. 1966. Chittagong Hill Tracts Soil and Land Use Survey 1964–1966. 9 vols. Vancouver.
Government of British India/Pakistan/Bangladesh. The Chittagong Hill Tracts Regulations 1900 (I of 1900). (Reissued several times with new amendments, but difficult to locate and retrieve).
Grierson, G.A. (ed). 1904. Linguistic Survey of India, III 3. Calcutta.
Henes, U. 1981. The Secret War in Bangladesh. (International Fellowship of Reconciliation, Report). Alkmaar.
Hughes, W.G. 1881. The Hill Tracts of Arakan. Rangoon.
Hunter, W.W. 1876. A Statistical Account of Bengal, Vol. 6. London.
Huq, M.M. 1982. Government Institutions and Underdevelopment. A Study of the Tribal Peoples of Chittagong Hill Tracts, Bangladesh. Birmingham.
*Hutchinson, R.H.S. 1906. An Account of the Chittagong Hill Tracts. Calcutta.
*Hutchinson, R.H.S. 1909. Chittagong Hill Tracts. (Eastern Bengal and Assam District Gazetteers). Allahabad.
Jana Samhati Samiti. 1987. Persecution of Human Rights in Chittagong Hill Tracts. s.l. (Chittagong Hill Tracts).
Kamaluddin, S. 1980. 'A tangled web of insurgency'. Far Eastern Economic Review 23. 5. 80: 34.
Kauffmann, H.E. 1934. 'Landwirtschaft bei den Bergvölkern von Assam und Nord-Burma'. Zeitschrift für Ethnologie 66: 15–111
*Kauffmann, H.E. 1960. 'Das Fadenkreuz, sein Zweck und seine Bedeutung'. Ethnologica N.F. 2: 36–69.
Kauffmann, H.E. 1962. 'Observation on the agriculture of the Chittagong Hill Tribes'. In: J.E. Owen (ed.), Sociology in East Pakistan.(Occasional Studies of the Asiatic Society of Pakistan 1). Dacca.
Kauffmann, H.E. 1969. 'Die Nouka auf dem Sangu, ein

Bootstyp in Ostpakistan'. Zeitschrift für Ethnologie 94: 15–32.

Kauffmann, H.E. und L.G. Löffler. 1959. 'Spiele der Marma'. Zeitschrift für Ethnologie 84,2: 238–253.

Khan, R.K. and S.I. Choudhury. 1965. 'Some tribal house types of the Chittagong Hill Tracts'. The Oriental Geographer 9,1: 17–32.

Khan, R.K. and A.L. Khisha. 1970. 'Shifting cultivation in East Pakistan'. The Oriental Geographer 14,2: 22–43.

Konietzko, J. 1929. 'Die Konietzkosche Indienexpedition 1927'. Ethnologischer Anzeiger 2: 31–33.

Latter, T. 1846. 'Note on some hill tribes on the Kuladyne river, Arracan'. Journal of the Royal Asiatic Society of Bengal 15: 60–78.

Lévi-Strauss, C. 1951. 'Miscellaneous notes on the Kuki of the Chittagong Hill Tracts, Pakistan'. Man 51: 167–169. (No. 284).

Lévi-Strauss, C. 1952. 'Le syncrétisme religieux d'un village mog du territoire de Chittagong'. La Revue de l'Histoire des Religions 141,2: 202–237.

Lévi-Strauss, C. 1952. 'Kinship systems of three Chittagong hill tribes'. Southwestern Journal of Anthropology 8: 40–50.

Lewin, T.H. 1867. 'Diary of a hill-trip on the borders of Arracan'. Proceedings of the Royal Geographic Society 11,52.

*Lewin, T.H. 1869. The Hill Tracts of Chittagong and the Dwellers Therein; with comparative vocabularies of the hill dialects. Calcutta.

*Lewin, T.H. 1870. Wild Races of Southeastern India. London.

Lewin, T.H. 1912. A Fly on the Wheel, or How I Helped to Govern India. London.

*Löffler, L.G. 1958. 'Bambus, Lebensgrundlage eines hinterindischen Bergvolkes'. Umschau in Wissenschaft und Technik 58: 755–757.

Löffler, L.G. 1959. 'Die Khyang der Chittagong Hill Tracts'. Zeitschrift für Ethnologie 84,2: 257–269.

Löffler, L.G. 1960. 'Khami/Khumi-Vokabulare. Vorstudie zu einer sprachwissenschaftlichen Untersuchung'. Anthropos 55: 505–557.

Löffler, L.G. 1960. 'Carrying Capacity, Schwendbauprobleme in Südostasien'. Actes du VIe Congrès International des Sciences Antropologiques et Ethnologiques, Paris, 2,1: 179–182.

Löffler, L.G. 1964. 'Chakma und Sak. Ethnolinguistische Beiträge zur Geschichte eines Kulturvolkes'. International Archives of Ethnography. 50,1:72–115

*Löffler, L.G. 1966. 'L'alliance asymétrique chez les Mru'. L'Homme 6,3: 68–80.

Löffler, L.G. 1968. 'A note on the history of the Marma Chiefs of Banderban'. Journal of the Asiatic Society of Pakistan 13,2: 189–201 Dacca.

Löffler, L.G. 1968. 'Basic Democracies in den Chittagong Hill Tracts, Ostpakistan'. Sociologus N.F. 18,2: 152–171.

Löffler, L.G. 1972. 'Pitch and Tone in Bawm'. Ethnologische Zeitschrift Zürich: 285–289.

*Löffler, L.G. 1975. 'Mru Tu Long'. In: H. Berger (ed.), Mündliche Überlieferungen in Südasien. Schriftenreihe des Südasieninstituts der Universität Heidelberg 17: 8–28.

Löffler, L.G. 1985. 'A preliminary report on Paangkhua language'. In: G. Thurgood, J.A. Matisoff, D. Bradley (eds.), Linguistics of the Sino-Tibetan Area. Canberra, Pacific Linguistics C 87: 279–286.

Löffler, L.G. (ed.) 1988. Bedrohte Zukunft. Bergvölker in Bangladesh. Zürich.

Löffler, L.G. 1988. 'Bodenrechte in den Chittagong Hill Tracts'. Geographica Helvetica 43,4 : 177–183.

Löffler, L.G. und S.L. Pardo. 1969. 'Shifting cultivation in the Chittagong Hill Tracts, East Pakistan'. Jahrbuch des Südasien-Institutes der Universität Heidelberg 3: 49–66.

MacCall, A.G. 1949. Lushai Chrysalis. London.

MacKenzie, A. 1884. History of the Relations of the Government with the Hill Tribes of the North-East Frontier of Bengal. Calcutta.

MacRae, J. 1801. 'Account of the Kookies, or Lunctas'. Asiatick Researches 7: 183–198.

*Mey, A. 1979. Untersuchung zur Wirtschaft in den Chittagong Hill Tracts (Bangladesh). Veröffentlichungen aus dem Übersee-Museum Bremen, D 6.

Mey, W. 1980. Politische Systeme in den Chittagong Hill Tracts, Bangladesh. Veröffentlichungen aus dem Übersee-Museum Bremen, D 9.

Mey, W. (ed.) 1984. Genocide in the Chittagong Hill Tracts, Bangladesh. (International Work Group for Indigenous Affairs, Document 51). Copenhagen.

Mey, W. (ed.) 1988. 'Wir wollen nicht euch – Wir wollen euer Land.' Macht und Menschenrechte in den Chittagong Hill Tracts, Bangladesh. (Pogrom Reihe bedrohte Völker 1016). Göttingen.

*Mills, J.P. 1931. 'Notes on a tour in the Chittagong Hill Tracts in 1926'. Census of India 1931, Vol. 5: 514–521.

*Ohn Pe, U. 1931. 'The Awa Khamis, Ahraing Khamis, and Mros in the Ponnagyun Chin Hills, Ponnagyun Township'. Census of India 1931, Vol. 11,1:257–264.

Op't Land, C. 1966. 'Chakma and Sak: a Rejoinder.' International Archives of Ethnography 50: 281–301.

Organizing Committee Chittagong Hill Tracts Campaign. 1986. The Charge of Genocide, Human Rights in the Chittagong Hill Tracts of Bangladesh. Amsterdam.

Parry, N.E. 1932. The Lakhers. London.

Phayre, A.P. 1841. 'Account of Arakan'. Journal of the Royal Asiatic Society of Bengal 10: 679–712.

*Rajput, A.B. 1964. 'Les Murung de la forêt de Bandarban (Pakistan Oriental)'. Objets et Mondes 4,2: 119–148.

Rajput, A.B. 1965. The Tribes of the Chittagong Hill Tracts. Karachi.

Rashid, H. 1977. Geography of Bangladesh. Dacca.

Reichle, V. 1981. Bawm Language and Lore, Tibeto-Burman Area. (Europäische Hochschulschriften 21,14). Bern.

Risley, H.H. 1892. The Tribes and Castes of Bengal, Ethnographic Glossary. Calcutta.

Riebeck, E. 1885. Die Hügelstämme von Chittagong, Ergebnisse einer Reise im Jahre 1882. Berlin.

Serajuddin, A.M. 1971. 'The origin of the Rajas of the Chittagong Hill Tracts and their relations with the

Moghuls and the East Indian Company in the eighteenth century.' Journal of the Pakistan Historical Society 29,1.
Shakespear, J. 1912. The Lushei Kuki Clans. London.
*Shafer, R. 1941. 'The linguistic relationship of Mru. Traces of a lost Tibeto-Burmic language?' Journal of the Burma Research Society 31: 58–79.
Sopher, D.E. 1963. 'Population dislocation in the Chittagong Hills'. Geographical Review 53: 337–362.
Sopher, D.E. 1964. 'The swidden/wet-rice transition zone in the Chittagong Hills'. Annals of the Association of American Geographers 54,1: 107–126.
Spielmann, H.J. 1968. Die Bawm-Zo. Eine Chin-Gruppe in den Chittagong Hill Tracts (Ostpakistan). Heidelberg.
Survival International. 1984. 'Genocide in Bangladesh'. SI-Review 43: 7–28.
St. Andrew St. John, R.F. 1872. 'A short account of the hill tribes of North Arakan'. Journal of the Royal Anthropological Institute 2: 233–247.
Thom, W.S. 1910. Burma Gazetteer, Northern Arakan District (or Arakan Hill Tracts). Rangoon.

Glossary of Terms related to the Administrative Structure

Cross references are marked with *

Chief: British designation for the *raja under the principle of indirect rule. The Chiefs were authorized to adjudicate in tribal legal matters and to nominate the *headmen of the *mouzas within their respective *Circles. For his services a Chief was entitled to keep a quarter of all field taxes collected by the *headmen. Their rights were abolished in 1981, but revived in 1989.

Circle: a territory whose inhabitants were placed by the British (1873) under the subordination of a *Chief. In 1892 the borders of the Circles were definitively drawn, and in the following years the three Circles, which were named after the Chakma, Bohmong, and Mong Chiefs, were divided into *mouzas. Between 1891 and 1900 the Chittagong Hill Tracts temporarily had the status of a Subdivision; after they were re-elevated to the district level, they were again in 1919 subdivided into three areas roughly corresponding to the Circles. These *Subdivisions were named after the three administrative centers, Rangamati, Banderban, and Ramgor; and each was placed under the jurisdiction of a Subdivisional Officer of the colonial administration. When the political power and rights of the *Chiefs were done away with in 1981, the Circles were likewise abolished; and the Subdivisions were elevated to Districts (now known as Rangamati, Banderban, and Khagrachori District).

Deputy Commissioner: cf. *Superintendent

District: cf. *Circle

Headman: originally an English term for a *dewan* of the Chakma or a *ruatsa* of the Marma who was subordinate to the *raja; from 1892 on, the indigenous head of a *mouza*, appointed by the *Superintendent (Deputy Commissioner) upon the recommendation of the *Chief. He is responsible for the keeping of tax lists, the handing over of field taxes to the *Chief (part of which he is allowed to keep for himself), and the upholding of order. In legal matters, the headman is empowered to adjudicate in disputes according to customary law. The position of headman is often taken over by the headman's son.

Karbari: (Bangla) 'manager' — head of a hamlet, informally elected by the villagers and acknowledged by the administration; responsible to deliver the field taxes to the *headman; has no official power or authority and receives no renumeration for services rendered.

Mouza: (Bangla) smallest regional unit of fiscal administration; in the Chittagong Hill Tracts, under the authority of a *headman; conceived of as the equivalent of the 'village' on the plains, but normally made up of several small, independent villages (hamlets) administratively united irrespective of ethnic composition.

Raja: (Bangla) name of the traditional head of the Chakma, the Marma, and the Tippera; as *Chiefs, entrusted by the British with the collection of taxes and the adjudication of minor legal matters among the indigenous population of a *Circle; places of residence ("*rajbari*") in Rangamati (Chakma), Banderban (Bohmong) and Manikchori (Mong).

Ruatsa: (Burman) "village-eater" (in English literature, generally written 'Roaja' and described as *headman); old term for the tax collectors subordinate to the Marma *raja (Bohmong); in the meantime, however, only a title (devoid of function) which the Bohmong confers — for a fee — on the *headmen and the *karbari*.

Subdivision: cf. *Circle

Superintendent: 1860-1867 and 1900-1919, the title of the highest administrative official of the Chittagong Hill Tracts; between 1867 and 1891, and since 1920, title replaced by "Deputy Commissioner"; since the former Superintendent also commanded the police force, the term still designates the highest police official ("Superintendent of Police"). The office of the Deputy Commissioner was split into three with the upgrading of the former *Subdivisions to Districts; in 1989 the Deputy Commissioners formally ceased to be the administrative heads of the Districts, becoming rather the ex-officio secretaries (still appointed by the government) of the newly instituted local councils.

Glossary of Mru Terms

Mru is a tonal language; however, no indication of the tones is given. *k*, *t*, and *p* are not aspirated (they are pronounced approximately as in French); wherever an aspiration occurs, I write *kh*, *th*, *ph* (*ph* is, therefore, not spoken like /f/), and *tsh* (often spoken like /hs/); *r* is always rolled; *y* and *w* are pronounced as in English; vowels have the Italian quality, but *e* and *o* are always open (*e*, therefore, like the German /ä/). In addition, Mru has two vowels for which we have no signs: I use *ö* and *ü* to indicate these vowel sounds. Like o and u one forms them in the back of the mouth cavity, but without rounding the lips.

bong-kom: the ceremony of binding (*kom*) a thread around the right wrist (*bong*) of all family members
hom-noi: a mixture of water and cooked rice (*hom*); serves as a substitute for beer on ceremonial occasions
kimma: literally "main house;" the smaller room of the house which serves as a bedroom for the married couple and small children; also used as a storeroom for possessions and food supplies; off-limits for strangers
kim-tom: the larger room of the house; common living room where the family cooks and eats, and where tools are kept; sleeping quarters for the older children; room in which guests are accommodated
klai-puk: a standing basket of the smaller type, without a lid; used daily and in ceremonies
köm-pot: small portions of food wrapped in pieces of leaves which are offered to the spirits
kua: hamlet, settlement
long: a length of bamboo; a verse of poetry (sung or played on an instrument)
meng: song; a modern, short piece of sung poetry or a long, traditional ballad
pen: "descendants" from the female point of view; members of the wife-takers' clans, particularly a man's sister's son or a man's son-in-law
plai: dance, in particular the ritual circumambulations of offering places, performed on specific occasions only: harvests, funerals and cattle feasts; for young people larger cattle ceremonies are the only occasions for dancing
plong-rau: lovesickness, lit. "liver pain"
plung: a wind instrument, so-called cheng or mouth organ (not to be mistaken for the harmonica); of various types, all consisting of a number of pipes inserted in two rows into a gourd bottle; similar instruments are to be found in Thailand, Laos, and southern China, as well as with the Dayak of Borneo.
sra: (word borrowed from Burman) master of certain activities, usually in the area of religion
tai-nau: older (*tai*) and younger (*nau*) siblings of the same sex; in a broader sense, also the members of clans which are considered to be in sibling relationship
tsar: open platform of the village house or field house
tu: single-pipe, gourd mouth organ; according to the dictates of certain poetic verses, a set of three *tu* is blown for funerals and larger cattle feasts; used also as a ceremonial item on other festive occasions, although it is not played
tur-tut: ritual spot on a slashed and burnt field; here field cultivation is begun and sacrifices are offered
tutma: "ancestors" from the female point of view; members of the wife-givers' clans, particularly a man's mother's brother or a man's father-in-law
tshai-ria: in former times the chieftain of an important clan with the southern Mru groups
tshüng-nam: spiritual beings who control the traditional order of life in the hills; they are called upon to participate in feasts and to partake of sacrifices in case of illness
üa: swidden; field under slash-and-burn cultivation
wak: a corpse
wan-klai: woman's skirt, consisting of a double layer of homespun material 10 inches wide

Picture Credits

All maps, as well as the following pictures and drawings, are by L. G. Löffler: Pages 6, 28, 30 right, 35 left, 38 right, 63 above, 64 right, 68, 69 above, 85, 111, 113, 116 left, 117, 118, 119 below, 120 below, 121 below, 127 right, 131, 135, 143 left, 170, 171, 172, 176, 182, 183, 184, 189, 192 above right, 193 right, 194 below, 195 above, 196, 197, 199, 227 above, 229, 232 left, 233 right, 234 above, 236, 237, 239. The same author also supplied the photographs taken by H. Löffler-Wolf (pp. 33 left, 114 above), A. Mey (p. 32 right), H. J. Spielmann (p. 35 right), and J. P. Mills (p. 24), as well as those taken by H. E. Kauffmann and published by courtesy of the Institut für Völkerkunde, University of Munich, on pages 30 left, 34 right, 137, 226, 234 below.

The pictures on pages 31, 32 left, and 188 are taken from publications of A. B. Rajput; those on pages 33 right and 39 were published by institutions of the Government of Bangladesh.
All other photographs and drawings are by Claus-Dieter Brauns. His drawings on pages 74/75, 138/39, 140, 180/81, and 232 below, as well as the reproduction on page 136 below, are based on photographs of objects collected by L. G. Löffler in 1964 for the Linden-Museum (Staatliches Museum für Völkerkunde), Stuttgart. These photographs were kindly made available by the museum. The drawing on page 193 above left and the reproduction on page 136 above are based on objects in the private collection of L. G. Löffler.